Rol

C

The finest walks on the coast and in the mountains

65 walks

ROTHER • MUNICH

ROTHER Walking Guides

Preface

»I hope for nothing. I fear nothing. I am free.« (Nikos Kazantzakis)
»Crete in front of me – the whole world behind me.« (Mikis Theodorakis)

Walking in the mountains, living by the sea! Crete has the perfect combination ready at hand. After a full day of touring the mountains or the coast, what could be better than taking a swim in the sea or simply starting off the evening in a seafood taverna and ending it in a *kafenion* watching the old men let a string of clacking beads slide through their fingers, as if time doesn't mean a thing? With the exception, perhaps, of the hectic metropolis of Heraklion, Crete is an island just made for winding down. *Sigá, sigá,* »slowly, slowly«; these are the words you will hear time and again on the island. Crete is Greece in its purest form, and yet, life is very different here than on the mainland. What amazes you the most is Cretan hospitality; visitors are given a welcome here as if they were old friends. Especially outside of the summer high tourist season, in spring and in late autumn when walking is ideal, the people of Crete have plenty of time to spend on their guests.

Crete is an extremely multifaceted walking region with very different landscapes. Many areas of the island are still rugged and pristine, which you would not necessarily expect for such a fully developed holiday destination. The island's terrain is dominated by three mighty mountain ranges, furrowed by deep gorges. Vineyards and vast groves of olive trees lie sprawling in the foothills and in the valleys. Plenty of worthwhile walking destinations can be found here. Among the peaks, you will also find many challenging alpine climbs of more than 2000 metres in altitude. If you prefer to keep to the lower altitudes, you can take a coastal trail to a quiet bathing cove or walk along ancient cobbled paths to secluded monasteries and chapels. Gorge walkers and cave enthusiasts will be thrilled by breathtaking canyons and dripstone caves; Crete offers a selection not to be beaten by any other Mediterranean island. Classic routes include not only Samaria Gorge, designated as a national park and extremely popular for hordes of walkers, but also Dead's Gorge (Zakros Gorge) where the site of a Minoan palace is located at the exit, bearing witness to five thousand years of Cretan history.

In one or two weeks of walking here, you will discover many attractive routes, but that doesn't mean you have »ticked off the whole list« that Crete has to offer; a good reason to return! The guide presented here has been thoroughly researched to the best of the authors' knowledge. If you should find any changes to the trail network, we would be very grateful if you would contact the publisher. It only remains for us to wish you many relaxing and eventful days on the Med!

December 2017   Rolf Goetz

3

Contents

Κ Ρ Η Τ

Kriti (Kreta)
Κρήτη

Όρμος Almirou
Όρμος Αλμυρού

Panormo
Πάνορμο
Bali
Μπαλί
Akr. Stavros
Ακρ. Σταυρός
Αγ. Pelagia
Αγ. Πελαγία
Kolpos
Κόλπος

Rethimno
Ρέθυμνο
M. Arsaniou
M. Αρσανίου
Angelliana
Αγγελιανά
Melidoni
Μελιδόνι
Sises
Σίσες
Fodele
Φόδελε
Ahlada
Αχλάδα
IRAKLIO
ΗΡΑΚΛΕΙΟ

λη 4
Geraki
Γεράνι
Episkopi
Επισκοπή
Adele
Άδελε
Viranepiskopi
Βιρανεπισκοπή
Perama
Πέραμα
Agia
Αγιά
Drosia
Δροσιά
Damasta
Δαμάστα
Rogdia
Ρογδιά
Gazi
Γάζι

ήρουπόλη
θουπόλη
Armeni
Αρμένοι
Gonia
Γωνιά
Eleftherna
Ελεύθερνα
Ag. Ioannis
Αγ. Ιωάννης
Axos
Αξός
Gonies
Γωνιές
Marathos
Μάραθος
Knosos
Κνωσός

37
Chromonastiri
Χρωμοναστήρι
Zoniana
Ζωνιανά
Anogia
Ανώγεια
Sklavokampos
Σκλαβοκάμπος
Kavrohori
Τύλισος

Koumi
Κούμοι
Selli
Σελλί
M. Arkadiou
M. Αρκαδίου
Apostoli
Απόστολοι
39
Psiloritis
Ψηλορείτης
Anria
Κορφές
Korfes
Κορφές
Stavrakia
Σταυράκια

Αγ. Ioannis
Αγ. Ιωάννης
57
Karines
Καρίνες
Patsos
Πάτσος
38
Ideo Andro
Ιδαίο Άντρο
Krousonas
Κρουσώνας
Pano Arha
Πάνω Αρχ

Sellia
Σελλία
Koxare
Κοξαρέ
Spili
Σπήλι
Gerakari
Γερακάρι
Amari
Αμάρι
40
Fourfouras
Φουρφουράς
A. Asites
Κ. Ασί
43
Venerato
Βενεράτο

Plakia
Πλακιάς
33
Mourne
Μουρνέ
A. Meros
Α. Μέρος
Nithafris
Νιθαύρη
Sp. Kamaron
Σπ. Καμάρων
Vorizia
Βορίζια
41
Gergeri
Γέργερι

34
Sfakoro
Σφακόρο
35
Akoumia
Ακούμια
N. Kria Vrisi
Ν. Κρύα Βρύση
Kamares
Καμάρες
Zaros
Ζαρός
59
Ag. Varvara
Αγ. Βαρβάρα

Piso M. Preveli
Πίσω Μ. Πρέβελη
Keramés
Κεραμές
Melambes
Μέλαμπες
Klima
Κλήμα
Galia
Γαλιά
Moroni
Μορόνι
A. Mouia
Α. Μούλια
Larani
Λαράνι
Tefeli
Τεφέλι

Akr. Melissa
Ακρ. Μέλισσα
Ag. Galini
Αγ. Γαλήνη
Lagolio
Λαγόλιο
Gangales
Γκαγκάλες

44
Timbaki
Τυμπάκι
Vori
Βώροι
42
Gortys
Γόρτυς
Ag. Deka
Αγ. Δέκα
Asimi
Ασήμι

Ormos Mesaras
Ormos Μεσαράς
Festos
Φαιστός
Mires
Μοίρες
Moires
Μοίρες
Vagionia
Βαγιονιά
Loures
Λούρες

N. Paximadia
Ν. Παξιμάδια
46
Matala
Μάταλα
Pigaidakia
Πηγαιδάκια
Μεσαρά
Μεσαρά

45
M. Odigitrias
Μ. Οδηγήτριας
M. Apezanon
Μ. Απεζάνων
Andiskari
Αντισκάρι
Krotos
Κρότος
Loukia
Λούκια
Param
50

47
Kali Limenes
Καλοί Λιμ
Peramata
Περάματα
48
Lendas
Λέντας
49
M. Koudouma
Μ. Κουδούμα

Akr. Lithino
Ακρ. Λίθινο

P E L A G O S

K Ρ Η Τ Ι Κ Ο

ti (K r e t a)

Κ ρ ή τ η

Akr. Stavros
Ακρ. Σταυρός

Dia
Δία

Panormo
Πάνορμο
Bali
Μπαλί
Sises
Σίσες
Ag. Pelagia
Αγ. Πελαγία
Kolpos Irakliou
Κόλπος Ηρακλείου

Akr. Hersonisos
Ακρ. Ηερόνησος

Kolpos Ma
Κόλπος Μα

Agia
Αγία
Melidoni
Μελιντόνι
76
Ahlada
Αχλάδα
Rogdia
Ρογδιά
Roudia
Ρούντια
IRAKLIO
ΗΡΑΚΛΕΙΟ
Gazi
Γάζι
N. Alikarnassos
Ν. Αλικαρνασσός
Limin Hersonisou
Λιμήν Χερσόνησου

Perama
Πέραμα
Fodele
Φόδελε
Damasta
Δαμάστα
Marathos
Μάραθος
Apori
Ανώπολη
Stalis
Σταλίς

Ag. Ioannis
Αγ. Ιωάννης
Axos
Αξός
Drosia
Δροσιά
Gonies
Γωνιές
Knossos
Κνωσός
Elea
Ελαία
Haraso
Χαρασό
31
Potames
Ποταμιές

Zoniana
Ζωνιανά
Anogia
Ανώγεια
Korfes
Κορφές
Tilisos
Τύλισος
Vasilies
Βασιλιές
Episkopi
Επισκοπή
Smari
Σμάρι
Krasi
Κράσι

Psiloritis
Ψηλορείτης
39
38
Ιδη

Krousonas
Κρούσωνας
K. Asites
Κ. Ασίτες
Stavrakia
Σταυράκια
Pano Arhanes
Πάνο Αρχάνες
Ag. Paraskies
Αγ. Παρασκιές
Kastelli
Καστέλλι
K. Metohi
Κ. Μετόχι
51

Fourfouras
Φούρφουρας
Venerato
Βενεράτο
Kato Arhanes
Κάτω Αρχάνες
Arkalohori
Αρκαλοχώρι
Geraki
Γεράκι
Dikti

Nithafris
Νιθαυρίς
Vorizia
Βοριζιά
40
41
Gergeri
Γέργερι
Ag. Varvara
Αγ. Βαρβάρα
Panorama
Πανόραμα
Partira
Παρτίρα
Kasanos
Κασάνος

59
Zaros
Ζαρός
Galia
Γαλιά
Moroni
Μορόνι
A. Moulia
Α. Μούλια
Larani
Λαράνι
Tefeli
Τεφέλι
Garipa
Γαρίπα
Inio
Ίνιο
Panagia
Παναγία
Katofigi
Κατοφύγι

Lagolio
Λαγολιό
44
Vori
Βώροι
42
Gangales
Γκάγκαλες
Asimi
Ασήμι
Kalivia
Καλίβια
Martha
Μάρθα
A. Viannos
Α. Βιάννος
Pefkos
Πεύκος

Timbaki
Τίμπακι
Mires
Μίρες
Moires
Μοίρες
Ag. Deka
Αγ. Δέκα
Loures
Λούρες
Mesohorio
Μεσοχώρι
Amiras
Αμιράς

Kalamaki
Καλαμάκι
Pigaidakia
Πιγαϊδάκια
46
Pigra
Πλώρα
Vagionia
Βαγιωνιά
Pirgos
Πύργος
Demati
Δεμάτι

Matala
Μάταλα
45
Andiskari
Αντισκάρι
Krotos
Κρότος
Parani
Παράνι
50
Mournia
Μουρνιά
Ahendrias
Αχεντριάς
Keratokambos
Κερατόκαμπος
Tsoutsouros
Τσούτσουρος

Kali Limenes
Καλοί Λιμένες
47
Perama
Περάματα
Lendas
Λέντας
48
49
M. Koudouma
Μ. Κούδουμα

Akr. Lithino
Ακρ. Λίθινο

Mesara
Μεσαρά

ΠΕΛΑΓΟΣ

Ν Λ Α Γ Ο Σ

Kolpos Mirambellou
Κόλπος Μιραμπέλλου

O. Sitias
Ο. Σητείας

Ormos Grandes
Όρμος Γράντες

Dragonada
Δραγονάδα

Gianisada
Γιανισάδα

Akr. Sideros
Άκρ. Σίδερος

Elasa
Έλασα
Ελάσα

Italos
Τρανός

Vai
Βάι
58

Amigdalia
Αμυγδαλιά

Mironikitas
Μυρωνικήτας

Skinias
ΣΚΙΝΙΑΣ

Akr. Ag. Ioannis
Άκρ. Αγ. Ιωάννης

Vrouhas
Βρουχάς

Spinalonga
Σπιναλόγκα

M. Areliou
Μ.Αρετίου

Notaras
Νοφαλιάς
Νοφαλιάς

Fourni
Φούρνοι

Elounda
Ελούντα

Lenika
Λένικα

Psira
Ψείρα

Piskokefalo
Πισκοκέφαλο

Sitia
Σητεία

Akr. Plaka
Άκρ. Πλάκα

Ag. Fotia
Αγ. Φωτιά

Palekastro
Παλαίκαστρο
59

60

Ag. Nikolaos
Άγ. Νικόλαος

Mohlos
Μόχλος

Staka
Σφάκα

Exo Mouliana
Έξω Μουλιανά

Maronia
Μαρωνιά

Mitato
Μητάτο

Azokeramos
Αζόκεραμος

Lato
Λατώ

Ammoudara
Αμμουδάρα

Tholos
Θόλος

Orno
Ορνό

K. Kria
Κ. Κριά

Karidi
Καρίδι

63 **64**

61

Zakros
Ζάκρος

62

K. Zakros
Κ. Ζάκρος

Kroustas
Κρούστας

Pahia Ammos
Παχειά Άμμος

Kavousi
Kavousi

53

Krtsa
Κριτσά

1237

Thripts
Θρύπτης

Hrisopigi
Χρυσοπηγή

Handras
Χανδράς

65

Prina
Πρίνα

Kalo Horio
Καλό Χωριό

51

Lithines
Λιθίνες

Kalo Horio
Καλό Χωριό

Xerokambos
Ξερόκαμπος

30

Vasiliki
Βασιλική

Onno
Ορεινό

56

·818

M. Kapsa
Μ. Κάψα

Goudouras
Γούδουρας

Kalamafka
Καλαμαύκα

1476

55

Makrigialos
Μακρύγιαλος

Ag. Triada
Αγ. Τριάδα

57

Anatoli
Ανατολή

Gra Ligia
Γρά Λυγιά

Koutsouras
Κουτσουράς

Akr. Goudoura
Άκρ. Γούδουρα

Ierapetra
Ιεράπετρα

Ferma
Φέρμα

Koufonisi
Κουφονήσι

ΠΕΛΑΓΟΣ

Hrisi
Χρύση

Walking on Crete

Grade

Most of the walks presented here follow distinct paths and trails. This should not obscure the fact, however, that some routes demand sure-footedness and good route-finding ability. It also should be noted that in inclement weather, difficulties could increase significantly. To better assess the particular demands of the individual routes suggested here, the walks (walk numbers) are colour-coded. The meaning of the colour codes are as follows:

Easy These trails are usually sufficiently broad and only moderately steep, so that even during inclement weather, they are relatively easy to negotiate without difficulty. They may also be undertaken by children and older people without any great danger.

Moderate These paths and steep ascents are usually narrow and may include short, somewhat precipitous, stretches. For these reasons, they should only be undertaken by sure-footed walkers. Some short sections may even demand a higher degree of route-finding skill.

Difficult These paths and mule tracks are often narrow and steep. Some sections may be precarious or, alternatively, may traverse slopes that are dangerously slippery underfoot. In some cases, scrambling may be required where even the use of hands is demanded. Therefore, these trails should only be undertaken by sure-footed, physically fit and experienced mountain walkers with good route-finding skills.

In gorges, sometimes rugged boulder fields must be crossed (here in the Samaria Gorge).

Walking times and height differences

The times given reflect only the actual walking time and do not include rest stops or taking photos. The total walking time is noted in the walk header. The height differences given encompass the total of the height differences during the walk, including intermediate ascents and descents.

Refreshment

The possible stops for refreshment on the way are noted in the short information blocks for each of the individual walks. A symbol is used to indicate if a taverna, snack bar or a similar locality is to be found en route.

Seafood taverna in Loutro.

Dangers

Most of the walks follow distinct trails. Sections without a distinct path, with scrambling or with precipitous stretches demanding an excellent head for heights, will be specifically noted. In high mountain areas, clouds may suddenly gather, severely limiting visibility. Alpine walks in the White Mountains and the Psiloritis massif should only be undertaken when weather conditions

Symbols

🚌	accessible by bus/boat	⭫	church, chapel, monastery
✕	refreshment along the way	∴	archaeological site
🏃	suitable for children	⬧	castle, ruins
⬩⬟	settlement with bar/restaurant	☼	water mill
⬛	bar/restaurant	∩	cave
⬠	mountain hut, shelter	△	campsite
P	official car park	⅀	picnic area
🚌	bus connection	)(	bridge
⚓	pier, wharf	✺	viewpoint
†	peak	✿	monumental tree
)(	pass, saddle, col	◉	spring
⌐	turn-off left	○	reservoir, cistern
⌐	turn-off right	▭	swimming spot

Signs warning of rock fall are not always posted.

are absolutely stable. Heavy rainfall during the winter months can turn a usually dry stream bed running through a gorge into a raging river in no time at all. Also, in the gorges, there is the constant danger of falling rock, triggered by rain or grazing goats.

Fields of old snow should be skirted around whenever possible because there is the danger of breaking through a concealed hole caused by erosion or to sustain injuries caused by sharp jagged rocks hidden under the snow cover. While traversing slopes, there is also the danger of slipping. In summer, be sure that you do not underestimate the heat. If longer walks lacking in shade near the coast are planned, we strongly suggest that you start off at sunrise. Especially in the Samaria Gorge, it is quite common for less experienced walkers to suffer from exhaustion and circulatory problems on the way – the rescue personnel have their hands full; even fatal accidents have occurred.

Walking regions

Crete's dramatic mountain and coastal landscapes provide the framework for an extraordinarily diverse walking area. On the northern coast, between Rethymno and Kissamos, four peninsulas projecting into the Cretan Sea offer attractive areas for walking; even Akrotiri on Souda Bay, with a naval

GPS tracks

For each of the 65 walks contained in this walking guide, GPS tracks are available for download without charge at www.rother.de; also available are the alternative routes for Walks 5, 38, 56 and 57. You need to use the following user name: **gast** / password: **wfcregb02zw1kg**

All of the GPS data was recorded in situ by the author and some have been revised, especially those in the narrow gorges where GPS reception cannot be completely relied upon. The author and publishers have conscientiously reviewed the relevant GPS tracks and waypoints to the best of their knowledge. However, the physical properties of the area may have changed between times. GPS data is certainly a great help for planning and navigation, but still requires meticulous preparation and a certain degree of orientation skill as well as expertise in judging the (geographical) situation at hand. You should never depend solely on GPS devices or GPS data for orientation.

You can expect leftover snowfields well into the month of June (here on Melindaou).

base, an international airport and a NATO base, boasts of surprisingly quiet and pristine spots. Easy walks can be found, particularly in the walking region around Vamos on the Drapanos peninsula, and a long circular route can be undertaken on the Rodopou peninsula, an area that is almost completely deserted. In the southern interior of Kissamos, you will also discover some gorges and in the White Mountains, between Chania and the southern coast, you are guaranteed to experience the ultimate thrill of a high summit when reaching the end of a long climb on one of the two-thousand-metre peaks.

Southwestern Crete boasts of being one of the island's top walking regions. On the equally sparsely populated coastline here, the White Mountains drop ruggedly down to the Libyan Sea. Along the long-distance walking trail, *E4*, leading along the coast, you can tackle rewarding one-day stages between Paleochora and Chora Sfakion; in the evening, return to the starting point by ferry. Several attractive gorges can be explored on foot, especially the Samaria Gorge which attracts up to 3000 walkers daily in the high season. Because of this number, the route must be ripe for entry into the Guinness Book of Records as the most popular walk in the entire Mediterranean region. If you prefer to avoid crowds, the gorges of Imbros, Aradena and Agia Irini present more than enough alternative choice.

Walking reaches a peak, in the truest sense of the word, in the Ida mountain range in central Crete: if you are in good physical condition, you can scale the island's highest summit, the Psiloritis, at 2454 m. On the southern slopes of the range, you'll also find plenty of metres of altitude to negotiate when

The best walks on Crete

Gorges

Samaria Gorge

This classic tour is one of the most popular walks in Europe. If you feel uncertain about the long descent (1200 m along the »normal« route), you can choose the route from the seaside entrance to reach the famous bottleneck, the »Iron Gates«, faster and with relatively less effort (Walk 11, 5.40 hrs; Walk 22, 2.00 hrs).

Aradena Gorge

Right at the outset, the entrance from the tiny marble rock bay is spectacular. In its upper reaches, exit the gorge via a cobbled trail that ascends in zigzags to the abandoned village of Aradena (Walk 28, 6.15 hrs).

Rouwas Gorge

Above the spring-fed lake near Zaros, a breath-taking gorge opens up which can be climbed to an altitude of almost 1000 m. After the walk, a restaurant specializing in trout is an invitation to a rest stop (Walk 41, 4.00 hrs).

Kritsa Gorge

This very popular gorge is not particularly long nor does it boast very high walls, but indeed, you will be surprised by its narrow, bizarrely- eroded, bottlenecks (Walk 53, 1.30 hrs).

Mesonas Gorge

This panoramic circular walk leads through the Thripti Mountains and crosses over a spectacular bottleneck of the Mesonas Gorge. A botanical highlight is a monumental olive tree – boasting an estimated age of over 3000 years, the tree is one of the oldest of its kind in existence (Walk 54, 5.00 hrs).

Coastal trails & bathing bays

Agia Roumeli

Located at the seaside entrance of the Samaria Gorge, here is the starting point for a spectacular walk along the southern coastline. The destination is the car-free village of Loutro, situated in a stunning location at the foot of towering coastal cliffs (Walk 24, 5.00 hrs).

Damnoni Beach

This short circular walk around Cape Kako Mouri to Damnoni Beach promises captivating views of the Plakias bay and the coastal mountains on the other side (Walk 34, 1.50 hrs):

Preveli Beach

Perfect beaches can't be kept a secret for long, however, in the off-season, the onslaught of day trippers to this lagoon beach is somewhat less than usual – you can choose between bathing in freshwater or in sea water (Walk 35, 2.40 hrs).

Summits

Gingilos, 2080 m

With a north face exceeding 1000 m in height, this 2000 metre-peak is one of the White Mountains' most striking. You don't necessarily have to climb all the way to the top; already from the Afchenas saddle at 1700 m, a spectacular downwards view opens up of the southern coast (Walk 12, 5.40 hrs).

Psiloritis, 2454 m

From Crete's highest peak, enjoy a bird's eye view of the Libyan Sea to the south, as well as the Cretan Sea, facing the Aegean. Westwards, take in the White Mountains, and to the east, the Dikti Mountains (Walk 38, 7.50 hrs; Walk 39, 4.10 hrs).

Ancient sites & monasteries

Moni Katholiko

On the Akrotiri peninsula, a cobbled trail connects two monasteries to one another. Visit the »Bear Cave«, boasting beautiful stalagmites (Walk 9, 1.00 hrs).

Lissos

The best route from the little seaside resort of Sougia is the trail to the ancient Asclepeion temple where, amongst other finds, a mosaic floor has survived the ravages of time. A picturesque pebbled bay for bathing can also be found here (Walk 16, 3.00 hrs).

Moni Koudouma

At the foot of the Asterousia Mountains, an attractive coastal path leads to the Koudouma Monastery. Be absolutely sure to take the excursion to the Agios Antonios chapel cave (Walk 49, 3.20 hrs.).

Dead's Gorge (Zakros Gorge)

More than 3000 years ago, the Minoans placed their dead in the cave-like niches of this gorge. A palace was constructed at the mouth of the gorge. The »normal« route is not complicated but the circular walk through the secondary gorge of Xeropotamos is a little more demanding (Walk 62, 4.00 hrs; Walk 63, 3.40 hrs).

ascending to the Kamares cave or climbing through the Rouwas Gorge. South-eastwards from the Ida massif, discover even more rewarding destinations located the Asterousia Mountains. But you really don't have to climb so high; relatively easy coastal walks, especially in the Matala region, have their charm. In eastern Crete, walkers are usually drawn to the Lassithi Plateau. The fertile alluvial plain is surrounded by the Dikti mountain range, with peaks of over 2000 metres in height. Eastwards from there, the somewhat lower altitude Thripti Mountains boast some worthwhile routes.

Rather unjustly, the east coast of Crete is overshadowed by the other walking regions. The mountains here only reach altitudes of up to 800 m, accommodating just about any walker not necessarily interested in conquering greater heights. Dead's Gorge near Kato Zakros is a very popular destination, as is the famous palm-surrounded beach of Vai, but apart from those, you can follow coastal paths and discover bays for bathing that are still serene.

Trail network and waymarking

Ancient cobbled trails are called *kalderimia* in Greek. These are usually former connecting trails between villages. Apart from that purpose, they lead anywhere someone needed to go – to chapels, monasteries and fortresses, through gorges and up to alpine pastureland. Normally, the trails are about two metres, and even up to four metres, in width, so that two fully laden mules could pass each other without much difficulty. These trails have been carefully paved with stones that are as flat or rounded as available and are laboriously reinforced with retaining walls along the slopes; some are even given additional support with fieldstone walls. Originally, all of Crete was criss-crossed by a network of *kalderimia* which totalled several thousand kilometres, but only a fraction of these remain. Most were destroyed during modern road construction, although the original courses of the routes were often availed upon. Others fell victim to erosion or have become overgrown by *macchia* and prickly *phrygana*. Unlike, for example, in Mallorca, where similar trails have been recently restored to accommodate walking tourism, on Crete, the ancient trail network has yet to be acknowledged as part of the island's historical heritage, let alone recognised for its touristic potential. As far as individual initiatives for the preservation and maintenance of the *kalderimia* are concerned, they are immediately confronted with another serious problem: the painstaking restoration and maintenance work that is needed simply lacks the necessary financing. There are some exceptions, though, such as the breathtaking *kalderimi* from Anopoli to Loutro (Walk 29), which was overhauled with EU funding. The famous *kalderimi* through the Aradena Gorge (Walk 28) is also well-preserved, as are some intact stretches along the connecting trail between Agia Irini and Omalos (Walk 21). In addition, many more of the suggested walks in this guide lead, at least sometimes, along ancient cobbled trails.

As if drawn using a straight edge, the cobblestone kalderimi in the Aradena Gorge.

Aside from the *kalderimia*, there is also an extensive network of mountain paths, coastal trails and gorge trails. Many of these have also been way-marked in the meantime. However, the waymarking system is still in its infancy here and cannot be compared to the waymarking found in the Alps or in the secondary mountain ranges of Western Europe. At the starting points in many locations, you can usually find a trail board presenting an overview of the walking region and, on the way, coloured waymarkers, as well as the traditional cairn, being used for orientation. These makeshift markers are naturally subject to the winds of change. Coloured dots painted on rocks and directional arrows fade quickly under the Mediterranean sun and the life expectancy of a cairn can be even shorter. Brushwood and phrygana only need a few years to produce enough impenetrable undergrowth to choke off a path. Occasionally, you will need a little route-finding ability to remain on the right track because even good route description has its limits.

Wind and weather

Boasting about 300 days of sunshine annually, Crete is the sunniest and warmest destination to be found on the Med, next to Cyprus. The Mediterranean climate is characterised by hot, dry summers and cool, wet winters. The change of the seasons can bring about fickle weather conditions. Prevailing northerly and westerly winter winds bring relatively large amounts of rainfall which can turn into snowfall in the higher elevations. The snow line is located at about 700 m above sea level. Most precipitation occurs in December and

January. The amount of rainfall decreases from the west towards the east, so that in Chania, it rains more often and for longer periods than it does in Sitia and Palekastro; the least amount of rainfall is in Ierapetra. Prevailing winds are from the northwest; on the southern coast, the occasionally turbulent *sirocco* carries hot air and reddish dust from the Sahara along with it. In summer, on the northern coast, the *meltemi* wind provides some refreshing coolness. Generally, it is about 2 °C warmer on the southern coast than in the north.
Weather forecast: www.meteo.gr/stations/chania/crete.htm

Walking weather throughout the seasons

March and April: For walkers interested in botany, this is a very good time to visit and to enjoy the mild temperatures; however, you can expect fickle weather and occasional rainfall. Walking is limited to the coastal routes and lower altitudes in the mountainous areas since snow is still lying at heights of over 1000 metres above sea level.

May to mid-June: This is the very best time for walking, with pleasant air temperatures and very little rainfall. Water temperature lies at about 20 °C. The island is already covered in green vegetation. Above 1800 m, into the month of June, you may still run into snowfields left over from winter.

Mid-June to mid-September: Stable, hot, mid-summer weather. Because of the intense heat, these months are more suitable for a beach holiday; in August, temperatures can climb up to 40 °C on the coast. Longer walks are only recommended in the mountainous areas starting at altitudes of 800 m and further up. Conditions are ideal for ascending a two-thousand-metre peak.

Mid-September to late October: The relaxed off-season with initially very warm weather and the best conditions for swimming. Above all, October is a very good month for walking. The landscape is fairly arid and burned-out as an aftermath of the summertime heat, but this does not play much of a role in the mountainous areas, which are usually barren anyway.

Climate table for Heraklion

	Month	1	2	3	4	5	6	7	8	9	10	11	12	Year
Day	°C	15	15	16	20	23	27	29	29	27	24	20	16	21,8
Night	°C	9	9	10	12	15	19	22	22	20	17	14	11	15
Water	°C	16	15	16	16	19	22	24	25	24	23	20	17	19,8
Sunshine/hrs		3	5	6	8	10	12	13	12	10	6	6	4	7,9
Rainy days		14	9	10	6	4	1	1	1	2	6	11	14	79

November: Days are still pleasantly mild, but occasionally, autumn storms and heavy rainfall can spoil a walking tour. On the south coast, weather is still good for swimming.

December to February: This is Crete's rainy season, but that does not necessarily mean that it is pouring down with rain every day. Snow may fall in mountainous areas above 700 m. On the comparatively arid southern coast, temperatures rarely drop below 15 °C, thus offering pleasant walking weather. At night, however, it can get quite cool and not all of the hotels that are still open can boast effective heating.

UNESCO World Biosphere Reserve, Samaria Gorge.

Samaria National Park

The most famous gorge on the island of Crete was designated a national park in 1962. In 1981, UNESCO had the area declared a Biosphere Reserve. Not only taking into consideration the extraordinary beauty of the towering gorge walls, the ancient trees and the rare wildflowers, the creation of the national park was especially targeted to establish a protected area for the Cretan Ibex, which was an endangered species at the time.

The gorge begins at about 1200 m in the high country in Omalos, crosses through the White Mountains and, 17 kms later, merges into a broad delta which empties into the Libyan Sea. Xyloskalo, the starting point in the mountains, takes its name from a wooden stairway constructed by goatherds in the 19th century, afterwards expanded to provide a convenient access trail in the upper reaches of the gorge. In the sometime village of Samaria, ancient houses built of quarried stone were restored to create a popular haven for walkers from all over the world.

The E4 long-distance walking trail

A section of the *E4* European long-distance walking trail (in Greek: Monopati Epsilon Tessera) starts off at the harbour in Kissamos and traverses the entire length of the island to arrive in Kato Zakros on the east coast. Posts with diamond-shaped waymarkings and with yellow/black blazes are set along the trail. The signposting, however, leaves a lot to be desired. In many cases, finding the trail is very difficult since it is not well maintained and many of the posts have gone missing in between times. Several of the diamond-shaped markings have been riddled with bullet holes – the Cretans see them as perfect targets. Starting from Kissamos, the *E4* leads at first along the west coast to the south coast and on to Paleochora. In Sougia, it divides into a coastal stretch or a mountain alternative; the two routes merge again near Imbros. Some stages are extensive stretches through uninhabited territory, making it necessary to spend a night outdoors. Water isn't available everywhere, so carry sufficient amounts of drinking water along with you. For the 320 km-long trek, plan at least three, or even better four, weeks to walk it.

Mountain huts

The only staffed mountain hut is the Kallergi hut, 1592 m, in the White Mountains (tel +30-28210-44647, mobile +30-6976-585849, www.eoshanion.gr, www.kallergi.co). Access is from Xyloskalo, at the rim of the Omalos high plateau, via a 5 km-long gravel track (Walk 13). The hut sleeps up to 50 persons and costs €10–€14 per night and per person. In addition, breakfast and dinner can be booked. The hut is open from the middle of April until the end of October. Advance reservations are requested.

Apart from the Kallergi hut, two others exist in the White Mountains: the Volikas hut, 1300 m, and the Katsiveli hut, 1970 m; the latter is the starting point for climbing Pachnes, 2453 m. Information available through the EOS Mountain Climbers' Club in Chania (tel. +30-28210-44647, www.eoshanion.gr).

On the western slopes of Psiloritis, the EOS/Section Rethymno (tel. +30-28310-57766, www.eosrethymnou.gr) manages the Stoumbotos-Prinos hut, 1600 m. Starting at the village of Fourfouras, about a 3.5-hour ascent along the *E4* takes you there. Information for the Prinos hut, 1050 m, on the eastern slopes of Psiloritis is available from the EOS/Section Heraklion (tel. +30-2810-227609, www.eos-her.gr), from Ano Asites, the hut can be reached in about a 2-hour climb (Walk 43).

Maps

■ The best selection is the Anavasi walking maps in the scale 1:25,000; these cover the most important walking regions. The tear-resistant maps are available locally (e.g., in the Bookshop Matala) and many souvenir shops. In addition, you could purchase maps in leading map stores or order them through the internet (e.g., directly from www.anavasi.gr). The following maps have been published so far: 11.11 Lefka Ori/Sfakia, 11.12 Lefka Ori/Pachnes, 11.13 Samaria/Sougia/Paleochora, 11.14 Mt. Ida/Psiloritis, 11.15 Mt. Dikti, 11.16 Zakros/Vai, 11.17 Frangokastelo/Plakias and 11.18 Asterousia/Phaistos.

■ Also published by Anavasi is the »Crete Atlas« (1:50,000) in book form. The atlas covers the entire island and also contains some interesting detailed maps for the individual walking regions. It is too heavy and impractical to carry along, however, many of the old cobbled trails are also included in it.

The Kallergi hut is precipitously enthroned on a ridge above the Samaria Gorge.

- The Harms-ic-Verlag offers the maps »Crete – Eastern Part« and »Crete – Western Part«, both with a scale of 1:100,000. Aside from the *E4*, most of the other important trails are marked in, but for an exact orientation in situ, these maps are limited in their reliability.
- A good road map is »Crete« (1:150,000) from Freytag & Berndt; the long distance trail *E4* is also marked on this map. A city index is included and is very useful.

Field guides
- Anastasios Sakoulis: »Amphibians, Reptiles and Mammals of Crete«, Mystis Editions. The island's most important birds of prey are described in this guide (only available locally).
- Vangelis Papiomitoglou, »Wildflowers of Greece« Mediterraneo Editions: this field guide encompasses around 600 different species of Cretan flora and special consideration is given to the numerous endemic species (available in many local book stores).
- Horst and Gisela Kretschmar: »Orchids: Crete and Dodecanese«, Mediterraneo Editions. Includes about 100 species of orchids, occurring on Crete and the Dodecanese.

Landscapes and natural areas

The Greeks call their southernmost and largest island Megalonisos. After Sicily, Sardinia, Cyprus and Corsica, Crete is the fifth largest island in the Med. About half of its population lives in the urban centres of Heraklion, Chania and Rethymno; one in four live in the greater metropolitan region of the capital.

Mountains

The island's land relief is determined by four major mountain ranges. Western Crete is dominated by the White Mountains (*Lefka Ori*). These mountains, the island's largest in area, live up to their name in winter when an uninterrupted blanket of snow lies over them. About 40 of its peaks reach an altitude of over 2000 m, the highest of which is Pachnes, at 2452 m. The karst mountains drop abruptly southwards to the Libyan Sea and are sliced by about 20 major gorges, the most notable being the Samaria Gorge which, with a length of somewhat more than 17 km, counts as one of the largest and most impressive canyons in Europe. Crete's geographical centre is formed by the Ida Mountains (also known as the Psiloritis massif). With Psiloritis (also called Timios Stavros) at 2454 m, the highest peaks on the island are found here. Deforestation and overgrazing has left a rugged mountainous terrain, overgrown with thorny cushion scrub. On the southern slopes, the mountain villages of Kamares and Zaros offer attractive walks; on the northern slopes, Anogia is a good starting point for ascending Psiloritis.

The Nida high plain at the foot of Psiloritis.

The counterparts to the White Mountains in the west are the Dikti Mountains in the east. These are not quite so extensive, but indeed, the summit trio of Dikti, 2148 m, Lazaros, 2085 m, and Afendis Christos, 2141 m, can be also counted among the 2000- metre peaks. Easiest access is via the Lassithi plateau. Situated even further to the east, the Thripti Mountains and the adjacent Orno range are not quite as high; the most elevated summit in this group is Afendis Stavromenos at 1476 m.

In addition to the four major mountain ranges, quite a few smaller mountainous regions can be mentioned. Interesting for walkers are the Asterousia Mountains, towering above the southern coast and surmounted by the striking summit of Kofinas, 1231 m. Shielded by the Psiloritis massif, the range receives relatively little rainfall and, accordingly, the entire region is characteristically dry and barren.

High plateaus and lowlands

Some extensive high plateaus are sprawling between the mountain ranges; most of them are used as pastureland for sheep and goats. For the walker, the high plains are starting points for walks in the surrounding mountains. Thus, setting off from the Omalos plateau, you can climb a number of 2000 m peaks in the White Mountains. The Nida high plateau in the Ida Mountains is the starting point for an excursion to the island's highest summit. The only highland inhabited year-round is the Lassithi plateau in eastern Crete; with an area of 48 sq.kms, it is also the largest on the island.

The most extensive lowland is the Messara plain. 40 km long and up to 12 km wide, it is shielded by the Psiloritis massif and the Asterousia Mountains and counts as one of the island's most important agricultural regions. Not only olives, but also citrus fruit and winter vegetables are cultivated here. The capital is Mires, where a major market is held every Saturday.

Gorges and caves

Perhaps no other island in the Mediterranean can boast such a large number of gorges, a total of 125, only counting the major ones. The beauty of it is that many of these are open to walkers. The Samaria Gorge is a must, so to speak; also high on the list, is the gorge located in Imbros on the southern edge of the Askifou high plateau and Dead's Gorge on the easternmost end

The Gulf of Kissamos with the Gramvousa peninsula (view from Walk 3).

of the island. In addition, there are many more easily accessible and less known canyons that are also worth visiting. For avid gorge walkers, this guide presents more than 20 walks of this kind.

There are about 3400 caves on the island. The Minoans used many of them as places of worship. The most famous one is the Dictaean Cave (Dikteon Andron) in Lassithi; according to Greek mythology, Zeus was born here. Visitors can climb 84 m down into the illuminated cave where, in the up to 20 metre-high chamber, fascinating stalagmites and stalactites can be seen. Also claiming to be the birthplace of Zeus is the Cave of Zeus (Ideon Andron) in the Psiloritis massif. Although easily accessible via a tarmac road, the cave has not yet been developed as a tourist attraction. The Kamares Cave, on the southern slopes of Psiloritis (Walk 40), is only accessible on foot. Thin shards of ceramic found here from so-called »eggshell pottery«, dating back to the period 2000–1700 BC, are considered representative of a unique style. Somewhat more modest in significance, but even so historically noteworthy in part, and also only accessible on foot, are the dripstone caves of Agios Georgios, Arkoudiotissa, Polifimos, Agios Antonios and Pelekita (Walks 9, 15, 19, 26, 49 and 64).

Peninsulas, coastlines and beaches

In the northwest, Crete draws attention to itself visually through its extensive peninsulas, some stretching far out to sea. Despite claiming only a modest geographical area, the coastal mountains on Gramvousa and Rodopou tower almost 800 m out of the water. These peninsulas are virtually uninhabited and are ideal for walking. The northern coast is edged with broad, sweeping bays with miles of gently sloping, sandy beaches. In summer, the sprawling beaches attract millions of sea-loving tourists looking for relief from the intense heat. Extremely popular and crowded is the »Cretan Riviera« between Limenas Chersonisou and Malia. However, Crete's most beautiful and unspoilt beaches are to be found elsewhere, such as in Vai and in Xerokambos towards the east or in Elafonisi and Balos westwards. On the southern coast, with a few exceptions, you will only find small bathing bays, usually with pebble beaches. Kommos Beach on the Gulf of Messara is the longest beach and is, for the most part, unspoiled. The general quality of the waters is good to very good and the Blue Flag waves over almost 100 individual beaches, but occasionally, beach tar, and in unmanaged bay areas, jetsam and plastic flotsam, can blemish the joy of bathing.

Nature and the environment

With the creation of the national park in the Samaria Gorge a good 50 years ago, an important step was taken to protect some of the natural terrain on Crete. However, considering the total area allotted to nature reserves, it's negligible. Designating a conservation area on Crete doesn't necessarily mean that everything will actually be running splendidly. Environmental awareness is still in its infancy here. Dumping refuse in the countryside, polluted beaches, untreated sewage flowing into the sea and the widespread agricultural use of pesticides and fertilisers compose only the tip of the iceberg. Centuries of deforestation have also left their mark. Reforestation programs have failed so far, not only because of lack of interest, but also because of animal husbandry – grazing sheep and goats have stripped many areas of the island completely bare.

Unfortunately, not always taken to heart.

Funds are unavailable for just about everything and investment in a sustainable environmental policy is hardly feasible for the foreseeable future. At least, you can do your part, no matter how insignificant it may seem, to avoid contributing to the island's problems and to leave things as they were before you came.

8000 years of island history

Quite a few researchers and archaeologists consider Crete the cradle of European civilisation or, at least, the first civilised culture on European soil. The first traces of settlement from the Neolithic Era date back to 8000 years ago. Over the millennia, many invaders and conquerors have left their »footprints« on the island.

The legacy of the Minoan Culture

Before the Englishman, Sir Arthur Evans (1851–1941), began his excavations at Knossos in 1900, no one knew of the island's incredible history. In the ruins of 4000 year-old Knossos, Evans found traces of a vanished culture. With a lot of imagination and concrete, he resurrected columns and walls and turned Knossos into a kind of archaeological Disneyland where visitors to this day are presented with a conceptual realisation of such quarters as the Throne Room or the Queen's Bath, as well as brightly coloured frescoes, which are, for the most part, based on figments of Evans' imagination. Evans created a personal vision of a highly developed culture. Many of his theories were groundbreaking for researchers, but others are pure speculation. Even today's usual term for this cultural period »Minoan« is actual one of Evans' inventions. Minos is a legendary figure in Greek mythology, whose father was claimed to be Zeus and his mother, the Princess Europa, who was kidnapped by Zeus and taken to Crete. Whether a King Minos actually existed, remains completely unknown.

In Evans' footsteps, countless archaeologists journeyed to the island and excavated other major settlements and palaces, such as Festos, Malia and Kato Zakros. It is a real mystery that these places were apparently not fortified. Did the Minoans live in peace for thousands of years? Was it thanks to their position as the leading naval power that they had no fear of enemies? Nobody can say what ultimately led to the downfall of the Minoan empire.

Transient rulers

After the fall of the Minoan empire, the rise of the Hellenistic culture, with their centres in Athens, Olympia, Corinth and Sparta on the mainland of Greece, caused Crete to become quite isolated. Beginning in 67 BC, the Romans were the impetus for a modest revival of the island. The new province, including the North African region of Cyrenaica (today's Libya), was governed from the capital city of Gortis where the Roman Culture set down roots through temples, theatres and spas. The new rulers invested heavily in infrastructure, building roads and aqueducts, and turning the Messara plain into a granary for the Roman Empire. The Apostle Paul landed on the southern coast of Crete in 59 AD, probably making landfall at Kali Limenes, and began spreading Christian teaching to the island.

After the division of the Roman Empire in 395 AD, Crete became a part of the Byzantine Empire and was governed by Constantinople until it was conquered by the Arabs in 826 AD. The Arabs were only able to hold out for a short time, and in 961, Crete became Byzantine once again. After the fall of the Byzantine Empire, Crete fell to the city-state of Venice which was controlling a large part of the Mediterranean as a new hegemonic power. The Venetians came to Crete in 1204 and remained for four and a half centuries. They surrounded the cities of Chania, Rethymno and Heraklion with fortress-

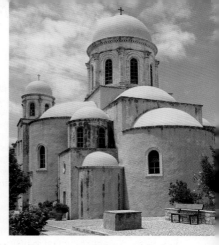

Venetian monastery Agia Triada.

es, constructed pompous aristocratic palaces and fountains and built monasteries in the Renaissance style. A relief of the Lion of St. Mark graces some fortifications even today.

The Venetians were followed by the Turks in 1669. There is very little good to say about their reign. The new conquerors ruled the destiny of the island with an iron hand, converted churches into mosques and struck down Cretan rebellions with much bloodshed. Following the Greco-Turkish War in 1913, Crete finally aligned with Greece.

World War II

Another dark chapter in the history of the island was brought about by the Second World War. As the crossroads for Europe, Africa and the Middle East, Crete became the plaything of strategic military interest. The German invasion began on May 20, 1941 with »Operation Mercury«, as 8620 paratroopers were dropped on Cretan soil. In battles against allied British forces stationed on Crete, the German battalions suffered heavy losses, but were still able to set up an occupation force on the island within ten days. The Cretan resistance was, however, far from broken. Partisans perpetuated acts of sabotage time and again and the Germans struck back with brutal reprisals. During the four years of occupation, about 40 villages were razed to the ground and the entire male population living in them were summarily executed. The bloody war claimed about 8000 victims. In the mountain villages of Anogia and Kandanos, as well as on other sites of the resistance, monuments have been erected to commemorate the times.

Cretan flora

A walk on Crete is a feast for the senses. Already starting at the end of January, the almonds are flowering above the Gulf of Mirabello; in early spring, daisies, yellow-flowering Jerusalem Sage and bright red poppies cover the slopes. Delicate orchids duck their heads, seeking shelter under prickly Cushion plants. The pungent scents of oregano, wild sage and thyme fill the air. Around Easter time, Crown Daisies carpet the areas of fallow land and, just in time for Pentecost, peonies unfold their lovely flowers. Somewhat later, on the high plains and the alpine meadows, white-flowering Cyclamen, dark-pink wild tulips and the iris, named after the messenger of the gods, appear. In the sub-alpine mountain areas, spring begins in June. After the snow melts, glory-of-the-snow and bugloss break out into the sunlight and on the summit of Gingilos, at 2080 m, the Spreading Cherry is blooming. Only in the arid summer months do the flowers take a breather, but indeed, only a few days after the first rainfall in autumn, they are brought back to life, so to speak, in a second spring. Among the approximately 1800 wild species of flora, there are about 170 endemics, that is, species that are only found on Crete and nowhere else in the world.

In the right place at the right time: the Lassithi Plateau in May.

Forests and characteristic trees

In prehistoric times, the entire island was covered by dense forest, but today, woodland takes up only about five percent of the total terrain. One of Crete's characteristic trees is the cypress (Cupressus sempervirens). »Tuscan« cypress trees can also be found here, but when comparing the differences between the two, the Cretan cypress usually grows asymmetrically and takes on bizarre contortions. The oldest specimens can be found in the Samaria Gorge, some of which date back to the Middle Ages.

Extensive stands of Turkish pine (Pinus brutia) can be found as well in the Samaria Gorge. This conifer, which can reach heights up to 30 m, also puts in an appearance at the foot of the Asterousia Mountains and in the Thripti Mountains. In addition to using the pinewood, the Greeks have also found a use for pine resin – they take it to »rosin up«, what is perhaps, their best known wine, *retsina*.

One of a kind is the Cretan Date Palm (Phoenix theophrasti), which thrives in only a few locations, mainly on the beaches of Vai and Preveli. Otherwise, these can only be found on Rhodes and on the Turkish Mediterranean coast. The tree's botanical name is taken from the ancient Greek naturalist and student of Aristotle, Theophrast (about 371–287 BC), who first described this palm tree in a botanical compendium.

Cypress (above), Turkish pine (centre), Cretan Date Palm (below).

Compared to the true Date Palm, the Cretan Date Palm seldom reaches heights of over 10 m, however, it can develop multiple trunks. The fibrous fruits it produces are not edible. The Oriental plane tree (Platanus orientalis) has existed on Crete since ancient times. According to the myth, Zeus is supposed to have copulated with the kidnapped Europa under the plane tree from Gortyn. Plane trees thrive in wet areas; their preferred habitat, in the company of oleanders, is on the banks of rivers. With their broad tree-tops, they are a popular shade tree adorning many a village square. One of the mightiest specimens of this deciduous tree, which reaches heights of up to 30 m, is located on the *platia* of Krasi and is an estimated 2000 years old.

Macchia and phrygana

On cleared forest land, a typical mixture of Mediterranean scrub, called *macchia*, composed of evergreen sclerophyllous plants, has taken up residence. Compared to other Mediterranean islands, its allotment in Crete is relatively modest. This brushwood, which can grow to heights up to 6 m, is primarily made up of mastic (Pistacia lentiscus), myrtle, arbutus, juniper and terebinth (Pistacia terebinthus). This botanical community also embraces a number of evergreen oaks; the kermes oak (Quercus coccifera), for example, is wide-spread. Superb specimens of this tree, growing up to 15 m in height under favourable conditions, can be found, for example, at the starting point for the ascent to the Kamares Cave (Walk 40).

In addition to the kermes oak, there are also holm oaks (Quercus ilex) and Downy Oaks (Quercus pubescens), also, to a lesser extent, Valonia oaks (Quercus macrolepis). An ancient stand of these oaks can be found on the road between Rethymno and Koxare.

Prickly juniper

Terebinth.

In the present day, Phrygana is the most common form of vegetation found on Crete; about a quarter of the island is covered in it. This plant community is regarded as degenerate scrubland; the bushes only grow to a maximum of about one metre in height, but are rarely shorter than knee-high. Many of the evergreen plants sport leaves of a leathery texture, thereby reducing evaporation and allowing the plants to survive well through periods of summer drought.

Sea squill.

Your first acquaintance with phrygana may be a somewhat prickly affair. Most of the plants are armed with thorns to protect them from grazing goats. At second glance, phrygana is revealed as a plant community with a diversity of dwarf shrubs and cushion scrub. A dominant species is the prickly burnet (Sarcopoterium spinosum), whose squarrose bracts are to be found everywhere. A member of the rose family, in spring, the plant produces fleshy fruit about the size of a cherry pit.

During the summer in the coastal areas, maritime squill (Urginea maritima) accentuates the landscape with stems bearing white flowers; a member of the lily family, the plant's flowering shoots form on

Pink rock rose.

a bulb, almost completely protruding from the ground, which can weigh in at one or two kilos.

Among the four members of the rock-rose family found on Crete, the pink rock rose (Cistus creticus) plays a unique role. The plant is easy to spot due to its pink petalled flowers which always bear a somewhat »wrinkled-look«. The resin, called »labdanum«, excreted from the epidermal stomata of the leaves, has been revered for its healing properties since time immemorial. In days gone by, to harvest this resin, leather straps were swept over the plants, so that the sap would collect on the straps' surfaces.

Autumn croci (Colchium macrophyllum) are often flowering in the understory of olive groves.

Among the most striking flora of the phrygana community is Cretan ebony (Ebenus cretica). From April to June, this member of the legume family creates dense mats of flora, covering road embankments, rocky slopes and fallow land in the middle elevations in a pink sea of flowers. In times gone by, the thick-haired tassels were collected for use as a filling for pillows.

The phrygana plant community also includes wild herbs, such as thyme, sage, oregano and rosemary, as well as various species of mint. Enjoying the protection provided by a cover of cushion shrub and of the ever-present gorse, grape hyacinths, wild tulips, and top lavender can be found. In terrain composed of chalky soil, Jerusalem sage (Phlomis fruticosa) flowers from April until June.

Seaside plants, crevice flora and cushion scrubland

Some examples of seaside plants are sea spurge, sea daffodil and star thistle just to name a few. Mostly found on the eastern coast, Spiny Rush grow in extensive thickets and, on rocky coastlines, one can spot Sea Lavender and rock samphire. In areas near the coastline, Chasteberry (Vitex agnus-castus) has taken root. Of the family lamiaceae, these produce lilac-coloured flowers from which fruit the size of peppercorns are brought forth. The plant is often referred to as Monk's Pepper and, in the Middle Ages, it could be found in many a monastery garden and was used by monks as an anaphrodisiac against »sins of the flesh« to make it easier for them to adhere to the vow of chastity. Monk's Pepper grows wild near freshwater lakes, streams and especially in gorges, for example, at the outflow of the Aradena Gorge and Dead's Gorge in Kato Zakros; it flowers continuously from summer right into the autumn.

In the gorges, largely protected from human intervention and browsing goats, a unique colony of flora has taken root in the rocky crevices. One of the more well known species is the dittany of Crete (Origanum dictamnus), which gets its name from the Dikti Mountains. Since ancient times, the Cretans have considered the plant, which is related to wild marjoram, a miracle cure for relieving not only nagging aches and pains, but also serious diseases.

The tree line is situated at about 1700 m above sea level in Crete. Above it, a sub-alpine, thorny cushion plant scrubland covers the rough and rocky limestone terrain. A rare endemic found in the White Mountains is the Anchusa cespitosa. This plant, belonging to the borage family, thrives in altitudes between 1200 and 2200 m, where it grows close to the ground and presents its dark blue flowers in the spring. You can find it, for example, during the ascent to Melindaou (Walk 13).

Up to altitudes as high as of 2000 m, the glory-of-the-snow flower (Chionodoxa nana) can also be chanced upon. With its small, bright-blue flowers, it is also known as Cretan star hyacinth. Not long after the snow begins to melt, various species of Crocus pop their heads up, seeking the sunshine; one of the most beautiful is Sieber's crocus (Crocus sieberi) whose domain, like Anchusa cespitosa, is restricted to the White Mountains.

Sea daffodil (above), Cretan star hyacinth (centre), Sieber's crocus (below).

Oleander, arum lilies and orchids

Oleander is the typical Mediterranean plant to crown them all. It is one of Crete's most common shrubs and displays its flowers throughout the entire springtime until well into summer. In the wild, it serves as a decorative ornamental bush, growing along stream courses and in the outflow of gorges. In addition, oleander is cultivated everywhere you look; in the park grounds of hotels and along the roads, such as the National Highway between Chania and Agios Nikolaos, where its rose and white-coloured flowers delight the eye for over two hundred kilometres. As fragrant as the flowers of the oleander are, the plant itself is equally as poisonous. The leaves contain a highly toxic alkaloid, so that even goats shun them.

Red-flowering oleander in Lissos valley.

Among the most striking of Crete's natural flora are members of the arum family of plants. An elongated spathe grows out of an arrowhead-shaped, yellow bract and, colours depending on the specimen, encloses a spike-like spadix boasting tiny flowers. The island lays claim to two endemic species, the Cretan arum lily (Arum creticum) and the Ida arum lily (Arum idaeum) which takes its name from the Ida Mountains, although it also occurs in other mountain ranges. It is somewhat smaller than the Cretan arum lily and produces a white/green spadix with a purple and black coloured spathe. Also belonging to the arum family is the Dragon Arum (Dracunculus vulgaris), also known as the Snake Lily. The violet-coloured spathe with the same colour spadix can reach a height of up to one metre. The plant attracts insects for pollination with its pungent smell and only releases them after they have done their work. Extensive stands of Dragon Arum can be found, for example, in the gorges of Samaria and Agia Irini.

Cretan arum lily.

Dragon Arum.

Crete is an island of orchids as well, boasting around 70 species. The main period of flowering is in March. In macchia and open grassland, the Italian orchid (Orchis italica) and the Pyramidal orchid (Anacamptis pyramidalis) are widespread. The Four-spotted Orchis (Orchis quadripunctata) can often be found growing along many trails. This delicate orchid can be easily identified by four spots on the lip of the pink flower. In bloom from the end of March until mid-May, the orchid usually appears in terrain in altitudes of up to 1200 m, for example, in the Rouwas Gorge, in the Thripti Mountains and on Jouchtas, where other rare species, such as the Sawfly orchid (Ophrys tenthredinifera) and Ariadne's ophrys (Ophrys cretica), occur. Threatened with extinction is the Hooded helleborine (Cephalanthera cucullata): with a fair amount of luck, walkers may spot these at the upper reaches of the Rouwas Gorge.

Settlements and attractions

With over 50 major seaside resorts on Crete, you are truly spoilt for choice. While on the northern coast, the majority of tourists are on a package tour, on the southern and eastern coasts, there are many independent travellers wending their own way. In places like Agia Galini, Plakias and Paleochora, the choice of small family-run guesthouses and holiday apartments is huge; even without a reservation, you normally have a good chance of finding a room. Only during the high season in summer, should you make arrangements well in advance. Looking for accommodation on site not only gives you the advantage of choosing location and amenities in your own sweet time, but you will also be able to change locality and walking region as you wish. Given the size of the island, this makes perfect sense. For example, Agios Nikolaos is, indeed, too far away from the White Mountains for a day trip and, the other way round, no one would think of exploring the eastern coast from their location in Chania, a good 4 hour's drive away, so as to walk through Dead's Gorge.

Kissamos (Kastelli)
The provincial capital, situated in the wide sweeping Gulf of Kissamos, hasn't really been discovered by tourists. From the harbour located westwards from the city, car ferries service the mainland (Peloponnese) and, in season, excursion boats bring day-trippers to the rock island of Gramvousa and to the lagoon at Balos.

Guests at the Hotel Galini Beach (Kissamos) have direct access to the beach.

Excursions: The beach of Falasarna on the west coast counts as one of the most attractive bathing spots on the island. In the southwest, the former nunnery of Chrissoskalitissa perches spectacularly at the top of a rocky cliff, about 140 m above the sea.

The earth pyramids at Potamida near Kissamos.

Walking: Kissamos is a good starting point for exploring the northwesternmost corner of the island. Very attractive are the walks along the Gramvousa and Rodopou peninsulas (Walks 1–4). In the hinterland, there are numerous gorges to explore (Walks 5, 6 and 8) and also, starting at the eco village of Milia, you can enjoy nice walks (Walk 7). Additional walks in the area: 9 and 10.

Accommodation: Hotel Galini Beach, tel. +30-28220-23288, www.galini-beach.com. This family-run hotel (25 air-conditioned rooms with balconies) is situated directly at the beach on the eastern village limits. Manolis Sergentakis and his team welcome new guests as if they were old friends. Good value for the money (DR starting at €48).

East of Kissamos and on the western side of the Rodopou peninsula, we can recommend the Ravdoucha Beach Studios, tel. +30-69399-95465, www.ravdouchabeachstudios.gr (2 persons for €45–60); excellent location on a pebble beach and, at the end of a narrow access road, absolutely quiet.

Info: www.kissamos.net.

Chania

The second largest city on the island, with about 55,000 inhabitants, is the most urban and, because of the ferry port of Souda and the Daskalogiannis International Airport on the Akrotiri peninsula, is also western Crete's public transport centre. With the White Mountains providing a backdrop, the Old Town presents one of the most picturesque cityscapes in the entire eastern Mediterranean. Don't expect to find a sleepy little town here however; during the day, outside of the car-free pedestrian passageways, traffic is congested and hectic.

Worth seeing: Chania possesses a magnetic attraction for tourists. The Old Town, surrounding the picturesque harbour, has been largely influenced by the Venetians and the Ottomans and, thus, many a restored Venetian *palazzo* has been converted to a hotel serving tourism. In the Old Town, you will find chic boutique-style hotels located next to small and humble pensions. The major beach hotel complexes for package holiday guests are located on the seaside road to the west of Chania in the settlements of Agia Marina, Platanias and Gerani. Some of the landmarks include the Venetian lighthouse, the

A little textile arts shop in Anogia.

castle at the harbour and the domed Janissary mosque.

Walking: Chania is an excellent starting point for walking in the White Mountains. The main attraction is the Samaria Gorge; in the high season, numerous busses drive up to the Omalas Plateau daily. From there, you can descend into the gorge or climb peaks, such as Gingilos and Melindaou (Walks 11–13). The peninsulas of Akrotiri, Drapanos and Rodopou are also close at hand (Walks 2, 3, 4, 9 and 10), even some single day excursions along the southern coast starting at Chora Sfakion and Sougia as well as through the Imbros Gorge are possible (Walks 22–24 and 27–31).

Tourist information: EOT, Kriari 40, tel. +30-28210-92943, www.chania.eu.

Rethymno

Crete's third largest city with about 28,000 inhabitants is located between Heraklion and Chania. In the last few years, the miles of beaches stretching westwards and eastwards from the Old Town have been built up into major tourist centres which are exceeded only by the Malia Bay in the number of beds available. Also attractive for tourists are the little seaside resorts of Panormo and Bali to the east, as well as the major package holiday centre of Georgioupolis to the west, located on a large estuary.

Worth seeing: Both the Venetians and the Turks have left their mark in the genial Old Town. Many of the old *palazzi*, as well as the castle, are Venetian, for example, and within the walls of the castle, both a church and a mosque have found a home.

Walking: In the hinterland, numerous worthwhile walks can be undertaken, for example, in the Valley of the Mills or the little circular walk around Argyroupoli (Walks 36 and 37). The Drapanos Peninsula is also not far away (Walk 10). If you have a car, both the walking regions of the White Mountains, as well as of Anogia on the northern side of the Psiloritis massif, are relatively easy to reach. Plakias, Preveli and Agia Galini can also be approached by bus (Walks 11–13, 33–35, 38, 39 and 44).

Accommodation: Youth Hostel Rethymno, Tobazi 41, tel. +30-28310-22848, www.yhrethymno.com. A simple hostel with dormitory rooms located in the Venetian Old Town; an international clientele (€12, per person).

Tourist information: Prokima Eleftherios Venizelou (on the seaside promenade), tel. +30-28310-29148, www.rethymnon.gr.

Heraklion

The American writer, Henry Miller, wrote in 1940: »Every inch of Heraklion is worth being painted«. Today, many holiday makers would disagree; most of them give the island's metropolis and fifth largest city (173,000 inhabitants) a wide berth and only a few want to spend some time here. There are reasons for this. Crete's most urban centre exudes the typical chaos which one expects from a Greek capital – noisy arterial roads, dreary residential areas and cheerless suburbs are not everyone's cup of tea.

Worth seeing: If you are interested in Minoan culture, a visit to the archaeological museum is a must. Amongst the outstanding exhibits are the faience statuette of a snake goddess, votive double axes cast in bronze with a golden shaft and the Phaistos Disc, bearing hieroglyphs arranged in a spiral; the disc remains one of the many unsolved mysteries of the Minoan civilisation. The Minoan Palace at Knossos, 5 km south of Heraklion, counts as the most important tourist attraction on the island. Whether the reconstruction of the palace, which dates back to the third millennium BC, has been true to the original, lies in the judgement that each visitor must make for himself.

Walking: We do not recommend Heraklion for a longer sojourn. If you plan on making good use of the bus transport system, however, you will find excellent service to all parts of the island. Matala and Agia Galini could easily be taken in as day trips and the mountain villages of Anogia and Zaros are included in the bus service (Walks 45, 46, 38 and 41).

Tourist information: EOT, Odos Xanthoudidou 1 (across from the archaeological museum), tel. +30-2810-246299, www.heraklion.gr.

Argyroupoli in the hinterland of Rethymno.

Malia Bay

With room for 30,000 overnight guests, the bay situated to the east of Heraklion counts as the largest holiday centre on Crete. The two main towns along the broad, sandy beaches are Limenas Chersonisou and Malia. These can only be considered for a longer sojourn by those who can come to terms with the excesses of mass tourism. In the holiday catalogues of tour operators, Malia is colourfully described as a »lively holiday resort«. Indeed, the pubs, discos and music clubs along the rumbustious nightlife strip are open until the wee hours of the morning. In Hersonissos, you must expect aircraft noise.

Excursions: West of Hersonissos, the Cretaquarium (www.cretaquarium.gr) in Gournes displays the diversity of the Mediterranean underwater world.

Walking: Malia Bay is an excellent starting point for walks to Lassithi (Walks 51 and 52). Additional walks in the area: 53 and 54.

Agios Nikolaos

The small town (19,000 inhabitants) on the Gulf of Mirabello is the administrative centre for eastern Crete and a renowned tourist resort. Meanwhile, the town's tiny, sandy beach cannot accommodate all the bathing guests coming here during the high season, but in comparison to other dreary holiday resorts along the northern coast, the little town has retained its charm. The range of accommodation suiting every pocket is huge, but the vast majority has been pre-booked by holiday package tours or last minute ticket agencies. Several of the beachfront hotels are now getting on in years and are located on the traffic-congested coastal road. If you are looking for comfort, north of Agios Nikolaos, your dream will come true in the luxury district of Elounda.

Worth seeing: Agios Nikolaos shows its brightest side when viewed from the shores of Lake Voulismeni, which has been connected to the sea by a canal since 1870. Tavernas and the terraces of cafés line the shores of the freshwater lake, 64 m in depth. 4000 year-old tombs are on display in the archaeological museum and also, a few years older, and the star of the collection, is the so-called Goddess of Myrtos, a crude ceramic vessel sporting a long neck and attached breasts.

Excursions: To the north of Agios Nikolaos, starting from Elounda or Plaka, you can take a boat over to the island of Spinalonga, with its former Venetian fortress. Until 1957, a village housing an isolated leper colony was situated here.

Walking: The Kritsa Gorge (Walk 53), a classic walker's destination in eastern Crete, is very close at hand and, in addition, for walks in the Lassithi and the Thripti Mountains, Agios Nikolaos makes an excellent starting point (Walks 51–54). For walking regions along the eastern coast, you have to reckon about 1.5 hrs drive, to Kato Zakros, a good 2 hrs drive. Somewhat less time is needed to reach the gorges on the southeastern coast (Walks 55–57).

Tourist information: On the bridge near Lake Voulismeni, tel. +30-28410-22357,www.aghiosnikolaos.eu.

Lake Voulismeni in Agios Nikolaos.

Lassithi Plateau

Two winding mountain roads climb up to Crete's most expansive high plain; the first one starts at Malia Bay via Mochos, Krasi and the Ambelos Pass, 1050 m, the other one, from Agios Nikolaos via the Nikifordiou Pass, 1000 m. From both of the passes, you can enjoy a wonderful panoramic view taking in the ring of the Dikti Mountains surrounding the plain. 21 villages are scattered around the edges of this completely flat plateau, connected to one another by a ring road. After the winter rains and the melt water period, the plateau takes on the appearance of a great lake. The water seepage is slow and is pumped back up to the surface to irrigate the fertile fields. In days gone by, more than 1000 canvas-sailed windmills performed this task, but they have all been replaced by motor-driven pumps – nowadays, windmills can only be found on postcards, yellowed by age.

Walking: A panoramic circular walk climbs up onto Karfi, where a late-Minoan mountain settlement is to be found near the summit (Walk 51). In addition, an easy gorge walk can be undertaken through the Havga Canyon (Walk 52). The village of Koudoumalia is the starting point for demanding alpine walks onto the summits of Dikti, 2148 m, Lazaros, 2085 m, and Afendis Christos, 2141 m, – for each of the three two-thousand metre peaks, you can reckon walking times of about 9 hours, there and back.

41

Palekastro and Kato Zakros

Up until now, the east coast has only been slightly developed for tourism, but the selection of small holiday apartments is constantly growing, especially appealing to tourists looking for tranquillity who prefer to keep far away from the normal touristic hurly burly. A refuge for independent travellers is Xerokambos, south of Zakros. For mobility around the east coast, you will need a hire car.

Worth seeing: The major destinations for day-trippers are: the palm beach at Vai and the 3600 year old Palace at Kato Zakros.

Walking: With a mere maximum height of about 800 m, the mountains in the far east of the island cannot compete with Crete's highest peaks, but nevertheless, this region, criss-crossed with gorges and blessed with lovely beaches, is a very good area for walking. Thanks to private initiative, a number of routes have been signed and waymarked. A very popular classic route is the final stage of the *E4* from Zakros through Dead's Gorge (Walk 62). Additional walks in the area: 58–61 and 63–65.

Accommodation: Stellas Traditional Apartments, Kato Zakros, tel. +30-28430-23739, www.stelapts.com. Stella Ailamaki is renting tastefully decorated studios and apartments in rustic stone-built houses. The complex, including a garden, has been created with great attention to detail and is situated in a panoramic location above the bay of Zakros. Stella's husband, Elias, has waymarked several trails in the area. Double occupation starting at € 60 .

Info: www.palaikastro.com.

Stellas Apartments in a panoramic location above Dead's Gorge (Kato Zakros).

Ierapetra

Cucumber Coast is the not-so-flattering name given to the southern coast near Ierapetra (12,000 inhabitants). It is indeed true that the plastic-covered greenhouses along this coastline are not necessarily attractive. The southwestern coast is the warmest region in Crete; in summer, it might be considered just a tad too hot, but the daytime temperatures in late autumn are pleasantly warm. The main tourist centre, Makrigialos, lies to the east of the cucumber

Bathing cove at the foot of the Asterousia Mountains.

capital. A popular meeting place for independent travellers is Mirtos, west of Ierapetra, where there are numerous little family-run guest houses (www.mirtos.de).

Walking: Along the southwestern coast, you can find adventurous routes through the gorges of Dasaki, Pefki and Perivolaka; also the Thripti Mountains are easy to reach (Walks 54, 55–57). The walking region on the eastern coast is a good one and only a half hour drive away.

Lentas

It could hardly get more remote; you can only reach this little settlement on the southern coast via a winding road through the Asterousia Mountains. Lentas, with pebble beaches close at hand, is especially attractive to independent travellers looking for peace and quiet. The landmark here is the Weeping Lion: a rocky ridge, dropping steeply down to the sea, which, with a little imagination, is said to resemble a reclining lion (see photo on p. 205).

Walking: Walk 48, leading to the beaches of Petrakis and Tracholuas, starts at your doorstep and the starting points for walks in the Asterousia Mountains can be quickly reached (Walks 49 and 50). Additional walks nearby: 43–47. Lentas is not suitable for those using public bus service.

Info: www.lentas-online.com.

Matala, Pitsidia and Kalamaki

In the 1960s, hippies from all over Europe were trying to live out their ideals for a better world here in Matala. Today, in the high season, the beach in front of the renowned caves is fairly crowded, but Red Beach and Kommos Beach present good alternatives. If you find Matala to be already too crowded or too loud, you can try the farming village of Pitsidia or, instead, Kalamaki.

Ferry offshore from Chora Sfakion.

Excursions: Highlights in the hinterland include, amongst others, the Minoan Palace of Festos and the archaeological digs at Gortis with the early-Christian basilica of Titus.

Walking: In the low season, Matala is a good location for attractive walking tours in the immediate vicinity (Walks 44–47). In addition, Kamares and Zaros, to the south of Psiloritis, and the Asterousia Mountains, are relatively easy to approach from Matala (Walks 40–43 and 48–50).

Accommodation: In the Old Town centre of Matala, you can find many family-run guest houses and, inland, somewhat larger accommodations. A good choice is the little hotel Neos Matala, tel. +30-28920-45157. www. hotel-matala.com, DR, € 38–58, depending on the time of year. This is situated in a quiet area at the village limits, somewhat away from the road; with a garden. Walk 46 begins almost right at the door of the hotel.

Info: www.matala-kreta.eu and www.visitmatala.com.

Agia Galini

Despite its name (in English: Holy Silence), Agia Galini is no longer quite as quiet as it was; the resort town counts as one of the largest on the south coast. However, when compared to the sprawling tourist towns in the north, this harbour town, with an old centre surrounded by pensions and holiday apartments, remains idyllic even today. Especially younger tourists feel at home here.

Walking: A delightful walk begins at the harbour and leads to Kommos Beach near Pitsidia (Walk 44). Agia Galini is also a good starting point for the walks in the Matala region (Walks 45–47), as well as for Preveli and Plakias (Walks 33–35). On the southern side of the Psiloritis massif, the ascents to the Kamares Cave and through the Rouwas Gorge (Walks 40 and 41) are worthwhile. In addition, the routes in the hinterland of Rethymno are within easy reach (Walks 36 and 37).

Info: www.agia-galini.com.

Plakias

The popular seaside resort on the south coast lies at the foot of a magnificent mountain backdrop. In addition to a large number of pensions, holiday apartments and a popular youth hostel, a number of major complexes have been established in recent years where package holiday tours can be booked.

Walking: Starting right in the village, two short but delightful walks set off (Walks 33 and 34). 10 km to the southeast, the »Venetian« bridge is the starting point for a walk to Preveli Beach (Walk 35). The walking region of Chora Sfakion is not quite an hour's drive away (Walks 24–28).

Accommodation: Youth Hostel Plakias, tel. +30-28320-32118, www. yhplakias.com. The popular low-budget hostel proudly lays claim to being the southernmost youth hostel in Europe and is situated only a five minute walk from the beach. Very Spartan dormitory rooms; open from Easter to the end of October. During the high season in summer, be sure to reserve well in advance (€12 per person).

Chora Sfakion

The main town of the municipality of Sfakia, which consists of 21 villages in total, is the most important hub for sea-going vessels on the southern coast due to its ferry port. Passenger boats and water taxis provide service to and from Chora Sfakion, Loutro and Agia Roumeli. Every day in the high season, thousands of day-trippers and walkers coming from the excursion through the Samaria Gorge are funnelled through the little harbour and are bussed back to their accommodations on the northern coast. Nevertheless, the atmosphere of the town itself has hardly suffered because most of the crowds flock from the harbour directly to the bus station. In the Old Town, not far from the harbour, you can find several small hotels and holiday apartments.

Walking: Chora Sfakion is an excellent starting point for walkers and includes worthwhile destinations in the immediate area, such as the gorges Imbros and Aradena as well as the villages of Loutro and Anopoli (Walks 22–31). If you have a hire car, Preveli and Plakias are also within range (Walks 33–35).

Info: www.sfakia-crete.com.

Chora Sfakion, the »capital« of the Sfakia region.

Daybreak ambience on Sweet Water Beach between Chora Sfakion and Loutro.

Loutro

No roads, no cars – Loutro, to the west from Chora Sfakion, is Crete straight out of a picture book. You can only reach the little settlement by boat or on foot along the *E4* or along the ancient trail connecting the village to Anopoli. On the narrow beach, inviting tavernas and chic cafés have placed their tables facing the sea, so that their customers can watch the coming and going of the ferries.

Walking: Thanks to the excellent ferry connections, Loutro is a very popular place for a longer stay. Along the *E4*, you can walk towards Chora Sfakion or Agia Roumeli, climb up to Anopoli, explore the Aradena Gorge starting at Marmara Beach, or take a short ramble into the Samaria Gorge (Walks 22–30).

Accommodation: Rooms can be rented in practically every house in the village. The best bet is Porto Loutro, tel. +30-28250-91433, www.hotelporto-loutro.com, DR €40–60).

Info: www.loutro.gr.

Agia Roumeli

The settlement at the mouth of the Samaria Gorge is only accessible by boat or on foot. The few permanent residents here are making a living almost exclusively from day-trippers or walking tourism. In the afternoon, a certain amount of turbulence rules as up to several thousand walkers and day-trippers swoop down upon the tavernas and the pebble beach.

Walking: If you spend the night in Agia Roumeli, early mornings, you can enjoy the Samaria Gorge virtually alone all the way to the Iron Gates since the droves of walkers start at the upper end and don't begin to drift in until near noon (Walk 22). Along the *E4*, your choice is between heading east or heading west along the breathtaking coastal cliffs (Walks 18, 23 and 25). In the summer, ferries provide daily service from Agia Roumeli to Chora Sfakion, Loutro, Sougia and Paleochora. The possible combinations are manifold.

Sougia

If there is still an insider's tip to be had for walkers on Crete, then it must be Sougia. It's true that the village, situated between Paleochora and Agia Roumeli, lives almost exclusively from tourism, but indeed, especially in the off-season, you can easily spend a couple of relaxing days here.

Walking: Directly from your doorstep, you can begin long coastal walks, either westwards towards Lissos and Paleochora or eastwards towards Cape Tripiti and to the Polifimos Cave (Walks 16–19). You won't need a hire car in Sougia since it is so easy to fill a week with walking tours without having a set of wheels. There is bus service to the starting points for the gorges of Samaria, Agia Irini and Figou (Walks 11, 20 and 21); ferries provide service from Sougia to Agia Roumeli and Paleochora.

Accommodation: Until now, the family-run pensions and little holiday apartments have been booked exclusively by independent travellers. A good bet not far from the beach is Captain George, tel. +30-28230-51133, www.sougia. info/hotels/captain_george/index.htm, DR €40–45 . The owner is glad to transport walkers to Lissos and to the Tripiti Gorge with his water taxi.

Info: www.sougia.info.

Paleochora

40 years ago, this settlement was a fishing village. Meanwhile, Paleochora (2000 inhabitants) has sprawled out all over the promontory and, with its excellent beaches, is the largest seaside resort in the southwest island.

Excursions: In summer, boats set sail to the island of Gavdos, the geographical southernmost point in Europe; in addition, the marvellous beach of Elafonisi can be visited by boat.

Walking: Along the *E4*, you can walk to Sougia via Lissos (Walk 16); to the west, a short walk to the Agios Ioannis Chapel is worthwhile (Walk 14) and inland, to the Zoures cave (Walk 15). Ferrys connect Paleochora via Sougia to Agia Roumeli at the mouth of the Samaria Gorge; there is bus service to Omalos, which makes this village a starting point for a complete walk through the gorge (Walks 11 and 22). You can also reach both Sougia and Agia Irini quickly by road with a vehicle (Walks 17–21), but there is, unfortunately, no direct bus service.

Info: www.paleochora.com.

Tourist information

Getting there

By plane: Both of the international airports at Heraklion and Chania are serviced from mid-March to the end of November by all of the major airports all over Europe (flight time about 3.5 hrs). In the winter, there are no direct flights to Heraklion and Chania, so you have to change planes in Athens and, on rare occasions, in Thessaloniki. From Athens, there are also connecting flights to the national airport in Sitia on eastern Crete.

By ferry: If you wish to travel here by boat, you have to allow a lot of time. The usual route is from Ancona – Patras; fast ferries make the journey in 18 hours. From Patras, a toll motorway runs to Piräus, 200 kms away. The journey from Piräus to Crete takes an additional 6 hours. On Crete, the ferry ports are located in Heraklion, Chania, Kissamos and Sitia (only in the summer). For schedules and prices, check with the shipping companies: www.anek.gr, www.minoan.gr and www.superfast.com.

Information

■ Greek National Tourism Organisation, 4 Conduit Street, London, W1S 2DJ, tel. +44-2074959300, www.visitgreece.gr

Equipment

Apart from some easy walks along gravel trails, sturdy footwear with treaded soles is required for all routes. Light beach footwear may also prove useful – as early as June, the sand can be so hot that walking barefoot can be torturous. For longer breaks on the beach, a small shade sail could also come in handy. Telescopic trekking poles are a possible additional aid for longer ascents and descents. Absolutely essential to take along: sufficient drinking water, rain and sun protection as well as a warm jumper or fleece jacket for cool days. Especially in the mountainous areas over 1500 m in altitude, temperatures can be surprisingly chilly even into the month of May. If you plan on paying a visit to a monastery, be sure to wear appropriate clothing (long trousers, long-sleeved blouses). Mosquito repellent is good to have against the possible onslaught of pests.

Bus transport

Intercity coaches connect the larger cities on the northern coast hourly along the National Road. The most important north to south routes are the stretches between Heraklion – Mires – Matala, as well as Rethymno – Agia Galini and Chania – Chora Sfakion. On the southern coast, due to the sometimes rough and steep drops of the White Mountains, there is no continuous road along the coastline. If you want to take a bus, for example, from Plakias to

Ferry landing in Chora Sfakion.

Sougia or Paleochora, you would have to go first to Chania on the northern coast and then back across the island to the southern coast (by car, the situation is, naturally, the same). If departure times are especially noted in the individual walk description, these refer to the summer schedule which is valid from May until October; in winter, especially on the southern coast, but also between the seaside resorts on the northern coast, you have to expect a serious reduction in service.

Busses and schedules can be subject to change. Generally speaking, the information noted in this walking guide should be checked before every walk. Schedules, timetables and fares can be found at www.bus-service-crete.com.

Ferries

For the southwest coast, lacking in a developed network of roads, ferry service is the most important means of transport during the summer. From May until the end of October, the Anendyk Line (www.anendyk.gr, tel. +30-28210-95511) connects Chora Sfakion with Loutro, Agia Roumeli, Sougia and Paleochora; most important for walkers, these connections present some interesting linking possibilities. In stormy weather, the ferries are not in operation.

Internet

■ www.crete.tournet.gr: is a good virtual travel guide with tips for special events, as well as many videos concerning the island

- www.samaria.gr: the official internet site of the National Park Administration for the Samaria Gorge
- www.levka-ori.com: walking forum focused on the White Mountains

Car hire
Car hire is quite inexpensive here when booking through the international companies (Avis, Hertz and so forth). The price of petrol is noticeably higher than that in Central Europe. Most petrol stations are closed on Sunday. The condition of the roads, especially along some secondary routes, leaves a lot to be desired: potholes, unsecured construction sites, road blocks without detours, as well as herds of goats crossing the road, demand a high degree of alertness.

Youth hostels & campsites
On Crete, youth hostels are run privately and do not belong to the International Youth Hostel Federation. Thus, a youth hostel card is not required and there are no age restrictions (addresses can be found under Rethymno and Plakias).
You'll find a solid dozen campsites on Crete. Most of them are very simple and lacking in comfort; almost all of them are located at the seaside or not

Herds of sheep and goats always have the right of way.

far from it. Shady and relatively acceptable are: Camping Nopigia (www.campingnopigia.gr) on the Gulf of Kissamos, Camping Elisabeth (www.camping-elizabeth.net) 4 kms east of Rethymno and Camping No Problem (www.agia-galini.com) in Agia Galini.

Camping in the wild is not permitted but, nevertheless, you will find it on many isolated coves, for example, on Sweet Water Beach near Chora Sfakion. Along the *E4*, due to the lack of accommodation en route, you have no choice but to camp outdoors.

Season
Peak season for a beach holiday is the summer months from July to the beginning of September when you'll enjoy stable weather with plenty of sunshine and virtually no rain on the island. For walkers, the low seasons are ideal, from May until mid-June and from end of September until end of October. These periods are not only advantageous due to less heat and fewer crowds of tourists, but also because the prices for accommodation are reduced by about 20 percent. In winter, most of the hotels and tavernas are closed.

Crime
Crete is a safe island; violent crimes against tourists are virtually unknown and thievery is very rare, but like anywhere else, you should not leave any valuables in your vehicle. At the car park near Agiofarango (Walk 47) there have been repeated incidences of car break-ins.

Taxi
For the relatively inexpensive city taxi service, the taxi metre is used (official regulations); overland, fixed prices are set, but are not inexpensive.

Telephone
The country code for Greece is 0030. From Greece to Great Britain 0044 (the zero in the local area codes is dropped). The mobile telephone network is well established on the island; dead spots are usually only encountered in sparsely populated mountain areas and in gorges.

Time zone
On Crete, clocks are set according to Eastern European Time (EET): upon arrival, if you live in the Central European Time zone, you have to set your time forwards by one hour.

Photo p. 53: At Preveli Beach, the Megalopotamos empties into the Libyan Sea (Walk 35).

A few words in Greek for the journey

good morning	kaliméra	boat	karáwi
good day	kaliméra	bridge	jéfira
good evening	kalispéra	trough fountain	pigádi
greeting when coming and going	já sas	castle	kástro
		bus	leoforío
		village	chorió
thank you	efcharistó	fire	fotiá
please	parakaló	house	spíti
I want ...	thélo ...	hill	lófos
... water	... neró	island	nisí
... a taxi	... éna taxí	cape	akrotírio
... food	... fajitó	church	eklisía
... drink	... na pjó	cliff	skópelos
where is ...?	pou ínä ...	monastery	monastíri
... the way to	... o drómos ja ...	sea	thálassa
... a café	... éna kafenío	path	monopáti
... the bus stop	... i stási	cobbled path	kalderími
... the harbour	... to limáni	square	platía
here	edó	source	vrísi
there	ekí	beach	paralía
straight ahead	efthía	road, trail (general)	drómos
right	dexiá		
left	aristerá	drinking water	pósimo neró
below	káto		
above	páno	1, 2, 3	éna, dío, tría
close by	kondá	4, 5, 6	téssera, pénte, éxi
far away	makriá	7, 8, 9	eftá, ochtó, ennéa
		10	déka
viewpoint	théa	100	ekató
car	aftokínito	1000	chília
mountain	vounó		

The Greek alphabet

A, α	ah		N, ν	n
B, β	»v« as in »villa«		Ξ, ξ	x
Γ, γ	y before e, i otherwise soft, gargled gh		O, o	oh
			Π, π	p (soft)
Δ, δ	hard »th« like »this«		P, ρ	r (rolled)
E, ε	eh		Σ, σ	s
Z, ζ	»z« like Ouzo		T, τ	t
H, η	ee		Y, υ	ee
Θ, θ	soft »th« like »thanks«		Φ, φ	f
I, ι	ee		X, χ	soft, gargled ch like the sound of a cat's hiss
K, κ	k			
Λ, λ	l		Ψ, ψ	ps like PS »chips«
M, μ	m		Ω, ω	between »awe« and »oh«

Ramble across the Gramvousa peninsula to a splendid coastline

In Crete's extreme north-west, the uninhabited Gramvousa peninsula, covered only in a sparse scrubland with cushion plants, extends into the Cretan Sea like a pointing finger. Pirates once made landfall on the west coast of the peninsula and a Venetian castle, perched on a fortified island lying offshore, recalls the stirring history. Today, tourist boats lay anchor in the turquoise-coloured lagoon at Balos. It is best to arrive early in the morning when hardly anybody else is around, or in late afternoon, when almost everyone has left.

Trail at the foot of the coastal mountains.

First, cross through the settlement of Kaliviani. After not quite 3 km from the harbour, at the Balos Beach Hotel, an extremely rough and bumpy road starts off, running always along the eastern side of the Gramvousa peninsula and then passing the Agia Irini chapel. 8 km further on, the road ends at the car park for the taverna. In high season, you have to pay a toll of € 1 per person.

Height difference: 155 m in both ascent and descent.

Grade: short, easy walk along a well laid, sometimes cobbled, trail.

Refreshment: tavernas at the car park and on the beach at Balos' lagoon.

Worth seeing: in summer, from the ferry harbour in Kissamos, excursion boats are sailing several times every day into the lagoon and also offer an excursion to the fortress island of Imeri Gramvousa (www.gramvousa.com). From the boat landing, a steep footpath climbs up to the Venetian outpost, situated at a height of 138 m. Keep an eye out to see if the Lion of St. Mark, broken into four pieces, still lies in front of the portal to the fortress.

Starting point: car park on the Gramvousa peninsula, 155 m. Approaching from Kissamos, 1 km past the harbour, a narrow road forks away towards Balos.

Municipal Canteen (3) Balos (4)
1 m
(I) (2) (2) (I)
155 m P ⌂ ⌂ P 155 m
3.1 km
0   0.30 1.00 h

The lagoon at Balos.

The **car park (1)** in front of the taverna is bordered on its western side by a knee-high wall. The upper passageway leads to a viewpoint 400 m away. But instead, take the trail that begins just a few paces below this passageway; at the outset, the trail is flanked by stones. Not quite 15 mins later, the turquoise coloured lagoon and Cape Tigani, which is connected by a rocky isthmus, come into view as well as the offshore islands. The Greek word *tigani* means »frying pan«, the isthmus is, so to speak, the panhandle of the island. From the **panoramic viewpoint (2)**, climb down to the dunes along a sometimes stepped trail and meet up with the beach at Balos. Just above the lagoon, first turn right to reach the **Municipal Canteen (3)** and then continue along the lagoon to the **Taverna Balos (3)** on the southern end of the bay. From here, return back again to the **car park (1)**.

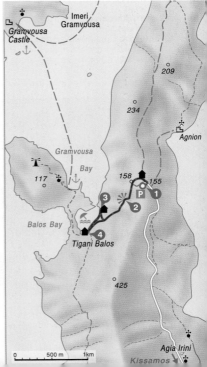

Grand circular walk crossing the Rodopou peninsula

Along panoramic trails to the pilgrimage chapel of Agios Ioannis Gionis

The northern part of the Rodopou peninsula is virtually deserted and the treeless terrain is extremely desolate. Nevertheless, this circular walk presents superb views of Chania bay and of Kissamos bay. After a rather unspectacular start along a road, descend via an ancient mule track to a secluded church, situated above the coast; every August, this is the destination for an important pilgrimage.

Starting point: Rodopos, 240 m. From the National Road between Chania and Kissamos, take the exit for Aspra Nera and then follow the signs into Rodopos, 5 km away. Parking possible at the village square.

Height difference: 540 m in both ascent and descent.

Grade: long circular walk on roads, trader trails and an ancient mule track. The first one and a half hours lead along a road which is tarmac at first, later gravel-surfaced, but with almost no traffic. If you wish to ascend onto the western side of the peninsula, you should be a sure-footed walker. The coastal trail past the turn-off to Agios Pavlos is waymarked, however, the sometimes rough path leading over karst rock is not always easy to follow. No shade and sometimes very windy.

Refreshment: nothing en route. A coffee house in the village square in Rodopos.

Fields and little vineyards surround the pilgrimage chapel of Agios Ioannis Gionis.

From the village square in **Rodopos (1)**, follow the main road of the village northwards and, a good 200 m on, pass a large domed church. A quarter of an hour later, the street ascends in two tight bends. Now walk through the entire length of a high valley where grapevines are being cultivated. After 40 minutes, the road becomes gravel-surfaced. The cultivated terrain is now behind us, and a treeless, rugged karst landscape begins, covered only in *phrygana* undergrowth. Eastwards, we have a view of the Chania bay, while to the left of the trail, a mountain range crops up with a height of a good 700 m; the White Mountains are behind us.

The roadway continues ascending steadily, but never unpleasantly steep. About one and a half hours after leaving Rodopos, keep an eye out to the left for a large, flat **cistern**

The pilgrimage church, Agios Ioannis Gionis.

(2) that is covered with two square metal flaps. At this point, turn left onto a path to leave the gravel track behind. The path, flanked by a low embankment, leads through a narrow valley. A good 250 m further on, the path crosses over a country lane and, three minutes after that, meets up with an intersecting trail. The cone-shaped Onichas mountain appears to the left, but we turn right instead and, at the fork not quite 100 m further on, bear slightly to the left while ascending. The gravel trail leads, after another 100 m, onto a windy **pass (3)**, 540 m. A couple of paces further on, reach a cottage with cattle watering tanks in front of it. With this to our left, head towards the sea while passing through a rocky notch in the terrain which leads, in two minutes, to a stonework viewing platform where a tiny church is located. Here, we get a wonderful view over the Kissamos Gulf, including the Gramvousa

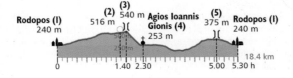

Rodopos (I) 240 m — (2) 516 m — **(3)** 540 m — Agios Ioannis Gionis (4) 253 m — (5) 375 m — Rodopos (I) 240 m — 18.4 km

0   1.40   2.30   5.00   5.30 h

View of the tiny church.

peninsula. Down below, a plain broadens out, filled with cultivated fields; on the right-hand edge of the plain, the pilgrimage church, surrounded with a wall, lies hidden by trees.

At the viewing platform, a cobbled mule track begins, descending sometimes roughly and in zigzags. In the lower reaches, the track has been destroyed, but orientation is very simple. At a little marble shrine, meet up with a road and take this by bearing right to reach the church dedicated to John the Baptist, **Agios Ioannis Gionis (4)**, 253 m. In this area, surrounded by a wall, two large tables have been placed which can accommodate several hundred people. It is always packed here on the 28th and 29th of August when a grand saint's day celebration is held to honour John the Baptist.

From the church, walk back to the marble shrine and then follow the road southwards along fields cultivated with grapes and olive trees, while heading in the direction of Agios Pavlos. The mountain ridge beyond the fields blocks the view of the sea at first, but a good 10 minutes later, the Kissamos Gulf appears once again.

About 40 minutes past the pilgrimage church, a downwards view opens up of a little church perched above the sea, **Agios Pavlos**, where the road ends. However, leave the trail behind a good way before then: in a sharp, right-hand bend, we head straight on along a mule track. At the outset, the track is rather indistinct as it runs at first, almost on the level, high above the coast; faded *red* dots and cairns lying 50 m further on are an assurance that we are on the right track. Below the mountain ridge, which divides the peninsula into two parts, we can spot a »white cottage«; the trail climbs up to the »cottage« after a final steep ascent. Arriving at the spot, the little house proves to be only a container. Now a track, ascending rather moderately, climbs up to a long, drawn-out **saddle (5)**, 375 m; from here, the Chania Gulf comes into sight once more. During the descent, the rooftops of Rodopos appear. Pass a football pitch and then meet up with an intersecting trail at the village limits. Turn right here and, a couple of paces further on, turn left to return to the village square of **Rodopos (1)**.

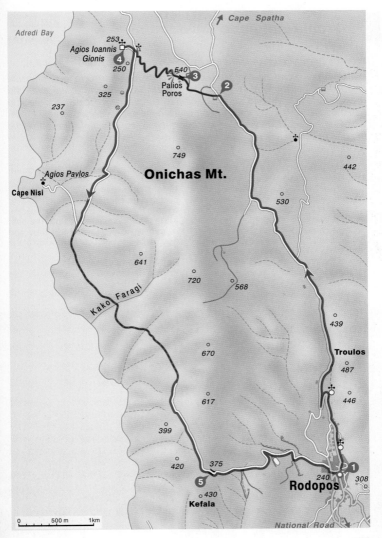

Adredi Bay

Cape Spatha

253
Agios Ioannis
Gionis
4
250
325
237
Palios
Poros
640
3
2

Onichas Mt.

749
442
530

Agios Pavlos
Cape Nisi

641
720
568
439

Kako Faragi

670
Troulos
487
446
617
399
420
375
5
430
Kefala
240
308
Rodopos

National Road

0   500 m   1km

Along a panoramic coastal path to the taverna Waves on the Rock

Between the grand bays of Kissamos and Chania, the Rodopou peninsula extends far into the Cretan Sea. On a hitherto little-known coastal path, the rocky west coast is open for exploration to some extent. Capes and pebble beaches are lying along the way and with a constant, lovely view of the Kissamos Gulf, boredom will certainly not come to the fore. The only drawback: the pebble beaches are marred somewhat by the flotsam and plastic waste washed ashore.

Starting point: the Nopigia campsite, 2 m. From Kissamos, take the National Road (New Road) towards Chania, passing the Mithimna campsite 4 km on. 1.5 km after that, take the turn-off for the Nopigia campsite. Arriving at the seaside, the campsite appears after another 300 m and, 150 m past the entrance gate, there's a little parking area at the side of the road. Nopigia is situated on the bus line Chania – Kissamos (ask the driver to stop at the turn-off for the campsite).

Height difference: 375 m in both ascent and descent.

Grade: this is not a difficult walk, leading along roads and coastal paths. The path is sometimes provided with cairns and waymarkers to point out the course of the route.

Refreshment: the taverna Waves on the Rock in Ravdoucha.

Flowering oleander in front of the silhouette of the Gramvousa peninsula.

From the **Nopigia campsite (1)**, follow the narrow seaside road in a north-easterly direction. After a few metres, the road becomes a gravel trail and then runs parallel to the waterline in a broad bend along the west coast of the Rodopou peninsula. The pebble beach gives way to a bizarre rocky coastline. Soon, a sweeping view opens up taking in the Kissamos Gulf, which is enclosed at the western end by the Gramvousa peninsula.

A good ten minutes later, reach a *panagia* **(2)**, a chapel, with a little bathing area in front of it. About 150 m past the chapel, leave the coastal trail behind (this ends shortly before reaching the steep coastline) by turning right onto a broad, eroded trail that climbs up the embankment. A cart track, bearing slightly to the right, leads over a small plateau to the foot of the coastal mountains. From here, the trail veers to the left, passing to the left of a couple of carob trees whilst heading northwards. Seven minutes later, at a fork, follow the vehicle tracks, at first rocky, but soon becoming a path, and descend to a pebble beach.

Now walking along the sea, head towards Cape Sideris lying ahead; offshore, two concrete posts are sticking out of the water. The path leads

through mastic bushes for a couple of metres, parallel to the pebble beach. Pass a circular threshing yard. Climb over two low walls built of gathered stones and, shortly after, reach the tumbledown, quarry-stone chapel of **Agios Vasilios (3)**, reconstructed in 2015 and dating back to the 15th century.

Not quite 200 m past the chapel, at a large thicket of oleander, keep your eyes sharp! Just past the first clump of oleander bush, waymarkers are pointing to the right (this spot is marked, a couple of paces on, by a square-shaped boulder, measuring about 30 cm in height). Along the path, head inland to skirt

61

Good Cretan cuisine is served in the taverna Waves on the Rock.

around the dense oleander thicket and then pass through a small wood and over a valley with a stream. Afterwards, ascend somewhat steeply up the slope (the path is slippery under foot) – in May, the gorse will be flowering here and, in October, the Mediterranean heath.

After a short ascent reach the rocky **Cape Sideris (4)**, 90 m. At the foot of the crag jutting out over the sea, on its northern side, you have a downwards view of the pebble beach of Ravdoucha; further northwards, the long boat landing at Ravdoucha, constructed over the water, appears.

The path now traverses a slightly precipitous stretch along a steeply dropping slope. Soon, we are joined by a chain-linked fence. Just when the fence begins an ascent to the right, continue straight on through a gate, entering a grove of olive trees. Afterwards, on a hairpin bend, meet up with a road, 133 m, and turn left (to the right, an ascent to the village of Ravdoucha).

After walking a good 200 m along the road, about 50 m before reaching a wash house, above which, the **Agia Marina (5)** chapel is perched but lies hidden (Walk 4), watch out for an ancient mule track forking off sharp to the left. This descends steeply and the last leg is fairly eroded, then it merges 10 mins later into a narrow road. Bearing left, soon pass the Agios Onofrios cave chapel and, at the end, reach the taverna, **Waves on the Rock (6)**, above the pebble beach. After enjoying a break, return along the approach route back to the **Nopigia campsite (1)**.

Cape Sideris (4)   Waves on the Rock (6)
            90 m   7 m   Agios Vasilios (3)
      Panagia (2)   Camping Nopigia (I)
Camping Nopigia (I)   3 m   (3)   (5)   (5)   (2)   2 m
      2 m   (4)   1 m   10.3 km
      0   0.55   1.45 2.20 3.15 3.30 h

On the Rodopou peninsula to the taverna Waves on the Rock

Ravdoucha, on the eastern coast of the Rodopou peninsula, is situated somewhat away from it all: the settlement, with a boat landing and a pebble beach, can only be reached via a narrow access road. Along this short circular walk, we will pass two churches and three chapels; the frescoes in Agia Marina are a delight for the art history fan. Lovely views and a good opportunity to take refreshment give the short walk its particular appeal.

Starting point: Ravdoucha, 175 m. From the National Road Chania – Kissamos take the exit Kalydonia/Aspra Nera and then follow the signs towards Rodopou. 2 km past Kamara, an access road forks off to the left towards Ravdoucha. In the centre of the little settlement, drive past the ancient church of Agia Triada and then descend for a good 200 m more until, at the new main church, Agios Georgios, the road forks; a car park is situated opposite the church. There is no applicable bus service available for the walker.

Height difference: About 200 m in both ascent and descent.

Grade: The descent usually follows farm tracks; a short stretch is negotiated over a tarmac road with little traffic. Starting from Agios Onofrios, a steeper, but short, intermediate ascent is made along a mule track which is, at the outset, extremely eroded. No waymarkers along the way but route-finding is simple.

Refreshment: Very good Cretan cuisine is served at Waves on the Rock (tel. +30-28240-23133, www.wavesontherock.eu).

Accommodation: You can rent a place with the sound of the surf guaranteed at Ravdoucha Beach Studios (tel. +30-69399-95465, www.ravdouchabeachstudios.gr).

The walk begins in **Ravdoucha (1)** at the fork opposite from the church Agios Georgios. From the car park, follow the concrete trail, broad at first, that leads above the cemetery. Not quite five minutes later, reach two benches under a carob tree; from here, you can gaze down at a boat landing where the descent will lead. To the south of the landing, Cape Sideris juts into the sea and, at the foot of the steep cliff, we can spot the destination for this walk, the taverna Waves on the Rock. Past the carob tree, ignore two trails

In the cave chapel of Agios Onofrios.

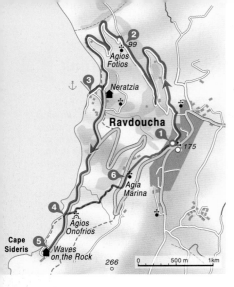

forking off to the right; the route heads straight on, descending slightly through a terraced plantation of olive trees. Just past a house with a bougainvillea-draped fence, meet a fork and bear left. The path veers sharp to the right after passing a elegant villa and, a couple of minutes later, reaches **Agios Fotios (2)**, 99 m.

The unadorned chapel, surrounded by olive trees, is dedicated to Photios I (died 891), erstwhile patriarch of Constantinopel, who is venerated as a saint. In front of the chapel, a picnic table is an inviting spot to take a break.

The cave chapel of Saint Onuphrios.

At the fork past the chapel, the trail bears left to descend in tight bends. Just above the boat landing, at two houses, turn sharp left and meet up afterwards with the access road for the harbour. Turn right and, a few more steps bring you to the **harbour (3)**, where there is a small beach and sunloungers. In low season, however, the spot usually gives the impression that it is somewhat ill-maintained.

From the harbour, the narrow road leads past the taverna Neratzia to a fork; turn right here. The road leads somewhat above the coastline and now heads towards Cape Sideris. Behind a crag, the cave chapel of **Agios Onofrios (4)** lies hidden. Onuphrios was an Abyssinian and an early Christian saint from the 4th century who lived as a hermit in a cave monastery in Cappadocia and, according to legend, subsisted exclusively on a diet of dates.

A few minutes past the cave chapel, reach the taverna **Waves on the Rock (5)**. Below it, there is a small pebble beach with offshore rock formations – a wild and idyllic setting.

The Ravdoucha bay.

Waves on the Rock (5) Agia Marina (6)
Agios Fotios (2) 7 m 114 m
Ravdoucha (I) (4) Ravdoucha (I)
175 m (3) 175 m
5.7 km
0 0.25 0.45 1.45 h

After taking some refreshment and a bathing break, return back to the Onofrios chapel and, just past it, turn off onto an ancient mule track, at the outset rather badly eroded, that ascends steeply along the slope. Pass two gates and then the trail leads to a road; by turning left, reach the wash house at Ravdoucha. Next to a towering plane tree, a couple of steps climb up to **Agia Marina (6)**. In the tiny inner sanctum, the Byzantine chapel, dating back to the 15th century, boasts several frescoes, well worth seeing, amongst which there is a portrait of Jesus; his eyes, in the depiction, were poked out by the Turkish occupation forces.

From Agia Marina, the mule track leads less steeply above the glamorous **Epavlis Villas**, one of Crete's most exclusive residential areas. A good five minutes later, the trail merges again with the road. Turn left and, 100m further on, meet up again with the church Agios Georgios in **Ravdoucha (1)**.

5 *Between Sirikari and Polyrinia* 2.45 hrs

Descent along a mule track in the Tsichliana Gorge

The wide gorge at Sirikari presents an opportunity for a very pleasant walk. This route is most obliging to anyone who wishes to ramble freely without constant path-finding, scrambling over boulders or crossing over stream beds via slippery fords. The path and an idyllic rest area, located in the middle of the gorge, were recently revamped and waymarked using EU funds; an excursion into the ancient site of Polyrinia makes for a fine alternative route.

In the Tsichliana Gorge.

Starting point: Agios Konstantinos, 505 m. At the eastern village limits of Kissamos, turn off onto the Old Road and then follow the signs to Sirikari, 18 km away. Drive through the village and, 0.5 km further on, head for the Agios Konstantinos church which could be seen from afar during the approach.

Height difference: 330 m in both ascent and descent.

Grade: a steep descent at the beginning along a well-laid mule track (be careful when wet). The trail is marked throughout with a *green* square on a *white* background.

Refreshment: nothing en route; tavernas in Polyrinia.

Alternative: just past the arched bridge, the houses of Polyrinia appear, although still quite a good distance away. 5 minutes later, meet up with a pump house. From there, ascend to a gate 30 m further on and then descend along a broad road while bearing slightly to the right. This road leads out of the gorge and then merges into a narrow, tarmac-surfaced secondary road a little later on. Follow the secondary road for not quite 20 minutes, bearing right at a fork (*E4*) and then, after another 5 minutes, meet up with the main road; turn sharp right here to reach the village limits of Polyrinia, 257 m. From here, you could climb up a hill, 417 m, to the modest remains of the acropolis of ancient Polyrinia, from which, you can enjoy a sweeping view over the Kissamos Gulf (walking time from the arched bridge to the village limits, is a good 30 minutes).

Opposite the **Agios Konstantinos (1)** church, two trails fork away. With your back to the church, take the right-hand path. A few paces on, this crosses through a gate and descends, at first quite steeply, along a slope which is covered in scrub. In autumn, the strawberry trees, bearing their bright red fruit, really catch the eye.

As soon as the scrubland thins out, the further course of the path can be scrutinised as it descends through

The fruit of the strawberry tree resemble ...

... those of the plane tree, almost to a T.

the Tsichliana Gorge. Now enter a grove of olive trees. Passing two gates, one following shortly after the other, the path merges into a concrete-paved trail. Turn right onto this trail and, 50 m further on, meet up with a little **farmhouse**. Immediately in front of the farmhouse, cross over the veranda and after a few paces, in front of a stall, turn right.

Just above the stream bed of the **Tsichliana Gorge (2)**, 322 m, meet

67

Plane trees provide shade for the rest area in the stream bed of the Tsichliana Gorge.

up with an intersecting path and turn right onto it heading down into the gorge. Along the dry stream bed, the usual flora is flourishing – plane trees, oleander bushes and Cretan maple, with some sweet chestnut trees mixed in. The western walls of the gorge tower more than 300 m in height, but they never close in to become very narrow. Afterwards, reach a **rest area (3)** right in the middle of the gorge's stream bed where picnic tables and even rubbish bins are there to use. Gnarled plane trees provide plenty of shade. If you prefer soaking up some sunshine, take the path another 200 m further on to reach a somewhat higher-lying **viewpoint** where there are also places to sit. The most beautiful area of the Tsichliana Gorge is now already behind us, however, you could continue along the path for another 15 mins to reach an ancient **arched bridge (4)**, 193 m. Several minutes past the bridge, the idyllic stretch comes to an end and a broad roadway begins. If you don't care to continue on to Polyrinia, the bridge marks your turn-around point. Return along the approach route to head back to **Agios Konstantinos (1)**.

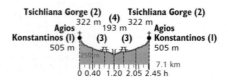

A two-gorge circular walk in the hinterland of Kissamos

The Topoliano Gorge is usually admired by most visitors from a viewpoint on the road along the way to the bathing paradise of Elafonisi, but indeed, you can also walk through it. The circular walk also takes in the less lengthy, but more pristine, Mouri Gorge. Between the two canyons, extensive groves of olive trees are traversed along pleasant country lanes and also, quiet villages are briefly encountered.

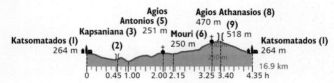

Starting point: the Taverna Archondas (Arxontas) in Katsomatados, 264 m. Approaching from Kissamos, take the Old Road at the eastern city limits and then follow signs towards Elafonisi/Topolia/Paleochora. Past Topolia and not quite 2 km past the tunnel that follows, in Katsomatados, turn sharp left onto a narrow road to the Taverna Archondas where parking is possible on the river bridge in front of the taverna. Katsomatados is the bus stop for the Chania – Elafonisi line (from Chania about 9.00; return from Katsomatados about 17.40).

Height difference: a good 500 m in both ascent and descent.

Grade: the circular walk leads mostly along broad, unpaved country lanes with no traffic. Narrow paths lead through the gorges, sometimes over very rocky terrain, and the most strenuous section of all is the short ascent through the Mouri Gorge. In the Topoliano Gorge, *yellow/black* waymarkers are a help in route-finding and, in the Mouri Gorge, very faded, *red* waymarkers. Otherwise, the route is not waymarked and it is important to pay close attention to a number of junctions. Outside of the gorges, expect very little shade.

Refreshment: the Taverna Archondas at the starting point; excellent Cretan home-made food at the Milia Mountain Retreat (10 km from Katsomatados; for the approach, see Walk 7).

Note: the circular walk is usually feasible starting from mid-June, but if undertaking the walk earlier than that, you must expect that the water level in the stream bed of the Topoliano Gorge is possibly still too high to negotiate.

Worth seeing: along the approach or during the return, it is worthwhile in Potamida (6 km south of Kissamos) to make an excursion to the bizarre earth pyramids (photo on p. 37). Approaching from Kissamos, shortly past the church at Potamida, a trail branches off (always follow the brown wooden signs). Also quite appealing is a visit to the Agia Sofia Cave Chapel in Katsomatados; from Café Romantza, you can reach the dripstone cave along a stepped trail in only a few minutes.

In **Katsomatados (1)**, a country lane begins in front of the taverna on the upper end of the river bridge. Follow the lane along the left bank heading downstream into the Topoliano Gorge. The lane leads at first through a grove of olive trees as it runs parallel to the secondary road down below. 10 minutes later, in the western rock face of the gorge, high above, we can spot the gable belfry of the Agia Sofia Cave Chapel.

Past the olive grove, the country lane becomes a path. Not quite a half an hour after beginning the walk, the path changes over to the right bank along a **concrete-paved ford**, sometimes somewhat overgrown with Jerusalem sage and spurge. Pass a cave in the left-hand rock face of the gorge where a cross is dangling from the ceiling.

Not quite ten minutes later, in front of a cubiform, concrete **water shaft (2)** cross diagonally left over the gorge's stream bed (waymarker). Past the utility hole, go through a gate and leave the stream bed behind by turning off onto a path ascending slightly. The path broadens to become a country lane. At the fork about 300 m past the utility hole, bear left (to the right is a possible excursion to an ancient arched bridge; 10 minutes, there and back). 75 m on, continue straight ahead (a sharp left would continue on to bring you to Topolia).

As the houses making up the village of **Kapsaniana (3)**, 91 m, meet up with a tarmac road. Bearing right, another bridge provides a river crossing. Immediately past the bridge, turn right again onto a narrow tarmac road and ascend. A few minutes later, the road becomes a dirt trail and continues along winding bends through terraces of olive trees while climbing eastwards up the slope of the gorge.

About 25 minutes past Kapsaniana, the trail forks in front of a vineyard hillside. Do not ascend by turning right here; instead, continue straight on. We are now at the same height as the striking church tower of Topolia, located on the western side of the gorge. 5 minutes past the vineyard, a chapel is situated below the trail with two tables in front of it, a nice place to take a break.

At the fork, 100 m on, continue straight ahead along the quarry-stone walls of an abandoned house; passing it by, catch a view of Kapsaniana, already lying far below. Not much later, at the village limits of **Latsiana (4)**, 193 m, meet up with a narrow tarmac road at a trough fountain; next to it is a gnarled plane tree and, down below, a chapel for the cemetery. Ascend along the narrow road which is no longer tarmac once past the houses of Latsiana.

Always keeping to the main trail, a good 10 minutes past the trough fountain, reach a major junction and, again, continue straight ahead. At the next signed junction, 200 m past the major one, opportunity knocks for a short excursion to the church of **Agios Antonios (5)**, 251 m. The church is situated

At the outset, a pleasant country lane leads through the Topoliano Gorge.

The Agia Sofia Cave Chapel in the rock face of the Topoliano Gorge.

panoramically at the terminus of a mountain ridge. From a bench on the square in front of the church, enjoy a sublime view, taking in extensive olive groves and, in a frame created by the Gramvousa peninsula and the Rodopou peninsula, the Kissamos Gulf. In the church's interior, take a peek at the vaulted ceiling, painted to portray a starry night.

Back on the main trail, turn left. 15 minutes later, reach a tarmac road at the village limits of **Mouri (6)**, 250 m. Turn right onto the road to pass through the almost completely deserted village and a *kafenion* which is usually closed. As soon as the road veers sharply to the right at the southern village limits, leave it behind by continuing straight ahead along a stony track. Once again, the route traverses extensive groves of olive trees.

Continue along the main trail about a half an hour past Mouri, during which, concrete-paved fords serve twice as a crossing over dry stream beds. Immediately after the second fording, a narrow path turns right into the **Mouri Gorge (7)**. The

In October, ivy-leaved cyclamen (Cyclamen hederifolium) is flowering in the Topoliana Gorge.

path ascends at first along the left bank of the rocky stream bed, but during the further course of the rather narrow and rocky gorge, we will be forced to change banks several times and scramble over boulders as well.

A good 10 minutes later, the rough spots of the relatively short gorge are already lying behind us. The path continues on to the left of a fence and then leads through a gate. Shortly before the **Agios Athanasios (8)** chapel, 470 m, climb down into an eroded gully, about 2 m in depth, and then, 30 m on, climb back out again by ascending the embankment to the right.

At the fenced-in chapel, cross the gully once again and pass through another gate. On the other side, now follow a gravel-surfaced track. Not quite 5 minutes later, turn right onto an intersecting trail and ascend. Immediately, a view opens up into the broad valley of Sasalos and across undulating hills cultivated with olive trees.

At the next junction, turn left and the trail now heads towards a saddle. Just before this, turn right to the **pass (9)**, 518 m. Once there, on the other side of a gate, meet a junction of three trails and take the middle one which is concrete-paved at the outset and, at the fork another 250 m or so further on, bear right. Now a long descent follows, during which we always keep to the main trail as it winds its way, in many bends, through treeless terrain of *phrygana*, descending towards the secondary road from Katsomatados; this road soon comes into view. Also appearing again is the Topoliano Gorge with the chapel of Agia Sofia, recessed in a cave.

At yet another **chapel**, enter again into a grove of olive trees and, 20 minutes later, return to the Taverna Archondas in **Katsomatados (1)**.

Photo on p. 74: The lower reaches of the Topoliano Gorge.

From an ecovillage through chestnut forests and remote villages

The one-time summer resort settlement of Milia is rather off the beaten track and hidden in a chestnut forest south of Kissamos. Today, Milia is a model project for sustainable tourism, driven by a committed community; the trip there is worthwhile, even if only because of the excellent taverna. A contemplative circular walk provides an insight into this peaceful region.

Starting point: the car park in Milia, 556 m. From Kissamos, at first take the Old Road for 2 km towards Chania to reach Kaloudiana. From there, follow the secondary road signed for Paleochora. A good 2 km past Katsomatados, turn off towards Vlatos; from there, follow the signs for Milia. The final 2.5 km is along a gravel road that is easy to drive.
Height difference: 380 m in both ascent and descent.
Grade: a circular walk that is not difficult, along paths and gravel-surfaced trails; the middle section follows a secondary

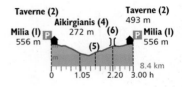

road with little traffic.
Refreshment and accommodation: a taverna in the Milia Mountain Retreat (tel. +30-28210-46774, www.milia.gr, DR €73–96).

From the car park in **Milia (1)**, a gravel trail, closed to cars, descends in 5 minutes to the houses of the ecovillage. At the **taverna (2)**, follow the trail that is cobbled at the beginning, descending slightly. About 100 m further on, before reaching a commercial building, turn left in the direction of Kato Milia. Another 30 m on, turn right to climb down over a couple of steps, cross through two gates, one after the other, and soon traverse a marvellous sweet chestnut forest via a slightly precipitous path. In **Kato Milia (3)**, at the junction 15 m past a quarry-stone house, turn left to descend. At

Trail signs in Milia.

Kalathenes

Aikirgianis

Milia Bk.

Kefala
477

272

Kissamos-

4

425

5

Tsourou-
niana

Topolia

Kria Vrisi
Milia Mountain
Retreat

1

P

Kato
Milia

Kastelos

Trapeza

556

2

3

6

581

Agia
Sofia

Milia

0   500 m   1km

Katsomatados

Arbutus trees near Milia.

the fork 30 m below the junction, bear slightly to the left. Now continue through a grove of olive trees whilst the trail keeps heading towards the prominent Kastelos. We will soon walk at its foot.

Pass a **chapel**; from time to time, arrows appear, pointing in the direction from which we came. The trail has become wide and gravel-surfaced as it descends along a stream course flanked by plane trees. Keeping to the main trail, it merges, a good 20 minutes past the chapel, into a secondary road. Turn right along the road and enter the hamlet of **Aikirgianis (4)**, 272 m. At the village limits, there is a trough fountain with good drinking water. Five minutes past that, leave the road behind by turning right onto a concrete-paved, stepped trail that ascends after a few paces to the church. Directly at

The cosy taverna in the ecovillage of Milia.

the bell-gable, turn right through a gateway then, just after, slightly right again and then immediately left to meet up with a dirt trail. Ascend along this through a grove of olive trees. At a cluster of houses continue straight ahead to reach a secondary road; turn right here to continue.

At the village limits of **Tsourouniana (5)**, reach a wash house and a memorial to the victims of the Second World War. Slightly set back from the street, a closed *kafenion* is standing. In front of the coffee house, turn left and meet up with a concrete-paved trail, 10 m further on. Climb up along the trail and, shortly afterwards, continue over a little stone stairway into the village. Once in the village, in front of a house (the house has a stepped entrance to the right) reach an intersecting, also concrete-paved, trail; turn left onto this trail and, 200 m on, meet up with a tarmac road. Turn sharp right onto this road. Continuing the ascent, the narrow road soon heads toward the mighty crag summit of Kastelos, to the left of which, we will descend again into the Milia valley after climbing a saddle. About 8 mins along the road, a dirt trail forks off; ignore this trail and instead, continue along the road another 10 m and then turn right onto a concrete-paved trail which becomes a rocky dirt trail after walking a few paces along it. To the left of Kastelos, the saddle also appears now. In a grove of olive trees, ignore all trails branching off from the main one. Now, pass through a gate. Shortly before reaching the saddle, the trail narrows into a path. In the **saddle (6)**, 516 m, we find ourselves standing at about the same height as Milia, but before we return again to the taverna, we must descend again into the valley. An ancient mule track, sometimes supported with laboriously-constructed walls, leads to a gravel trail. Along this, bearing to the right, descend past strawberry trees and heather trees to meet up again with the junction for **Kato Milia (3)** and, from there, ascend straight ahead to reach the **taverna (2)** and the car park at **Milia (1)**.

Through the Deliana Gorge

1.20 hrs

Simple ramble to a little chapel

Depending on the direction from which you approach the gorge, it bears a different name: if you are coming from Deliana, it is called the Deliana Gorge; in Mesavlia, it is called the Mesavlia Gorge. The short gorge is easily reached via a pleasant trail, yet it is little-known and rarely walked.

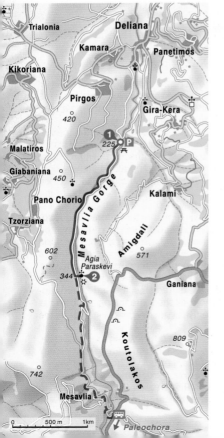

Starting point: Deliana, 225 m. From the National Road, take the Kolimbari exit and drive from there, via the villages of Spilia, Drakona and Episkopi to reach Deliana, 13 km away. Drive the whole way through Deliana and, shortly past the village limits, a sign to the left points out the direction to the gorge. Along a gravel road for 1.4 km, reach a large car park with a picnic area at the entrance to the gorge.
Height difference: 120 m in both ascent and descent.
Grade: the walk through the gorge follows a broad trail, pretty much the whole way on the level. Comfortable, mid-height footwear is more than adequate.
Refreshment: nothing en route. Tavernas in Deliana.
Alternative: if you are approaching by bus, begin the walk in Mesavlia. The settlement is on the bus line Chania – Paleochora (Mon–Sat, three times a day, twice on Sun.). From either location, the walk is feasible to tackle as a single day's tour. At the bus stop shelter in Mesavlia, a sign (Gorge of Mesavlia) points out a narrow tarmac road. In front of a cottage with a bread oven, the road veers to the left and ascends. 10 minutes later, in front of a cluster of houses, bear right and a good 5 minutes after that, the road leads to the right and then immediately to the left, passing between some houses. At a fork, 2 minutes later, leave the narrow road by turning right onto a gravel trail; descend along this into the gorge (walking time to the rest area at the gorge's exit and back again, 2.20 hrs.).

A pleasant gravel track leads through the Deliana Gorge.

From the **rest area (1)**, go past the WC, following a broad trail, and enter the gorge. The trail leads along a dry stream bed flanked by plane trees and oleander. Five minutes later, the trail changes over to the other bank of the stream for the first time, via a concrete-laid ford and, somewhat later on, reaches a wooden gate. Here, the walls of the gorge tower 150 m heavenwards. A little marble shrine with a cross is located to the right of the trail. After about 20 minutes, the trail, concrete-paved for a short stretch, begins to ascend gently along the right-hand side of the gorge; ignore another trail branching off to the right. Shortly after that, reach a large open area, to the left of which, the **Agia Paraskevi** chapel (2), 344 m, is situated.

The long picnic benches in front of it are only fully occupied once a year when the festival of the chapel's patron saint is celebrated. The chapel already marks our turning back point; return along the approach route to the **rest area (1)** near Deliana.

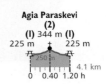

Agia Paraskevi
(2)
(l) 344 m (l)
225 m   225 m
250 m
4.1 km
0   0.40 1.20 h

From Moni Gouverneto to Moni Katholiko

To the monasteries on the Akrotiri peninsula

The peninsula lying north-east of Chania boasts of three monasteries worth seeing. The oldest of the three is Moni Katholiko, built picturesquely on a rock face perched over a little gorge; this can be reached via a delightful cobbled path. From the starting point of the walk, Moni Gouverneto appears strikingly like a fortress. Moni Agia Triada, which is a prime example of the style marking the Italian Renaissance, lies along the approach route; the museum within houses a valuable collection of icons. One of the highlights of this short walk is the Arkoudiotissa Cave (Bear Cave) – taking its name from a stalagmite that most certainly looks like a bear.

Dripstones in the Bear Cave.

Starting point: Moni Gouverneto, 254 m. From the National Road, near Chania, take the exit to Souda and then follow the signs for the airport. 1 km before reaching the airport, bear left towards Agia Triada and, from there, reach the Gouverneto Monastery after another 4 km.

Height difference: 180 m in both ascent and descent.

Grade: pleasant ascent along a sound cobbled path. To explore the Bear Cave and St. John's Cave, we recommend taking a torch along with you.

Refreshment: there are no opportunities to take refreshment en route.

Opening hours: Agia Triada Monastery (entrance fee) is open to visitors daily in summer from 8.00 until sundown, in winter, from 8–14.00 and from 16.00 until sundown.

The Gouverneto Monastery (there is an entrance fee) is open from Easter until mid-October, Mon, Tues and Thurs 9–12 and 17–19, Sat 9–12 and 17–20, Sun 5–12 and 17–20, in winter, closed an hour earlier in the afternoon.

Be sure to respect the dress codes of the monasteries (no shorts or sleeveless blouses). The areas outside of the Katholiko Monastery, as well as the Bear Cave and St. John's Cave, are always open to the public.

The former conventual church of Moni Katholiko is leaning directly up against a rock face.

From the large car park in front of the **Moni Gouverneto (1)**, pass through the wooden portal and into the monastery garden, planted with cypress and mulberry trees, then head for the monastery grounds enclosed by a fortification-like wall. With the monastery entrance to our right, past yet another portal, reach a saddle where you can enjoy a view of the Cretan Sea. To the right, a memorial commemorates those who fell during the Second World War. With the memorial also to your right, descend along the trail, which is gravel at the outset, but soon stepped and cobbled, into a valley. With the sea always in sight, reach a tumbledown quarry-stone house after a good ten minutes where the entrance to the **Arkoudiotissa dripstone cave (2)**, 188 m, is located.

In the middle of the cave, hanging from a soot-blackened ceiling, is a stalagmite, about 5 m high, which, with a little help from your imagination, looks like a bear. A little chapel is snuggling against the left-hand wall of the cave.

Moni Katholiko (3)
Arkoudiotissa (2)   Arkoudiotissa (2)
Moni Gouverneto (I)   Moni Gouverneto (I)
254 m   254 m
                            2.8 km
0   0.30 1.00 h

Archaeological finds have furnished evidence that the cave was already used as a sanctum in pre-Minoan times.

From the Bear Cave, continue descending along the cobbled trail and then pass a round house built of quarry stone, all the while, enjoying the splendid view of the rocky coastal landscape. Down below, a gorge opens up and already, a half an hour later, reach the **Moni Katholiko (3)**, 76 m. The former church of the monastery, which was abandoned in the 16th century because of repeated pirate raids, is embedded directly in a cave, however, the entrance is usually closed.

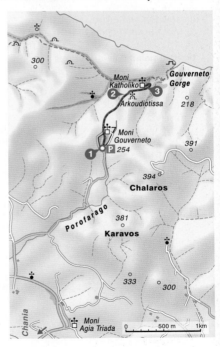

About 15 m before reaching the picturesque bell-gable (the bell has gone missing), the low entryway to the St. John's Cave appears to the left. The cave extends 150 m into the mountain; after about 40 m, reach two beautifully shaped stalagmites, one of which is almost 10 m in height. Past these, the cave narrows and you can only continue by ducking down.

Not long ago, it was possible to walk through the Gouverneto Gorge, situated below the monastery, and reach the sea. Now, however, the descending path into the gorge is closed – the monks do not want people passing through here and their wishes should be respected. Therefore, we head back from Katholiko to return to the **Gouverneto Monastery (1)**.

Along the cobbled trail to the Katholiko Monastery.

83

From a pearl of a village across the Drapanos peninsula

A cape projecting into the sea and capped by the 527 m high Drapanokefala lends the peninsula to the east of Chania its characteristic look. Between groves of olive trees and cypress woods, villages are in-

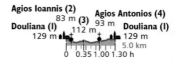

terspersed, peopled by immigrants who have settled here. Douliana is a peaceful hamlet with no through traffic. Near the kafenion on the little village square, a delightful path begins a descent into a verdant valley. Through brushwood and groves of olive trees, the route returns to the village. Before or after the short circular walk, you could take a ramble through Vamos.

Starting point: Douliana (on trail signs, also written as Ntouliana), 129 m. From

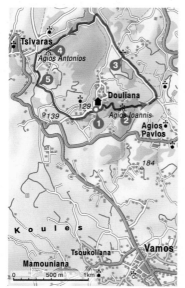

the National Road, between Georgioupolis and Chania, take the exit to Vamos. From there, drive in the direction of Kalyves; 3 km further on, turn off towards Gavalochori and, 0.3 km after the turn-off, bear left towards Ntouliana. Parking possible at the village limits in front of Natalias House.

Height difference: 140 m in both ascent and descent.

Grade: short, easy walk without any major ascents or descents along a path that is narrow at the outset and then along broad farm tracks. The circular walk is not waymarked; some junctions require a certain degree of attentiveness.

Refreshment: in Douliana, the *kafenion* on the village square. In Vamos, we recommend the traditional Taverna Sterna tou Bloumosifis, with excellent Cretan country cuisine (tel. +30-28250-83220), a part of the eco-project Vamos Village.

Worth seeing: in Vamos, which is the main settlement on the Drapanos peninsula, a ramble through the old town with its lovely, painstakingly restored natural stone houses is a worthwhile excursion. A focal point is the information office for the eco-project Vamos Village (www.vamosvillage.gr).

From »Natalias House« at the village limits of **Douliana (1)**, head into the little settlement. Immediately pass the *kafenion* on the tiny village square. 50 m past the coffee house, descend along the steep concrete-paved trail to the right; perhaps a wooden sign at foot level points out the way, in Greek, to Agios Ioannis. About 30 m further on, ignore a trail forking off to the left, and soon afterwards, pick up a cobbled trail that is flanked by fieldstone walls as it leads past carob and olive trees.

At the fork located on the valley floor, turn sharp left; the path follows the dry stream bed which is surrounded by lush greenery, as it leads to the cave chapel, **Agios Io-**

Furnished: the Agios Antonios Chapel.

annis (2), 83 m, leaning against the rock face. Shortly past the little church, the wood thins out and the idyllic path merges into a broader trail. Continue along this trail while crossing over slabs of rock and ignoring a fork to the right. Now meet up with a junction in front of a house with a flat roof; here, turn left along the gravel trail.

The trail ascends slightly, passing between olive trees and cypress trees. Now always keep to the main trail and, 10 minutes later, at the top of a height, pass by a **shrine to the Virgin Mary (3)**, 112 m. Once again gently descending, continue to ignore all forks. On the valley floor, not quite 15 minutes past the shrine, turn left onto a dirt trail. Take this trail, keeping always straight on, until reaching the **Agios Antonios (4)**, 93 m, a quarter of an hour later. This is also a cave chapel with an area in front of it for picnicking; even a trough fountain with potable water is provided.

Afterwards, continue on along the trail; this merges 100 m later into a narrow road. Turn left along the road and head towards the houses of Tsivaras. About 200 m further on, the tarmac road veers sharply to the left; at this point, leave the road behind by heading straight on along a gravel trail. Before reaching the first houses of **Tsivaras (5)**, 109 m, meet up with a junction; turn left here to descend and, at the fork 50 m on, turn right to ascend. The trail leads to a high ridge up above. In front of a vineyard slope, bear right yet again. At an electricity pylon, meet an intersecting trail. Turn right along this for a short stretch and then turn left to descend until reaching the access road to Douliana in front of a cemetery wall. Take the road to the left and, in five minutes, return back to **Douliana (1)**.

Samaria Gorge National Park

Classic tour through one of Europe's longest gorges

The Samaria Gorge is an absolute »must« – mind you, in the high season, up to 3000 walkers daily are thinking the same thing! So, don't expect a good deal of peace and quiet. From the high plateau of Omalos, 1200 m, in the centre of the White Mountains, an alpine path, very steep at the outset, descends through a beautiful valley designated as a national park, as it makes its way to the Libyan Sea. Along the 16 km stretch, leading through splendid pine and cypress forest, rest areas, equipped with trough fountains and toilets, provide excellent spots for a break. What is perhaps the most spectacular landscape that Crete has to offer is traversed here in the lower reaches of this Cretan Grand Canyon which includes the »Iron Gates«. In Agia Roumeli, at the mouth of the gorge, ferries are waiting to provide transport back to the resorts along the southern coast. The posted walking time of 5.40 hrs is rather generously calculated; experienced walkers can arrive at the ferry pier in not quite 5 hrs without taking long breaks. If you get an early start, you can descend to the sea without making haste; the first ferry for Agia Roumeli doesn't leave before 17.00.

Starting point: Xyloskalo, 1230 m. Approach by bus from Chania to Omalos/Xyloskalo (daily at 6.15 and 7.45; length of journey, 1.30 hrs.), Sougia (from mid-June, daily at 7.00, length of journey 1.30 hrs.) and Paleochora (Mon–Sat, 6.15, length of journey, 1.30 hrs.). Bus service from Rethymno and Kissamos with a transfer in Chania. Current schedule available locally and at www.bus-service-crete.com.
Return: ferry service from Agia Roumeli to Loutro/Chora Sfakion from May until October around 17.30, to Sougia/Paleochora also around 17.30 (current schedules available locally and at www.an-endyk.gr). The last bus to Chania from Chora Sfakion daily at 18.30 (waits for the ferry to arrive), from Paleochora daily at 18.15, from Sougia daily at 18.15. Walkers staying in Paleochora or Sougia enjoy the advantage of taking the ferry directly »home« without bus transfer.
Height difference: 1250 m in descent.
Grade: long gorge walk, demanding physical fitness, along a well-laid trail; the first 600 m of altitude follows a steep alpine path. Depending on the season and water level, you may have to cross the stream bed several times over sometimes slippery stones; some sections are loose underfoot and require sure-footedness.

For reasons of conservation, you must keep to the main trail. In the upper reaches, very shady, but in high summer, for the last 30-minute stretch to the sea, expect blazing sun and scorching heat which could lead

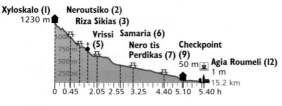

Xyloskalo (1) 1230 m — Neroutsiko (2) — Riza Sikias (3) — Vrissi (5) — Samaria (6) — Nero tis Perdikas (7) — Checkpoint (9) — 50 m — Agia Roumeli (12) 1 m — 15.2 km

0 0.45 2.05 2.55 3.25 4.40 5.10 5.40 h

Early morning callisthenics at the gorge entrance with Gingilos in the background.

to problems relating to heatstroke. Be sure to take enough sunscreen! At the half-way point, in the former village of Samaria, there is a first aid station. Camping and also bathing in the gorge are strictly prohibited, but nevertheless, bring along your bathing gear to enjoy the beautiful pebble beach in Agia Roumeli.

Opening hours: depending on the water level, the gorge is usually open from the beginning of May until the end of October daily from 6.00–16.00 (after 16.00, you can only walk to km 2; spending the night in the gorge is not permitted). The entrance fee is €5.

Refreshment: at the starting point, Xyloskalo, there is a cafeteria already open at 7.00; there is a variety of (expensive) snack bars at the Check Point near the gorge exit; numerous tavernas in Agia Roumeli. At the rest areas en route, several trough fountains provide fresh mountain spring water.

Accommodation: on the Omalos plateau, at 1050 m, is the Hotel Neos Omalos, tel. +30-28210-67269, www.neos-omalos.gr; numerous rooms to rent in Agia Roumeli at the gorge exit.

Linking tip: if you prefer not to return to your holiday accommodations on the same day as the walk, spend the night in Agia Roumeli. The next day, you could then walk the *E4* along the south coast to Chora Sfakion (Walk 24).

Starting from the car park at the cafeteria in **Xyloskalo (1)**, at first, enjoy the view of Gingilos, with its rugged rock face. At over 1000 m in height, it stands towering like a sentinel guarding the entrance to the gorge; during the first stage of the descent, the mountain will act as our steadfast companion. After buying an entrance pass at the ticket booth (this will be cancelled at the mouth of the gorge), descend along the stepped trail that is flanked by railings. Along zigzags, quickly put some metres of altitude behind you; many

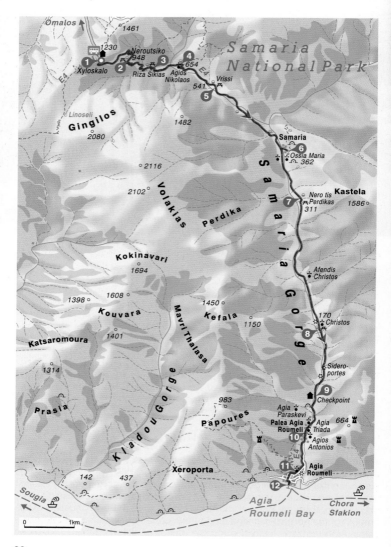

In the rocky upper reaches of the gorge.

sections are protected by chain link fencing which, at least, catches the smaller rocks as they fall down from up above. The path leads through a splendid mixed forest of mountain cypress, kermes oak and, in the lower reaches, Turkish pines. Every couple of hundred metres there are caches of water for fire-fighting in case a forest fire should break out. In shady spots, you'll find sizeable patches of the Cretan violet (Cyclamen creticum). Iron-wort (Sideritis syriaca) is also growing here; when the plant is dried, the finished product is sold throughout Central Europe as Cretan mountain tea.

Three-quarters of an hour later, the rest area, **Neroutsiko (2)**, 948 m, sheltered beneath a spreading plane tree, offers a good spot for the first break. There is a WC here and a trough fountain where you can refresh your drinking water supply. A good 20 minutes later, reach the rocky stream bed of the gorge for the first time; on the left bank of the bed, a trail leads to the rest area **Riza Sikias (3)**, where additional trough fountains can be found. In early spring, the rare Cretan helleborine is flowering here, but when the gorge opens in May, it is already withered. As compensation, walkers build hundreds of cairns at this spot to pay their respects to the gorge. Shortly past Riza Sikias, cross over the stream bed of the gorge (dozens of crossings will be made during the walk), big, smooth, round boulders fill up the bed. Oriental plane trees act as companions during the following, not quite so steep, descent.

Ancient cypresses, some as old as 600 years, tower above a cosy spot situated near the quarry-stone chapel of **Agios Nikolaos (4)**, 654 m. The chapel stands on the same site, legend has it, where an ancient sanctum dedicated to Apollo stood in the 6th century BC. In the clearing nearby, peonies, Cretan arum lily and Dragon Arum, some specimens growing to a height of 1 m, are flowering in May – from a botanical perspective, certainly one of the most spectacular spots in the entire gorge. From the chapel, cross through a stately cypress forest to continue on to the rest area of **Vrissi (5)**, and after a short intermediate ascent, climb back down again to **Samaria (6)**, 362 m. In front of the abandoned village, the stream bed of the gorge is crossed via a bridge. In the ancient, partially-restored, stone houses, you will find a first-aid station and toilets; a village trough fountain has also been included. Picnic tables, under fig and mulberry trees, are usually fully occupied around midday. A good half of the route now lies behind us. From Samaria, cross over the bridge again and continue descending along the right bank. 2 mins later, pass the **Christos Chapel**, which appears to seek protection by squatting under a rock face. On the opposite side of the gorge, you can spot the Ossia Maria Chapel (presumably the namesake for the gorge), peeking out through the cypress trees, as well as the ruins of **Kato Samaria**. The trail changes to the other side of the stream bed for the gorge (here, a good 20 to 30 m wide) via a bridge – you can well imagine the size of the torrent that rushes through here on its way to the sea after the winter rainfall. Past the rest area, **Nero tis Perdikas** (in English, »Partridge Spring«) **(7)**, 311 m, the actual gorge begins. Now continue directly along the stony stream bed, heading for the first bottleneck. The torrential stream is crossed several times via stepping-stones, some of which are slippery. Walk beneath rugged rock faces and scree slopes to the rest area **Christos (8)**, 170 m, snuggling under shady pines; a couple of paces above the rest area, is the chapel of the same name. This is the last major rest area along the stretch to the sea. A couple of minutes afterwards, a log-paved trail leads through **Sideroportes**, the »Iron Gates«. With a mere 3 m distance between the vertical and sometimes overhanging, gorge walls, towering 300 m above, this is the supreme bottleneck of the canyon. Afterwards, the gorge broadens once more. Along walkways and over bridges, the river is criss-crossed several times until finally reaching the national park border at the **checkpoint (9)**, 50 m, where your ticket will be cancelled. A row of kiosks are offering refreshment here. Now it's only another 3 km to reach the ferry. A cobbled trail leads soon along groves of olives and carob trees, passing the abandoned houses of **Palea Agia Roumeli (10)**. In spring of 1952, a flash flood carried away a part of the village and the inhabitants built a new village directly on the sea as a result. At the village limits, cross over a stone bridge to the Agia Triada church and the cemetery (if you are too tired to walk anymore, a shuttle bus for the ferry is available here in the high season). A concrete-paved road leads, in 20 mins, to the new village of **Agia Roumeli (11)**. At a fork on the village limits, continue straight ahead and, 3 mins later, bear slightly to the right. Finally, in the village centre, just past the Pension Sorbas, reach the ticket office for the ferry; keep left from there and a few paces will bring you to the **ferry dock (12)**.

Sometimes rickety wooden walkways – here, in front of the Iron Gates – aid in crossing the torrential stream.

The Xepitiras rock arch.

Vigorous summit climb onto a popular 2000-m peak

From Xyloskalo, the north face of Gingilos appears rugged and menacing; at first glance, an ascent does not seem easy, and what seems to be, is true indeed. From the west, however, a relatively negotiable ascent trail exists for the experienced mountain walker. From the more than three dozen 2000-metre peaks of the Lefka Ori (White Mountains)) Gingilos is the most popular, not only because of the magnificent view from the summit, but also due to the fact that the approach is easily accessible from the entrance to the Samaria Gorge.

Starting point: Xyloskalo, 1230 m. Approaching from the northern coast along the National Road, in Chania, take the exit to Omalos and, via Lakki and the Omalos high plateau, reach the car park, Xyloskalo, at the entrance to the Samaria Gorge. From Paleochora and Sougia, reach Omalos via Agia Irini. With the bus from Chania (during the summer season, daily at 6.15 and 7.45), from Paleochora (Mon–Sat 6.15) and from Sougia (June until Sept, daily at 7.00) to the car park at the entrance to the Samaria Gorge. For »bus travellers«, however, there is only a single return to Chania scheduled in the afternoon (13.30 and 19.30), otherwise, you must spend a night in one of the simple hotels in Omalos.

Height difference: a good 1000 m.

Grade: until reaching the Afchenas saddle, the route ascends along a well-laid alpine path which is, however, in the last section, fairly steep, sometimes way-marked with the *E4* waymarkings. At the saddle, the steep ascent continues, heading for the summit, waymarked with *yellow* markings and cairns; this stretch demands absolute sure-footedness. During easy stretches of scrambling, sometimes you have to use your hands. Slightly precipitous sections in the area around the rock arch. Into the month of May, expect snowfields between the Linoseli spring and saddle, as well as in both of the depressions between the secondary and the main peak. Hardly any shade!

Alternative: from the Afchenas saddle, you could descend the *E4* in a good 4 hrs to the Libyan Sea at Sougia. The route is well marked until Koustogerako; from there, follow Walk 19. From the saddle, continue along a path (sometimes precipitous); later on along pleasant gravel trails.

Refreshment: a cafeteria at the car park and, above it, the restaurant Xyloskalo with a panoramic view (daily, from 11.00).

The walk begins at the car park, **Xyloskalo (1)**, at the entrance to the Samaria Gorge. You can't miss the towering, rugged face of the mountain in front of you whose summit is your target. Also, the destination for the first stage of the walk, the Afchenas saddle between Gingilos and Strifomadi, is easy to spot. A few paces on, next to the entrance for the gorge, an *E4* sign points out the direction. The stepped trail, flanked by a railing at the outset, climbs in 3 mins above the car park to pass the entrance to the restaurant Xyloskalo. Shortly afterwards, pass through a gate. From here, you can already enjoy a fantastic backwards view over the Omalos high plateau and, soon after that, also catch a splendid panoramic view into the Samaria Gorge. The alpine path is stony, but well laid, and sometimes marked with *E4* posts and waymarkers. Weather-beaten cypresses flank the trail's edge.

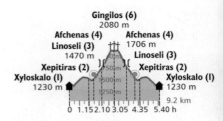

During the first hour of the ascent, the rocky summit of Gingilos keeps almost always in sight. At a good 1500 m above sea level, the Afchenas col appears once again in front of us. But before the ascent to the saddle begins, enjoy a relaxing level stretch and then descend slightly. During this section, walk along a narrow mule track to cross over the **Xepitiras (2)**, 1461 m, a natural vaulted gangway, 10 m in height, that looks like a Gothic arch standing in the middle of the landscape.

Lovely views of the Omalos high plateau open up at the beginning of the ascent.

Along the stretch to the Afchenas col, a steep, scree-covered slope must be climbed.

The route now takes on an alpine character as the trail traverses a scree slope and passes striking crags. Shortly past an overhanging rock face and a shelter situated there in case of a sudden change in the weather, reach the **Linoseli spring (3)**, 1470 m, gushing water into a bathtub-like trough. In midsummer, Bupleurum kakiskalae can be found flowering here. This wild-flower is found exclusively in the Linoseli region and is one of the rarest endemic flowers that Crete has to offer – entered on the Red List of Threatened Species, only a few hundred specimens of this member of the carrot family are known to exist.

The now steep ascent leads over the rocky, scree-covered slope to reach the saddle between Gingilos and Strifomadhi; until well into May, you must expect to cross over snowfields. Arriving at the **Afchenas col (4)**, 1706 m, the first thing to do is to take a deep breath. South-wards, a view opens up taking in the Tripiti Gorge, merging into the Libyan Sea, and of Gavdos Island, lying offshore from the south coast; to the north-east, the Kallergi hut (Walk 13) perches precipitously over the Samaria Gorge. When the *E4* leaves us behind by turning off to the right, turn left at the saddle and begin the ascent to Gingilos over slanted plates of rock. Sometimes along a well-trodden alpine path, sometimes over bare rock without a distinct path to follow (*yellow* waymarkers), finally reach the **secondary summit (5)**, 2075 m, of Gingilos which is only a few metres lower than the main summit.

At the pyramid-shaped cairn on the flat summit area, many walkers think that they have already arrived on Gingilos. The main peak, however, is actually the craggy knoll lying to the north-east. You may be able to spot a metal rod there which is actually a part of the former summit cross, now missing the cross bar. Waymarkers lead downward, at first, into a depression; skirt around this along the right-hand rim. A second, somewhat larger, depression is also skirted around along the right-hand rim via sharp-edged rocks. After some roundabout scrambling, finally reach the main peak of **Gingilos (6)**, 2080 m, a quarter of an hour later, where a little shrine is situated. The panoramic view is not much better than that from the secondary peak, but the view of the Omalos high plateau, lying down below our feet, is a pretty one. Seemingly close enough to reach out and touch, Volakias, 2116 m, lies to the south-east. Eastwards is Pachnes, 2453 m, Crete's second highest mountain. At the end of May, directly in the summit area, rose-coloured flowers appear on the Spreading cherry (Prunus prostrata), a small-leaved, ground-hugging shrub, which even the severe frost at this altitude, cannot cause any harm.

After taking a long look, descend again via the approach route to return to **Xyloskalo (1)**.

At the large cairn at the 2075 m point, you are already eye-to-eye with the true peak (far left).

Via the Kallergi hut into the heart of the White Mountains

Do not be put off by the relatively long walking times and the many metres of height! Melindaou is a relatively easy 2000-metre summit in the very centre of the White Mountains. The ascent leads for the most part along a pleasant and panoramic, traffic-free, gravel track; only the last third of the route, sometimes climbing a rocky alpine path, requires not only good physical fitness, but also sure-footedness. By spending the night in the Kallergi hut, you can extend the walk to a two-day trek.

Starting point: Xyloskalo, 1230 m. See Walk 12 for the approach. »Bus travellers« can take the early bus from Chania to Omalos (Xyloskalo), during the descent, spend the night in the Kallergi hut and, the next day, take the early bus back to Chania.

Height difference: 1250 m in both ascent and descent.

Grade: a long mountain walk demanding physical fitness. The first stretch to the pavilion is along a pleasant track, followed by a steep and rocky alpine path

to the summit. Expect snowfields up into May. The trail is sporadically marked with *E4* posts. Almost no shade at all!

Refreshment and accommodation: self-service cafeteria in Xyloskalo; Kallergi hut, tel. +30-28210-44647, mobile +30-6976-585849, www.eoshanion.gr; it is necessary to reserve in advance for accommodation and to participate in an evening meal.

Shorter walk: the pleasant ascent to the Kallergi hut alone is worthwhile; there and back, 2.20 hrs.

Kallergi: Crete's only catered mountain hut sits almost 1600 m above sea level.

From the car park in **Xyloskalo (1)**, next to the entrance for the Samaria Gorge, ascend for a few paces along the *E4*-signed path, stepped at the outset, towards the Kallergi hut. The path immediately crosses through a gate; please close this carefully behind you. Keeping at first parallel to the road, the path ascends the slope on the diagonal. 20 minutes later, enjoy a view of the mighty summit of Gingilos, 2080 m. To the left of the peak stands the somewhat higher summit of Volakias, 2116 m, and to the right of Gingilos, Psilafi 1984 m, with the Afchenas col between the two where the final ascent of Gingilos begins (see Walk 12).

Past yet another gate, the well-laid alpine path meets up with a **gravel track**, turn right onto this track to continue ascending. 10 mins later, at a left-hand bend, there is a possible short-cut along a meagrely-marked path that ascends along a steep, rough and rocky gully. At the end, however, we won't be saving much time by doing this, so instead, we continue along the pleasant track while enjoying a view of the Omalos high plateau.

The track climbs up to a saddle, and at the top, a shrine to the Virgin Mary is situated next to a round stone hut. Here, bear right to continue on to the **Kallergi hut (2)**, 1592 m, now within sight. The hut is perched precariously

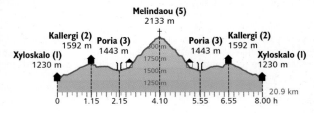

Barren mountain terrain during the descent from Melindaou.

on top of an alpine knoll, high above the Samaria Gorge. From the spacious viewing platform, enjoy a startling panoramic view of the 2000-metre peaks of the White Mountains, of Gingolos directly opposite, also of Melindaou (the final destination of this walk) to the east, and of Pachnes just to the south of it. At the rear of the hut, a couple of steps descend along a fence to return to the track down below. Follow the track for five minutes until it veers off to the left at an *E4* post; here, we could short-cut a zigzag along a stepped path. Returning to the track, continue on eastwards, more or less keeping on the level; to the north, cast your gaze into a valley and to the coastline far below. The rocky terrain is covered in low-growth *phrygana* with scattered cypress trees and Cretan maples punctuating the terrain.

At the foot of Psari, reach a junction in the **Poria col (3)**, 1443 m. Keep slightly to the left here, that is, keep to the track and then, three minutes later, ignore a track forking off northwards. The trail continues on along the foot of Psari to meet up with a battered **pavilion (4)**, 1512 m. Directly opposite to the pavilion, leave the track behind by turning right onto a rocky alpine path. The path is relatively well-marked with *E4* posts as it ascends steeply to a saddle at about 1750 m above sea level; from there, continue on through a long, broad basin to reach yet another col. Up until late spring, this notch can be covered with extensive fields of snow. Now arriving on the uppermost col, the trail veers to the left and, finally, ascends along a broad ridge to reach the summit of **Melindaou (5)**, 2133 m.

After a good, long look at the views, return along the approach route back to **Xyloskalo (1)**.

Along the long-distance trail westwards

A popular second choice to Paleochora's municipal beach, usually packed to the gills and especially so in summer, is the splendid sandy beach at Krios. From there, we could walk for a stretch via the well-marked E4 along the delightful coastline to reach a chapel and, if you so wish, even continue further to the excellent beach of Elafonisi (see Alternative).

Starting point: Krios Beach, 3 m. From Paleochora, follow the signs in the direction of Kountoura. At the junction for Voutas, continue straight ahead along the road running near the coastline, passing greenhouses, until reaching the Taverna Krios Beach; the last 0.6 km is a gravel road.
Height difference: 250 m in both ascent and descent.
Grade: a coastal walk along a well-marked path; a precipitous section will demand sure-footedness. Hardly any shade, be sure to take along your sunblock and bathing gear!
Refreshment: taverna on Krios Beach.

Alternative: if you make the approach from Paleochora by taxi (tel. +30-28230-41128, www.paleochora-taxi.com) to reach Krios Beach, from there, you can walk the entire stage of the *E4* to reach Elafonisi and, in the high season, take a ferry or a bus (normally leaving at 16.00) to return to Paleochora. The complete coastal tour is also feasible when using Chania as a starting point: take the early bus to Paleochora (travelling time 2 hrs.), then a taxi to Krios Beach and take the afternoon bus from Elafonisi (departure about 17.00) to return to Chania (walking time Krios Beach – Elafonisi 3.30 hrs.).

Jutting capes and little bays break up the coastline near Paleochora.

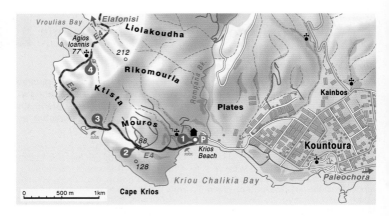

From the car park in front of the Taverna **Krios Beach (1)**, walk to the western end of the beach. There, scramble over a projecting rock, crowned by an *E4* post. A tiny, but very popular bathing cove (naturism), about 30 m in length, follows. At the cove's end, scramble up over the coastal rocks to yet another *E4* post.

After the first rough and tumble metres, soon continue along the well-laid alpine path which leads for a few paces above a track running parallel, to reach a **saddle (2)**, 88 m, at the top of Cape Krios. While the track now turns towards the interior, instead, follow a gravel trail from the saddle straight ahead for a good 100 m and then fork off to the left onto a path. Far in the distance, westwards, the view stretches all the way to the Elafonisi island. The path now drops to a **bathing cove (3)**, peppered with countless boulders and boasting tiny beaches in between. The last cove along the way, but also the prettiest, is something to note down for the return. In front of the cove, the still well-marked trail veers to the right and, passing a tiny church perched on a cliff 100 m in the distance, ascends again along the coastal cliffs. Skirt around the cape that lies in front of us. At the same height as a crag, a breathtaking panoramic view opens up over the wide sweeping bay with the offshore island of Elafonisi. For a short stretch, the path is slightly precipitous as it leads along striking cliffs. At the end, reach the little church

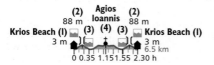

of **Agios Ioannis (4)**, 77 m. After taking a rest break on a stone bench in front of the chapel, return along the approach route back to **Krios Beach (1)**.

To the cave of the 99 fathers and an Ottoman Fortress

The adventurous descent via a ladder into the cave of the 99 fathers (also known as the Zoures Cave) is certainly guaranteed to be an unforgettable experience. According to one legend, the name refers to 99 hermits who immigrated here from Cyprus in the 12th century and who took a vow to all die on the very same day. After visiting the cave, we will continue along a high mountain trail to the ruins of an Ottoman Fortress. Set in an exposed location high above the southern coast, the site offers a marvellous view of the Libyan Sea and the resort town of Paleochora.

Starting point: Azogires, 380 m (8 km to the north-east of Paleochora), is quickly reached by car, taxi or the bus to Omalos (not daily and via Azogires; ask in Paleochora for the up-to-date schedule).
Height difference: 250 m.
Grade: the ascent to the cave is via a broad roadway; the path to the ruins of the castle is sometimes overgrown (long trousers recommended), the last section is cross-country. The descent into the cave along a ladder demands sure-footedness. Be sure to bring along a torch!
Short version: if you have a car that isn't built too low to the ground, you can take the 2.3 km long roadway from Azogires to the car park just below the cave (if you meet another car, then it becomes tight). The walking time is thereby shortened to a good 1 hr.
Refreshment: in the uniquely decorated Alfa Café, you feel like you have landed in

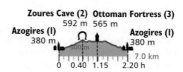

Zoures Cave (2) Ottoman Fortress (3)
Azogires (I) 592 m 565 m Azogires (I)
380 m   300m   380 m
7.0 km
0 0.40 1.15 2.20 h

a museum.
Worth seeing: as a bonus, you could descend from Azogires to the monastery church of the 99 fathers (Agii Pateres) nestled beneath a rock face. From the Alfa Café, follow the village street a good 200 m to the eastern village limits and then descend along a cobbled path following the untamed and romantic mill stream to the monastery (20 mins, there and back). Also worth seeing is the evergreen plane tree, venerated as sacred, located a few paces west of the monastery church.

From the village street in **Azogires (1)** and 50 m from the Alfa Café, at a tiny chapel, a road, at first concrete paved, ascends steeply to the upper part of the settlement. A good 5 minutes later, meet a fork and turn left. A good stretch after that and further above, pass a **church**, 492 m, painted blinding white.

Now on a stony roadway, ten minutes later, in a hairpin bend and after a metal gate, a path forks off to the Ottoman Fortress. We, however, first turn right to continue along the roadway until, 200 m on, it ends at a **cul-de-sac**. From here, you can spot a white cross perched on the jagged line of crags

Only some mighty walls of the Ottoman Fortress still remain.

where the entrance to the cave is located. A sound path climbs up above to it in a few minutes. The descent into the dimly-lit **Zoures Cave (2)**, 592 m, is actually more like a crevice in the rock and is negotiated by climbing down three steep metal ladders. About 30 m down, reach a little altar. From there, if you are equipped with a bright torch, you could penetrate about another 50 m into the cave.

Returning to the cul-de-sac, head back to the metal gate in the **hairpin bend**; we can pass through via a narrow opening. About 100 m further on, pass through a second gate. The *blue*-marked path, keeping on the level, leads above a little plain, formerly used as agricultural land. At the end of the plain, bear slightly right; at this point, the trail is sometimes overgrown with thorny burnet, but the old course of the trail can be spotted quite well as it leads along the foot of the rocky mountain ridge and opens up far-reaching views of the sea.

A good 10 minutes past the little plain, the path peters out; faded *yellow* waymarkers lead us to a fence that can be passed through by unhooking a

wire loop. Now continue along the fence until, at the end, in a few minutes, the **Ottoman Fortress (3)**, 565 m, appears in front of us. The last 300 m until reaching the ruins of the castle is negotiated more or less cross-country.

After taking a break, return along the approach route to descend back to **Azogires (1)**.

To an ancient spa and a pebble bay on the Libyan Sea

The walk to Lissos has all the ingredients that a top tour on Crete would need: a wild and romantic gorge adorned with bushes of oleander, a high plateau with a breath-taking panoramic view of the coast, and the archaeological site of the ancient Lissos, unearthed in the 1950s. In this secluded valley, there once existed an early-Helladic spa which was later maintained by the Romans. Even the Byzantines have left their tracks on this area which, just as in the past, is only accessible on foot or by small boats. Oh, by the way, a bathing cove with an inviting pebble beach is waiting here as well.

Starting point: Sougia, 1 m. Approach by car from the north coast via Agia Irini; with the early bus from Chania, Mon–Sat, 5.15 and 8.45, Sun, 7.30 (travelling time 2 hrs.); return from Sougia at 18.15.

Height difference: 310 m in both ascent and descent.

Grade: uncomplicated gorge walk, afterwards, along a well-trodden path to Lissos. The route constantly follows the waymarked *E4*. Take along your bathing gear!

Refreshment: nothing en route, several tavernas in Sougia.

Alternative: from Sougia, you can walk along the relatively well-marked *E4* via Lissos to reach Paleochora. The coastal route is an especially good choice for walkers staying in Paleochora. From there, take the early ferry (mid-May to end of Oct.) to Sougia and then walk the described route to Lissos. By the trough fountain at the rest area, keep the low building to your right-hand side and head towards the west along the path over the abandoned terraces. In a good hour, ascend to a high plateau, 250 m, while passing Cape Flomes situated to the south. From the plateau, descend again to the coastline and then take a relatively level path following the coast. The final stretch to Paleochora leads along a tarmac road (walking time, a total of almost 5 hrs.).

Small, but nice: the bathing cove of Lissos.

Byzantine chapel Agios Kyriakos with integrated ancient marble friezes.

Begin the walk in **Sougia (1)** at the Taverna Galini (bus stop) and ramble the seaside road along the pebble beach, heading westwards. From the ferry dock at the **harbour (2)**, turn right to pass the fishing boats. Past a large boulder lying directly in front of the steep coast and near a goat pen, look for the entrance to the **Lissos Gorge**. Not quite another 100 m further on, scramble over a smoothly polished boulder; in the further course of the route, several large boulders and bottlenecks must be skirted around, however, the trail through the gorge is always relatively easy to negotiate.

A good five minutes past a narrow passage between overhanging rocks (see photo page 107), keep an eye out for a *yellow/black* waymarker. Here, leave the gorge behind by turning left onto an ancient mule path which climbs up in zigzags to the uppermost edge of the gorge (Walk 17 continues straight on along the stream bed of the gorge).

Along the high plateau **Kandouni (3)**, the rust-coloured path now leads panoramically through undemanding, thorny cushion plant undergrowth. Soon the small, turquoise-coloured bay of Lissos appears. In tight bends, descend from the plateau while traversing a steep rock face and, after passing a grove of olive trees and just past a cave, meet up with an in-

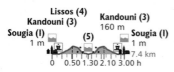

tersecting trail. Bearing to the right, reach the fenced-in grounds of ancient **Lissos (4)**. On the lower end of the fence, follow the fence further to the right to reach the entrance to the archaeological digs. A stone stairway ascends to a wall constructed from precisely dressed stone blocks, behind which, the **Asklepios Temple** lies hidden. This sanctum, dedicated to the Greek God of Healing, dates back to the 3rd century BC. The well-preserved floor mosaic was laid 200 years later by the Romans.

After visiting the temple, return to the entrance and turn right to follow the fence leading to a Byzantine chapel, a good 50 m on. In front of the chapel, the remains of another floor mosaic can be seen. A path descends slightly from the chapel to a low building, behind which, a tow-

Roman floor mosaic in Lissos.

ering eucalyptus tree is growing. Here, next to the warden's house, meet up with a shady **picnic site** with a trough fountain.

From the warden's house, it seems like a very good idea to pay a visit to **Lissos Beach (5)**. The path leads past ancient olive trees and, just before reaching the beach, also passes another Byzantine chapel (Agios Kyriakos, 14th century), whose construction includes ancient fragments of temples and marble friezes. After taking a bathing break at the pebble beach, return along the approach route back to **Sougia (1)**.

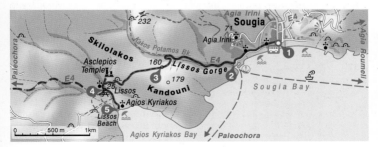

The little canyon at Sougia

For more than 2000 years, a path runs through the Lissos Gorge, and now, just as then, it is still the shortest route overland from Sougia to the ancient settlement of Lissos. This walk, however, does not have the early-Helladic Asclepius temple as its destination (see Walk 16), but instead, it continues for a stretch further through the accessible gorge and then cuts a wide arc across the pastoral hill country to return to Sougia.

Starting point: Sougia, 1 m. For the approach, see Walk 16.
Height difference: 250 m.
Grade: uncomplicated gorge walk; the

path that follows is well-marked with *red* dots.
Refreshment: there are several tavernas in Sougia.

The circular walk begins in **Sougia (1)** at the Taverna Galini (bus stop). From there, ramble westwards along the seaside road, passing other tavernas on the way, until reaching the **harbour (2)** 10 mins later. In front of

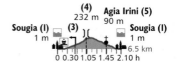

the ferry dock, bear to the right and pass a couple of fishing boats bobbing in the waters of the sea. Past a large boulder, directly at the edge of the steep coast, look for the entrance to the **Lissos Gorge**, located next to a goat pen. Not quite another 100 m further on, scramble over a smoothly polished boulder; in the further course of the route, along the stream bed of the gorge, choked with oleander bush, several large boulders and bottlenecks must be skirted around. The most striking section of the gorge is reached at an approximately 50 m high, slightly **overhanging rock face**; a narrow passage allows the walk to continue. Shortly afterwards, another bottleneck can be passed through via a path on the left. About 5 mins past the overhanging rock face, the **E4 (3)** cuts away to the left and climbs out of the gorge (*yellow/black* waymarkers), however, con-

tinue straight on here along the stream bed of the gorge which continues to be fairly easy to negotiate. From time to time, it is necessary to scramble over boulders between one and two metres in height. The gorge begins to open up slightly. About 25 mins past the point where the *E4* branched off, reach a boulder, about 2.5 metres in height, located in the dry stream bed. Cairns and *red* waymarkers draw attention to a path breaking away to the right; follow this to reach a **saddle (4)**, 232 m. From the saddle, descend slightly for a couple of minutes through a little valley, until it veers southward to the sea. Our path, however, continues to lightly ascend. Cairns and *red* dot waymarkers help to keep us on the right track.

Meanwhile, enjoy a view of the Libyan Sea. About 15 mins past the saddle, reach a dry **stream bed**. Follow the stream bed to the right, but soon after,

The overhanging rock face in the Lissos Gorge.

5 m further on, ascend again to the left. With the sea always in sight, traverse the slope above the stream bed along a path. In front of us, the beach at Sougia comes into view. At a goat pen, the trail merges into a farm road. Descend straight ahead along this road to reach the **Agia Irini** chapel **(5)**, 90 m, dedicated to the Virgin Mary. From the area in front of the chapel, enjoy a downwards view of the harbour. From the chapel, continue descending

along the trail. Below the chapel, in a bend to the left, there is a picnic table in the shade, next to a trough fountain. At the village limits of Sougia, the gravel trail merges into a street. Keeping to the right along this street, at the large village church, meet up again with the harbour road which brings us back to the village centre of **Sougia (1)**.

Lovely view from the Chapel of Our Lady, Agia Irini.

To a ringside view high above the Libyan Sea

From the seaside road in Sougia, we can already spot the destination for this walk: far to the east, a chapel is perched on a humpbacked cape. The ruins of a castle that was built by the Venetians are, however, not yet visible. The Venetians took advantage of the strategic location somewhat below the cape. The well-trodden path along the coast that leads there opens up a breathtaking panoramic view of the pristine and completely uninhabited coastline. The path is waymarked as a stage of the E4 long distance trail.

The ruins of a Venetian fortress.

Starting point: Sougia, 1 m. For the approach, see Walk 16.

Height difference: about 850 m in both ascent and descent.

Grade: a long coastal walk via the relatively well-marked *E4* with a steep final ascent onto the cape; some stretches are somewhat precipitous. The constant up and down walking should not be taken lightly. Bring along plenty of drinking water as the spring located a short distance before the cape has hardly any water in the summer months.

Refreshment: nothing en route, several tavernas in Sougia.

Alternatives: 1. Since the route there and back is rather strenuous, you may prefer to make it a linear walk by hiring a boat to take you from Sougia to the Agios Nikolaos Chapel at the mouth of the Tripiti Gorge (information at Captain George in the pension of the same name in Sougia, tel. +30-28230-51133, www.sougia.info/taxi-boats.htm). From there, a steep ascent along the *E4* will bring you, in 1 hr, to the saddle below the Tripiti fortress.

2. It is very adventurous, but very long, strenuous and demanding to tackle the entire stage along the *E4* from Sougia to Agia Roumeli. Even if you start off at sunrise, the route can only be done in one day by absolutely physically fit walkers (walking time is a good 10 hrs.). It would be better if you plan on a two-day trek, taking along a sleeping bag and plenty of drinking water (at least 5 litres per person). A popular place to spend the night is the beach at Domata, from which, on the following day, you will ascend steeply to the top of a 500 m high cape and descend as steeply to Agia Roumeli (many rooms to rent are available here). With the help of Captain George (see Alternative 1), you can also begin the walk to Agia Roumeli at the exit for the Tripiti Gorge, then the tour can be made in a single day without much effort.

If your eyesight is good, you can spot the Agios Nikolaos chapel (in the shade of the rock face) at the mouth of the Tripiti Gorge.

In **Sougia (1)**, at the Taverna Galini, turn eastwards along the seaside promenade and then, not quite 100 m on, turn left onto a concrete-paved trail heading towards the interior. Another 200 m on, a commercial sign points the way to the Taverna Polifimos; at the sign, cross diagonally over a broad, dry stream bed by following the traces of a path. On the opposite side, cross over a track and head straight for a house perched on the slope. Directly in front of the metal gate for the house, bear slightly to the left, heading towards a stone wall bordered by a chain-linked fence about 25 m away. Following the fence, pass through a grove of olive trees. After not quite 100 m, the trail veers to the right, still following the fence, and then becomes a path climbing up the slope. In front of a **goat pen** (*E4* post) bear slightly to the left to meet up with a gravel trail and then ascend along it. This merges 40 m further on into an unpaved road. Here, turn sharp right, continuing the ascent along the slope, and then 150 m further on, at the next fork, turn sharp left. The broad gravel trail climbs up onto a rocky headland while opening up a lovely backwards view of the bay at Sougia with its extensive pebble beach.

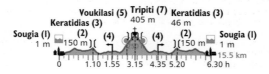

109

Arriving at the flat-topped **headland**, ignore a track forking off to the left; straight ahead, a view opens up once again of Cape Tripiti. After 75 m along the track, a well-marked coastal path breaks off to the right which sets the direction for following the coastline, which is punctuated by small coves and protruding capes. Sparse woodland, made up of pine trees and a couple of carob trees, provides a minimum amount of shade.

In front of us, little by little, a cliff with a rocky ridge appears, at the foot of which, a couple of seastacks rise up out of the waters. The path leads along the left side of the cliff to reach a **saddle (2)**, 150 m, up above. About 75 m before reaching the saddle, ignore a conspicuous *blue/white* waymarked path that ascends to the Polifimos Cave (see Walk 19). From the col, the trail drops in zigzags down into the deep cleft of the **Keratidias Gorge (3)**. Arriving in the dry stream bed, head downstream for a stretch into the gorge. About 2 mins after passing a cave, the path leaves the bed behind by turning left and ascending to a headland, from which, you can already enjoy a lovely view of the coastline towards the west. To the east, the view takes in the Agios Antonios Chapel, perched on a lonely spot on a rocky promontory.

The path continues in easy up and down walking, at a height not quite 100 m above sea level. At an *E4* waymarker on a pine tree, reach a **turn-off (4)** that leads to the Agios Antonios chapel (no longer in sight), but ignore this. Shortly after, traverse a scree-covered slope. Cape Tripiti appears now, seeming close enough to touch. To the left of the cape, you can spot a treeless col; this is the goal for our next ascent. The trail traverses more scree-covered slopes and drops down again into a little gorge at the foot of an almost 200 m-long, scree-covered slope; the last steps for this stretch require scrambling down a steep embankment. Now the steep ascent to the col begins. At first, this leads through a rocky ravine which will be left behind 5 mins later by turning to the right (cairn). The path is reinforced by supporting walls as it ascends along tight bends to a **stone pillar**, 2 m in height, with an embedded shrine at the top. Archaelogists speculate that this is the spot where the ancient settlement of Pikilassos once stood, however, no recognisable traces have been found to support this. From the pillar, a little later

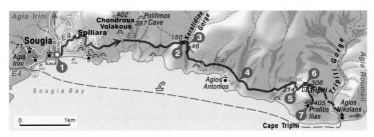

The rocky outcrops next to the trig point on the cape provide a spot to take a break.

on, reach the **Voukilasi spring (5)**, 214 m, where an oleander bush is clearly making good use of the water. A good 10 mins past the spring, finally reach a second pillar next to the **crest of the pass (6)**, 306 m. While the *E4* continues straight ahead, descending steeply to the mouth of the Tripiti Gorge, turn right instead at the pass. Somewhat higher up, you can't fail to spot the ruins of the Venetian Tripiti fortress. The path to the chapel at the cape's summit leads along the left side of the fortress, once put to use by the Turks as well. Past a square boulder about 6 m in height, keep to the left of the rocky summit relief and finally, a quarter of an hour later, reach the apex of **Cape Tripiti (7)**, 405 m, and the pilgrim's chapel of Profitis Ilias. The best panoramic view can be enjoyed from the tumbledown trig point located a few paces above the chapel. Especially striking is the downwards view of the Agios Nikolaos Chapel, situated at the mouth of the Tripiti Gorge.

After taking a break, return along the approach route back to **Sougia (1)**. If it be your pleasure, you can take an extra excursion, starting at the pine tree mentioned before, to the double-aisled **Agios Antonios Chapel** at the seaside. The rocky coast, however, is not suitable for bathing. On the flat plates of rock, water sandals would be an aid for footing; to enter the water, the best spot is at the boat dock. The excursion descending to the chapel and climbing back up again, takes about 25 minutes.

Along a panoramic circular trail to the lair of the one-eyed Cyclops

Like almost every Cretan cave, the Polifimos Cave, high above the bay of Sougia, is shrouded in »legendary« history. In the Odyssey, Homer tells of the one-eyed Cyclops, Polyphemos, a shepherd, said to be living in a cave on Crete, took Odysseus and his companions, who were on a raid of the island, as prisoners and ate several of the men. At the end, Odysseus thrust a wooden stake into the eye of the sleeping brute and so escaped. After the ascent to the Cave of the Cyclops, a panoramic, high-level trail ascends to the mountain village of Koustogerako, completely untouched by tourism.

Starting point: Sougia, 1 m. For the approach, see Walk 16.
Height difference: 550 m in both ascent and descent
Grade: easy walk along wide tracks and mule paths, in the middle section, along a relatively steep, sometimes rocky path. The route leads at first along the *E4*, then it ascends, well-marked, to the cave. Very little shade.

As with all walks starting in **Sougia (1)**, this one also begins at the bus stop opposite the Taverna Galini. As already described in Walk 18, at first follow the *E4* towards Cape Tripiti, along a promontory above the pebble beach at Sougia. On the mountain above it, a transmission tower is standing; the later

The ascent to the Cave of the Cyclops opens up sweeping views of the southern coast.

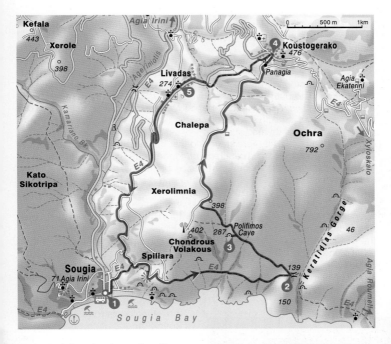

course of the circular walk will pass not far away from this tower. On the promontory, a delightful coastal path begins which leads in 40 minutes, at first on the level, later ascending, to a col. 50 m before reaching the col, leave the route to Cape Tripiti behind by turning left at a **turn-off (2)**, 139 m, onto a *blue/white* marked path heading towards Polifimos.

The ancient mule path, sometimes cobbled, is at first very indistinct, but way-markers simplify route-finding. At a striking crag, ascend steeply along the slope. Meet up with a signed junction and turn left, descending slightly for 100 m, to reach the **Polifimos Cave (3)**, 287 m, two minutes later. The roomy cave has two entrances; additional light pours in through an opening in the roof which is 8 m in height, so that you don't need to carry a torch. In the area to the

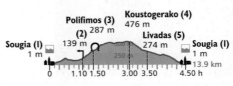

rear, there are stalagmites one to two metres in length. You can take a rest break on the rocky outcrops in front of the cave to enjoy a downwards view of the bay of Sougia.

Back on the main trail, continue by ascending further along the slope. The path soon reaches the same height as the mobile phone transmission tower, perched on a mountain ridge, which we already spotted from the seaside promenade. The path passes, however, about 500 m away from the tower and then merges, finally, into a partially concrete-paved, rust-brown **dirt road**. Turn right onto this road, ascending slightly through *phrygana* with aromatic clumps of thyme.

About 15 mins past a large cistern and just before reaching **Koustogerako (4)**, 476 m, pass by a trail branching off to the right. At the village square of the sleepy settlement, a couple of paces below the closed coffee house, there is a memorial to a resistance fighter and, behind it, a relief with a mule and a dog. Opposite the disused *kafenion*, the *E4* continues on to Gingilos and to Xyloskalo. We, however, between the terrace of the coffee house and the neighbouring low-rise building, continue along a path, marred by rubbish at the outset, leading through a grove of olive trees. Now we are following the trail, at the beginning shady, connecting the village with Livadas. At the edge of the trail, amongst others, rock roses, Jerusalem sage, Dragon Arum, Sword lilies and Mediterranean Spurge are flowering in spring; almond and pear trees are growing behind the field stone walls.

In the Polifimos Cave.

Before **Livadas (5)**, 274 m, the mule path merges into a secondary road. Turn left onto this road and descend through the handful of houses. The village church is hidden away a few metres below the road. A good 15 mins past the church, leave the secondary road behind at a sharp bend to the right by turning off onto a dirt trail. At the junction, 10 mins later, bear right, that is, do not follow the *red* dot waymarked trail which ascends. With a view taking in Sougia, pass a couple of new stone houses built into a rock face. A good 5 mins after that, meet up with an intersecting trail; turn left onto the trail and, 150 m further on, reach the goat pen already met during the approach route. From here, descend once again to return to **Sougia (1)**.

At the mouth of the gorge, the Oasis snack bar offers an inviting terrace for a break.

Through the gorge of Saint Irene

Compared to the impressive gorges of Samaria and Aradena, the Agia Irini Gorge seems rather modest. Nevertheless, boasting jungle-like vegetation in the upper reaches and several bottlenecks downstream, the gorge is indeed very attractive for the walker. The canyon can already be walked in April when the Samaria Gorge is still closed. Cretan Dittany is growing in crevices in the rock face and on the banks of the stream course, depending on the season, Dragon Arum, Anemones and Cyclamen are in flower. A trail that was established in the 1990s, with rest areas and trough fountains, leads pleasantly through the good 7 km-long gorge. At the mouth of the gorge, the Oasis snack bar offers a nice spot to take refreshment. From there, descend along the fairly traffic-free secondary road to return to Sougia. If you prefer to avoid walking along the road, the friendly proprietor of the bar will call a taxi to pick you up.

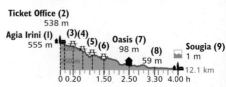

115

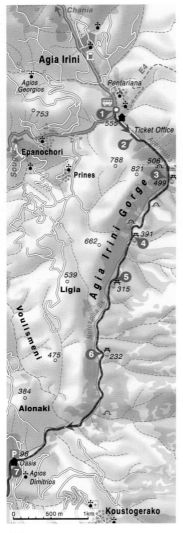

Starting point: Agia Irini, 555 m, is located on the bus line Chania – Sougia (from Chania, Mon–Sat, 5.15 and 8.45, Sun 7.30, travelling time 1 hr; from Sougia daily, 7.00 and 18.15, travelling time not quite 1 hr, in off-season, only three times weekly). The driver stops at the southern village limits of Agia Irini (approaching from Chania, about 1 km past the petrol station) directly at the entrance to the gorge. If you need to return to Chania or back to your car in Agia Irini, take the evening bus from Sougia at 18.15. If you are approaching by car, getting an early start and are staying in Paleochora or Plakias, you would avoid needing a bus ride back by parking in Sougia and, from there, taking the early bus to Agia Irini.

Height difference: about 70 m in ascent and 630 m in descent.

Grade: the sometimes rough path is relatively easy to walk; precipitous sections are protected by wooden railings. On some stretches, however, the path has been destroyed by rockfall. In the lower reaches of the gorge, you have to use your hands while scrambling over two steep, rocky outcrops. In the gorge itself, it is shady, but the last one and half hours of the route is very sunny. Route-finding is very easy.

Refreshment: there's a taverna at the entrance to the gorge; the Oasis snack bar is at the mouth of the gorge; there are several tavernas in Sougia. At the rest areas in the gorge, there are several trough fountains, but you can't be certain that they are always providing water.

Alternative: the gorge can be walked by starting at the lower entrance. If approaching by car, from the main road Chania – Sougia, turn off towards Livadas. Past the bridge spanning the Ageriniotis, turn left; there is a large car park in front of the Oasis snack bar. From there, ascend through the gorge until reaching rest area no. 4 and then return along the approach route back to the snack bar (there and back, a good 3 hrs).

Approaching from Sougia, the entrance to the gorge is situated at the sign for the village limits of **Agia Irini (1)**. At two information boards, the one providing info for the Samaria National Park, the other for the Irini Gorge, two trails begin, both marked with *E4* waymarkers. With your back to the boards, take the left-hand trail to descend (the right-hand trail leads to Omalos/Figou, see Walk 21). 150 m on, pass by the taverna Kri-Kri, equipped with tables outside (it is usually open early in the morning). The gravel trail leads straight on from there along the bank of the Ageriniotis through an ancient grove of olive trees, heading downstream. At the **ticket booth (2)**, 538 m, cancel your ticket (in the low season, the booth is usually unmanned). 200 m further on, cross over the river for the first time via a bridge. Towering plane trees

A rough section in the lower reaches of the Irini Gorge.

line the bank. In the stream bed, oleander is thriving and massive boulders are scattered about. The gravel trail becomes a path which leads to wooded slopes, some reaching heights of 300 m, lying in front of us. 20 minutes from Agia Irini, a path merges from the left, coming out of the **Figou Gorge** (a possible excursion, see Walk 21). Keeping straight ahead, reach the first **rest area (3)**, 499 m, shortly after, with a trough fountain. A couple of paces further on, a small sign posts the distance in kilometres already walked (to here, *km 1*, calculated with the ticket booth as starting point). The river begins to flow underground now and leaves behind a dry, stony stream bed that only carries water after rainfall.

Five minutes past the rest area, ascend along a sometimes stepped path on the left-hand rim of the gorge in order to skirt around a longer rocky section; a fence, sometimes battered by rockfall, accompanies the trail. Arriving back at the bed of the gorge, at *km 2*, reach the second **rest area (4)**, 391 m,

where picnic tables, located under plane trees, invite you to linger a while. In the continued course of the route, the path crosses over the stream bed numerous times; sometimes you have to hop over from stone to stone. On the rock walls, closing in on each other more and more, pine trees are desperately clinging; bizarrely-formed Oriental plane trees flank the trail. Past the third **rest area (5)** (boasting a WC hut), 315 m, the gorge opens up again for a short time.

In easy up and down walking, past a boulder field of sharp rock, reach the final official **rest area (6)**, 232 m, at *km 4*. Half an hour later, pass through the first bottleneck in the gorge; here, beneath an overhanging rock face, you have to scramble through a washed-out rock gully. At a second steep section, you also have to use your hands to scramble past this point. After a final stretch with an overhanging rock face, the gorge walls begin to level off. Now ramble through cultivated countryside with olive trees and, finally, reach the **Oasis snack bar (7)**, 98 m, at the mouth of the gorge. The lovely garden here is an excellent place to take a break before you tackle the final 5.5 km which will bring you to Sougia.

From the bar, follow the narrow road (during the week, there is hardly any traffic) to pass a large car park. To the right, the Ageriniotis River acts as our travelling companion, the banks of the river sports mullein, Spiny Starwort and other wildflowers. Arriving at a junction, bear right and cross over a bridge spanning the river. Quarter of an hour later, reach the main road Agia Irini – Sougia and a **memorial (8)**, 59 m, dedicated to the Cretans who were deported by the German *Wehrmacht* to the Austrian concentration camp, Mauthausen, and lost their lives there. The road descends in a good half hour to **Sougia (9)**. (As an alternative, starting from the memorial, follow a stony stream bed to the sea, but this will not save you very much time.)

Circular walk through a sometime Cretan hideaway

For most walkers, the mountain village of Agia Irini is the starting point for the transit of the St. Irene Gorge, named after the settlement (Walk 20). The route suggested here, along a lovely kalderimi, is taken almost exclusively by long-distance walkers who are ascending to the Omalos high plateau. From the well-preserved cobbled trail, pick up an ancient connecting trail through the short Figou Gorge into the canyon of Agia Irini. Like many other Cretan gorges, the Figou Gorge has a story to tell. The name is Greek for »flee« and refers to an event that took place in 1821 when many woman and children were brought to safety in the gorge before the onslaught of the Turks.

Starting point: Agia Irini, 555 m. To get there, see Walk 19.
Height difference: 340 m in both ascent and descent.
Grade: the ascent leads along a pleasant cobbled trail; the descent runs through the Figou Gorge along a sometimes steep mule track, in places loose underfoot, requiring some sure-footedness.
Refreshment: taverna Kri-Kri, near the end of the circular walk.
Linking tip: in the Agia Irini Gorge (4), you can use Walk 20 to descend to Sougia.

At the sign for the village limits at the southern end of the settlement, **Agia Irini (1)**, meet up with two information boards; one provides info relating to the Samaria National Park and the other relates to the Irini Gorge. Two trails lead away from this point; both are waymarked with *E4* markings. With your

The ancient kalderimi leads to the Omalos high plain.

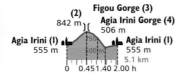

Figou Gorge (3)
Agia Irini Gorge (4)
506 m

(2)
842 m

Agia Irini (I)
555 m

Agia Irini (I)
555 m

5.1 km

0   0.45 1.40 2.00 h

back to the boards, take the right-hand trail to descend. Immediately after, cross over the stream bed of the Ageriniotis via an arched bridge. Then, the trail leads through a grove of olive trees. A good 150 further on, turn right onto a cobbled trail, broad at the outset (*E4* sign to Omalos).

We soon leave the open woodland of mountain cypress and holm oak down below. The trail is now overgrown in some sections with Thorny Primrose and ferns; sometimes the trail tapers down into a narrow path. As the higher altitudes are reached, superb views open up over the broad mountain valley of Agia Irini and the surrounding mountains. Down below, we can make out the forest-covered notch of the Agia Irini Gorge. The trail leads past a copse of Turkish pines and, 10 minutes later, meets up with a broad **col (2)**, 842 m. At this point, descend into a funnel-shaped basin and then continue on past a cistern with a watering trough. Shortly afterwards, reach a junction. While the *E4* continues straight ahead to the Omalos high plain, we descend to the right along a narrow mule track leading down into the Figou Gorge; the last stretch climbs down via zigzags.

Arriving at the dry stream bed of the **Figou Gorge (3)**, 708 m, pick up a path, sometimes rough, which, at first, traverses the foot of a scree-covered slope. Then the route continues, sometimes along the left bank, sometimes along the right, criss-crossing the stony stream bed. In the lower reaches, the path squeezes its way between huge boulders. At the remains of a wall for the sometime guard post of the Cretan resistance fighters against the Turks, bear slightly right (to the left, an excursion to the Xirotripa Cave is possible). Shortly afterwards, pass an open quarry-stone hut. 100 m below this point, the Figou Gorge merges into the **Agia Irini Gorge (4)**, 506 m. (To the left, you could walk a stretch into the gorge of St. Irene and after a few minutes, arrive at a rest area where a trough fountain with drinking water is located.) We turn

right instead along the broad trail and head north-west along the stream bed of the Irini Gorge, flanked by plane trees. Cross over the stream bed via a footbridge and, shortly afterwards, pass the **ticket office** at the entrance to the gorge where a fee for the Irini Gorge is paid. 250 m further on, in the shade cast by olive trees, a kiosk is an invitation for a break; a little later on, return back to the secondary road at the village limits of **Agia Irini (1)**.

Agia Roumeli, at the mouth of the Samaria Gorge.

From Agia Roumeli to the Iron Gates in the national park

The usual route through the Samaria Gorge descends from the Omalos high plateau down to the seaside (see Walk 11), however, you don't necessarily have to walk through the entire gorge. If you spend the night in Agia Roumeli and get an early start the next day, you even have the advantage (when taking the »easy version«) of enjoying a fantastic experience in this natural setting without having to share it with others, since most walkers descend from above and don't reach the Iron Gates until just before noon. Even without adding the overnight stay, you can walk the exploratory route comfortably as a day trip and still be certain to relish the high point of a »classic« visit to Crete – this begins with a sensational boat ride along the dramatic cliffs dropping down to the sea.

At the Iron Gates...

Height difference: 170 m.

Grade: relatively easy gorge walk along a well-laid trail. »Exploratory tour« doesn't mean, however, that the route is a piece of cake – the log-paved trail through the Iron Gates demands sure-footedness.

Opening times: the gorge is usually open from the beginning of May until the end of October; entrance fee is €5.

Refreshment and accommodation: tavernas and many rooms to rent in Agia Roumeli; snack bars at the Check Point near the gorge entrance; trough fountain with potable water at the Christos rest area.

Alternative: either before or after walking the gorge, you have the possibility of ascending to an Ottoman fortress, enthroned high above the mouth of the Samaria Gorge on the spur of a ridge. The fortress once secured the access to the gorge from the seaward side, although the Turks were never able to completely control the vast canyon since the Cretans held the Iron Gates firmly in hand. The ascent, not quite a half an hour to climb, leads along a zigzag path which begins behind the village church of Agia Roumeli, situated somewhat on the outskirts of the settlement. You can get there by starting diagonally across from the ticket office and taking the passageway towards the interior; when it ends, turn right. The short tour is rewarded with a spectacular panoramic view of the village and the river delta.

Starting point: Agia Roumeli, 1 m. Approach with the ferry (May–October) from Chora Sfakion, Paleochora and Sougia. The tour is also possible when starting from Chania; from there, with the early bus, daily at 8.15, to Chora Sfakion (transfer to the ferry at 10.30).

Return: with the ferry from Agia Roumeli to Chora Sfakion and Sougia/Paleochora around 17.30 (up-to-date schedules available locally and at www.anendyk.gr). Bus from Chora Sfakion to Chania, daily around 18.30 (the bus waits for the arrival of the ferry).

From the **ferry landing (1)**, reach the tiny village centre of **Agia Roumeli (2)**, only a few steps away. At the ticket office, meet up with the main street which is flanked by tavernas and apartment houses. Turn right onto the street and, in front of Apartments Sorbas, immediately turn left again.

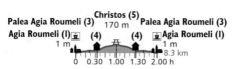

A concrete-paved road leads, at first, through the alluvial plain while heading into the gorge. A good quarter of an hour from Agia Roumeli, pass the Agia Triada church at **Palea Agia Roumeli (3)**; a bridge allows you to cross over the river bed. The houses here lie hidden behind the walls; the village was destroyed by a flood in spring of 1952 and has been abandoned ever since.

Past a row of kiosks, you have to cancel your ticket at the **checkpoint (4)** for the official entrance to the gorge, which has been designated a national park. Now you have to cross footbridges several times over the stream bed, flanked by oleander, Turkish pines and cypress trees. The walls of the gorge close in more and more; the log-paved trail through the **Sideroportes**, the

...the walls of the gorge allow only a narrow passage through.

Iron Gates, is simply fantastic as the steep rock faces, separated here by a mere 3 m of breadth, tower up to almost 300 m in height.

A few minutes past the bottleneck, reach the major **rest area**, **Christos (5)**, 170 m, where there are picnic tables, toilets and a trough fountain with potable water; a few paces above the rest area is the eponymous chapel. The most spectacular section of the gorge is now behind us, but that doesn't mean that continuing on would be uninteresting. If you want to continue further into the gorge, you can walk to the next rest area, Nero tis Perdikas, in a good hour. Otherwise, turn back again from Christos and take the approach route back to **Agia Roumeli (2)** and the **ferry dock (1)**.

The short circular walk from Agia Roumeli

To the Ottoman fortress perched above the mouth of the Samaria Gorge

The village of Agia Roumeli at the mouth of the Samaria Gorge is well-known amongst walkers throughout Europe. Whilst most walkers explore the gorge by starting from the ferry landing (Walk 22) or walk along the E4 to Loutro (Walk 24), a nearby walker's destination is often overlooked: above the settlement, the ruins of an ancient Ottoman fortress are enthroned, from which the erstwhile occupation force held watch over the mouth of the gorge. From the old walls, you can get a bird's-eye view of Agia Roumeli down below.

Starting point: Agia Roumeli, 2 m. The village is not connected to the road system; ferries provide daily service from mid-May to the end of Oct from Chora Sfakion (via Loutro) and Paleochora (via Sougia).

Return: ferry service from Agia Roumeli to Chora Sfakion (via Loutro) and Paleochora (via Sougia) at 16.30 or 17.30 depending on the season.

Height difference: 220 m in both ascent and descent.

Grade: easy circular walk with short stretches of intermediary ascents and descents along a well-laid mule track.

Refreshment: kiosk providing cold beverages and fresh-squeezed orange juice in Palea Agia Roumeli; a large selection of tavernas in Agia Roumeli.

Linking tip: the walk can be combined well with Walk 22. Returning back, out of the Samaria Gorge, before the arched bridge in Palea Agia Roumeli, turn right onto the mule track.

Kastro (3)
Agia Triada (2) 222 m
46 m (4) Agia Roumeli (I)
Agia Roumeli (I)
2 m
2 m
3.6 km
0   0.50 1.20 h

From the ferry landing in **Agia Roumeli (1)**, reach the village main street after walking a few paces. Turn right along the street and before the Apartments Sorbas, turn left. A concrete-paved roadway leads through the broad alluvial plain of the Samaria Gorge.

Just past the church **Agia Triada (2)**, in the abandoned village of Palea Agia Roumeli, cross over the river via an arched bridge and, before the kiosk on the other side, the trail forks: turning right leads into the Samaria Gorge, but we turn left instead onto a mule track heading towards Kastro. At first, this leads

A bird's-eye view of Agia Roumeli.

From the castle, the Turks once held watch over the mouth of the Samaria Gorge.

for a short stretch above the river bed and then begins to ascend leisurely. A good five minutes later, pass by the turn-off to the chapel Agia Paraskevi (a possible excursion; about 20 minutes, there and back). An open pine wood soon provides a little shade. The higher we climb, the better is the view of Palea Agia Roumeli in the estuary of the Samaria Gorge.

In zigzag bends, climb up a rocky ridge from which a couple of paces lead to the **Kastro (3)**, 222 m. From the ruins of the walls left over from the Ottoman fortress, enjoy a spectacular view of Agia Roumeli, with its long pebble beach, lying down below.

After taking a break, begin the descent, with a constant view of the village and the sea, down to the **Panagia (4)**, 38 m, at the village limits of Agia Roumeli. At the church, pick up a broad cobbled trail and, bearing right, return in 150 m to the village main street of **Agia Roumeli (1)**.

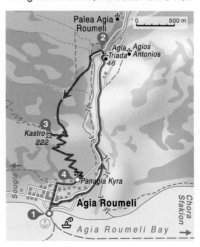

The classic walk on Crete's southern coast

The trail at the foot of the steep coastal cliffs offers one of the most impressive routes for southern Crete. During the walk, pass by several pebble coves, some small and some spacious, as well as a Byzantine chapel, well worth a visit. A small pine forest provides a splash of green and some shade, too. Inviting tavernas can also be found on the way. The route also provides an overview of what the region still has to offer in the way of other walks: along the trail, turn-offs and starting points for the walks to Agios Ioannis (Walk 25) and the Aradena Gorge (Walk 28), as well as the circular walk from Loutro to Finix (Walk 30).

Starting point: Agia Roumeli, 1 m. Approach with the ferry (May–October) three times daily from Chora Sfakion. The first ferry sets sail from Chora Sfakion at about 10.30 and reaches Agia Roumeli after about 1.15 hrs. Ferries to Agia Roumeli also set sail from Paleochora and Sougia, but you have to plan an overnight in Loutro or Chora Sfakion since you would be unable to return on the same day.
Return: between May and October, the last ferry from Loutro to Chora Sfakion sets sail at 18.10. The time needed for the walk is then more than adequate, but bathing or rest breaks, even for lively walkers, are limited to a total of one and a half hours at the most.
Height difference: a good 300 m in both ascent and descent.
Grade: this walk leads mostly along a well-laid coastal path; a short stretch between Marmara and Lykos demands being sure-footed and vertigo-free. Path-finding is very simple; the route is way-marked throughout with *yellow/black* markings and *E4* posts (without dia-

monds). The final 3 hours is almost completely lacking in shade and, in mid-summer, it is fairly exposed to the blazing heat. Be sure to take along your sunblock and bathing gear!
Refreshment: numerous tavernas in Agia Roumeli and Loutro; en route, near the Agios Pavlos church, is the Taverna Saint Paul (also with rooms to rent), as well as beach bars in Lykos Beach, Marmara and Finix.
Alternative: if you are staying in Loutro, you can start the walk from there and take the ferry back from Agia Roumeli in the afternoon. If you get an early start, you could also begin the walk from Chora Sfakion (at the outset, follow the instructions in Walk 27 to Loutro).
Linking tips: physically fit walkers could also reach Chora Sfakion on the same day by following Walk 27 in the opposite direction. Samaria Gorge walkers (Walk 11) can spend the night in Agia Roumeli and, the next day, continue on to Loutro, then by boat or using Walk 27, reach Chora Sfakion.

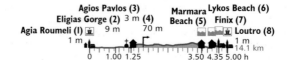

Agios Pavlos (3)
Eligias Gorge (2) 3 m (4)   Marmara Lykos Beach (6)
Agia Roumeli (I)   9 m   70 m   Beach (5) Finix (7)
1 m   1 m
                                             14.1 km
0   1.00 1.25   3.50 4.35 5.00 h

The southern coast between Agios Pavlos and Marmara Beach.

After a short visit to **Agia Roumeli (1)**, start off at the ferry dock to join the promenade, at the outset flanked by low walls, and head east. 150 m further on, the cobbled trail veers towards the interior and the seaside entrance to the Samaria Gorge. At the Taverna Rousios, leave the trail behind by turning right. Cross over the broad, dry stream bed and, at the eastern bank, reach a stone wall, which is reinforced by a chain-link fence. Follow the wall towards the sea until it ends; here, meet up with a coastal path, sandy at the beginning, waymarked with *E4* markings. At the outset, the path leads along a pebble cove. Half an hour later, pass bizarre boulders with a rock arch. A second, adjoining pebble cove, almost 500 m in length, comes next. Some minutes afterwards, reach the mouth of the **Eligias Gorge (2)**. If this point was not marked by two boulders towering out of the sea, it would be very easy to pass by without even noticing the inaccessible canyon.

At the rocky slope, Turkish pines now provide a little shade; it is also shady on the roofed terrace of the **Taverna Saint Paul,** reached not quite half an hour past the Eligias Gorge. Prior to that, reach another beach which is quite suited for a bathing break. Not far from the taverna, an in-depth visit to the little Byzantine chapel, **Agios Pavlos (3),** is well worthwhile; the chapel goes

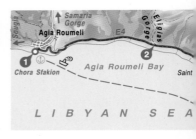

back to the 10th century (see photo, page 132). About 15 m below the chapel, the source for a fresh water spring can be found directly at the beach.

Directly in front of the chapel, scramble up the steep, rocky embankment. Up above, the coastal path continues, sandy at first, and soon ascends along a well-laid stretch, following tight bends and passing through a relatively dense pine wood until reaching the **turn-off for Agios Ioannis (4),** 70 m. Diagonally to the left, a spectacular, *red/white* waymarked alpine path climbs up the steep coastal slope (Walk 25), but we keep to the *E4* and keep heading straight on. In spring, the air is filled with the aromatic scent of thyme; in autumn, the metre-high, torch-like rosette of the sea squill appears here by the thousands.

Pass a round **cistern**. A good 10 minutes afterwards, reach a rock face with caves and again enjoy a lovely backwards view of the coastline peppered

Bizarre rocky cliffs at Marmara Beach.

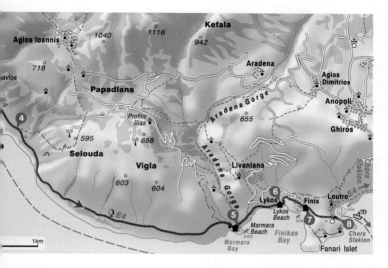

with pebble coves. Now we have left the shade behind us, since the Turkish pines have had to make way for a low-growth, cushion plant scrubland. The path leads along the foot of the sometimes sheer cliff belonging to the 600-m-high Vigla. Cross over a stony field of scree and then pass another rock slope, riddled with caves, as well as a solitary **olive tree**.

After a long stretch without any noteworthy features, finally a view opens up of the peninsula between the bays of Finix and Loutro, on which you can spot the watchtower of a Venetian castle. Down below, perched above the bay of Marmara at the seaside, a chapel and a handful of summer cottages appear. Starting in front of the chapel, pass through a gate and then, at an *E4* post, descend to a broad, gravel trail which leads into the Aradena Gorge (Walk 28). Turning right, only a few paces lead to **Marmara Beach (5)**, and if we haven't taken one already, we have most certainly earned a bathing break at this splendid cove, which offers sun loungers and parasols, as well as an inviting taverna situated up above the beach.

Afterwards, it's time to cut to the chase. From the little pebble cove of Marmara, climb up the rocky promontory (white marble!), which borders the beach to the east. 10 minutes later, pass by a waymarked turn-off heading towards Livaniana. In the further course of the route, the **mule track** becomes rather rough and somewhat precipitous with a cliff dropping vertically for 20 m. Past a cave-like overhanging cliff (see photo on page 138), descend again to the seaside; you may need to use your hands during the scramble.

Pure tranquility: the car-free holiday village of Loutro.

Passing goat pens and ancient olive trees, ramble on to traverse **Lykos Beach (6)**, where beneath salt cedars, the Taverna Akrogiali presents a place to take a break. Afterwards, cross the terrace of the Taverna Nikos Small Paradise, and immediately past it, climb up a flight of steps. Above Nikos, the trail, flanked by a chain-link fence, veers to the left, soon to reach a car park; then follow a stony access road towards the interior. 200 m on, the track turns to the right, leave it behind about 75 m further on at a sharp left-hand bend, but keep straight ahead (*yellow/black* waymarkers). Now arriving back at the coastal path, climb up to a rocky plateau. Arriving there, cross through a gate and then ignore another turn-off leading to Livaniana. Also ignore the signed path turning off to the right towards the Old Phoenix Restaurant (this is another very attractive place to take refreshment; see photo on page 142). 5 minutes later, cross diagonally over a gravel track and then our path leads for a couple of metres above the pretty chapel of **Finix (7)**, passing it by.

In a final short ascent, now climb up the peninsula situated between Finix and Loutro. First pass a couple of carob trees, then pass the Venetian **castle**; from here, enjoy a downwards view of the row of houses, belonging to Loutro, that appear just like a picture in a holiday brochure. At the junction, halfway down, turn right onto the seaside promenade of **Loutro (8)**; the ferry dock with a ticket office is located about 75 m further on to the right.

Panoramic descent to a Byzantine chapel on the sea

A descent as pretty as this one, taking in the turquoise-coloured Libyan Sea, can hardly be matched by any other. On top of that, it leads along a kalderimi, cobbled at the outset. The walk's destination is the thousand-year old church of Agios Pavlos. The church stands on the spot where the Apostle Paul, on his missionary journey to Crete in 59 AD, supposedly made landfall; no evidence exists to support the legend, however. Originally, Paul wanted to spend the winter somewhat further east in the harbour town of Phoenix (today's Finix). But as the ship cruised offshore from the Cretan coast, a north-easterly squall came up and drove the boat to Gavdos instead (as set down in the New Testament, Acts 27). Next to the St. Paul Chapel, we can also gather strength in the Taverna Saint Paul for the long return ascent and, in front of the chapel, there is a tolerable pebble beach.

Starting point: Agios Ioannis, 755 m. From Chora Sfakion, drive up the road to reach Anopoli and there at the roundabout (sporting a monument to the Cretan resistance fighter, Daskalogiannis), keep straight on and, 5 km past the Aradena bridge, reach the car park located at the village limits of Agios Ioannis.

Height difference: 770 m in both ascent and descent.

Grade: aside from a few slight precipitous and rough sections through scree fields, the ancient mule track is well-laid, as well as waymarked throughout (until reaching the *E4*, the descent is *white/red* and then, the *E4* is *yellow/black*). Be sure to take along your bathing gear! The lower third of the strenuous, steep intermediary ascent is lying solely in shade.

Refreshment: Taverna Saint Paul at the Agios Pavlos Chapel (you can also spend the night here).

Short walk: if a spectacular view of the coast is enough for you, only walk as far as the edge of the cliff (2), where you can take a break and enjoy the superlative panoramic view (there and back, 1.30 hrs.).

Alternatives: if you hitch a ride, or take a taxi to Agios Ioannis, or take the bus (end of May–end of Oct) from Chora Sfakion to Aradena (from there, an additional walking time of 1.15 hrs) and, because of that, you don't have to ascend again to the village after the descent, you can either walk the *E4* westwards until reaching Agia Roumeli or eastwards to reach Loutro/Chora Sfakion (Walk 24). The last ferry to Chora Sfakion from Agia Roumeli (May–October) sets sail at 17.30, from Loutro, at 18.10.

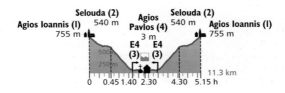

131

1000 years old: the Agios Pavlos Chapel.

From the car park at the village limits of **Agios Ioannis (1)**, descend along a narrow tarmac road. 75 m further on, a stony trail, flanked by field stones, starts off to the right (*white/red* waymarkings) and leads between two chapels (one to the right and another to the left, both situated somewhat off-trail) through an open wood of cypress and Turkish pine. A good quarter of an hour later, cross an intersecting trail and, 40 m further on, continue straight ahead along a narrow path. Some minutes later, cross through a valley notch. A short intermediate ascent climbs up to a karst plateau; here, cross a country lane again and finally reach the cliff's edge, called **Selouda (2)**, 540 m. A fantastic view opens up of the coastal countryside – far below, the Libyan Sea shimmers in various tones of green and blue; westwards, you can spot Agia Roumeli.

The descent begins along a cobbled trail, perfectly preserved at the outset, which was a very busy connecting trail between the highlands and the coast in the past. After some tight bends, traverse a stony scree slope, which is sometimes slightly precipitous. During the descent, the sea is almost constantly in view. After crossing over more scree slopes, the pine wood begins

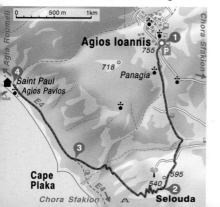

to provide more shade, a fact that we will especially appreciate during the return ascent. Located in the middle of the wood belt, meet up with the *E4 (3)*, 70 m, and turn right onto it. Soon the E4 follows sharp zigzags until it finally reaches the **Agios Pavlos** chapel **(4)**. Below the chapel, there is a long pebble beach and, 100 m further on, the shady terrace of the Taverna Saint Paul. After a good, long rest stop, ascend again along the approach route back to **Agios Ioannis (1)**.

Through the wooded highlands of Sfakia

The route to the cave chapel Kormokopos in the highlands of Sfakia has not been walked very much up to now. Since the forest doesn't allow for many grandiose views, you could also do this walk on a day when the weather isn't so great. Beyond that, the shady woodland path is a good alternative for an easy summer walk when, on the treeless coast, it is too hot to go walking.

Starting point: Agios Ioannis, 780 m. From Chora Sfakia, drive via Anopoli and the Aradena bridge to the entrance of the village of Agios Ioannis. Past the taverna (closed) at the fork just before the church, turn left. 300 m on, bear right and, after another 150 m, a country road forks off to the left; parking possible at the side of the road.
Height difference: 320 m.
Grade: easy-going, walkable, ancient mule track (except for the short, some-what bumpy descent to the cave) that is

never unpleasantly steep. The trail is well-marked with *blue* dots on a *white* square. Mostly shady.
Refreshment: kiosk on the Aradena bridge.

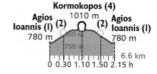

Starting point for the walk is the little scattered settlement of Agios Ioannis at the foot of the White Mountains.

Gnarled, huge trees act as companions...   *...to the entrance of the Kormokopos cave.*

From the tarmac road in **Agios Ioannis (1)**, turn off onto the waymarked country lane and pass through a metal gate; a good 100 m on, pass through yet a second gate. The trail descends into a small valley; on the other flank

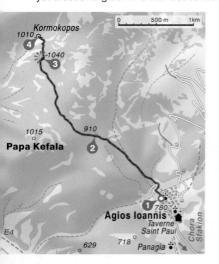

of the valley, an ascending path sets off, heading straight on.

Continue through a shady, mixed forest of Aleppo pines and cypress trees. At a clearing, meet up with a **cistern (2)**, 910 m. After a half-an-hour stretch of easy up-and-down walking, reach a **viewpoint (3)**, 1040 m, with a view of the cave, situated in a re-entrant. The path descends, winding down in tight zig-zag bends to reach the entrance to the **Kormokopos Cave (4)**, 1010 m. Ferns are growing on the ceiling of the cave, about 5 m above our heads, and water running from a spring is collected in a watering trough for goats.

After a rest break in front of the cave, return along the approach route back to **Agios Ioannis (1)**.

To the official insider's tip on the Libyan Sea

In peace and quiet, from the return trip by ferry, we can take another look at the walk we have left behind us. Sweet Water Beach is crouched in a spectacular spot at the foot of the towering coastal cliffs, more than 800 m in height. Thinking back, it is difficult to imagine that a path, and moreover, the popular long-distance trail E4, leads along there, in fact, it looks pretty dangerous (due to rockfall). In regard to Loutro itself: the setting of the car-free village, which can be reached only by boat or on foot, is simply sensational!

Starting point: Chora Sfakion, 7 m. Synchronised with the arrival of the ferry, a good bus connection to Chania.

Return: from Loutro, ferry service five or six times daily in the summer months to Chora Sfakion, the last one sets sail at around 18.10.

Height difference: about 200 m in ascent and descent.

Grade: the walk follows a coastal path that is sometimes not easy; precipitous sections demand sure-footedness and being vertigo-free. Beware of rockfall! The trail is along a stage of the *E4* and waymarked *yellow/black* throughout. No shade; bring along your sunscreen and bathing gear!

Refreshment: beach bar at Sweet Water Beach, numerous cafés and tavernas in Chora Sfakion and Loutro.

Linking tips: in Loutro, the route can be linked with crossing the Aradena Gorge (Walk 28) or with the circular walk to Finix (Walk 30).

The adventurous descent to Sweet Water Beach, as seen from the ferry.

Spectacular location: Sweet Water Beach.

Begin the walk in **Chora Sfakion (1)**, at the roundabout on the village limits where the tourist information booth is also located. At Taverna Nikos, follow the line of restaurants until reaching the Café Akrogiali, in front of which, a concrete-paved trail ascends to the right. Not quite 200 m on, in front of a couple of steps, the trail forks. Bear left (*blue* arrow) along the traces of a path and climb up a stairway to the main road leading to Anopoli and turn left. As soon as we leave the last house behind us, a picturesque downwards view opens up of the little beach at Vrissi. A quarter of an hour later, pass by the access road to **Ilingas Beach (2)**. Another 10 mins after that, at a sharp bend, the coastal path starts off (sign: *E4*/Sweet Water Beach). At the same time, enjoy a view of Sweet Water Beach at the foot of the steep coastal cliffs; behind it, you can spot the Timios Stavros Chapel, which our path will lead past.

First, descend along a rocky, but well-laid, alpine path climbing down in zig-zags. Soon traverse a somewhat precipitous rocky slope of scree (see photo on page 135) and continue descending, while scrambling under an overhanging cliff face, down to the sea. A few minutes later, reach **Sweet Water Beach (3)**. On maps, it is listed as in Greek as *Glika Nera* (sweet water) and

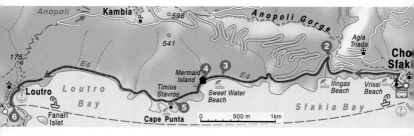

From Loutro (here in the photo), return to Chora Sfakion in comfort by ferry.

takes its name from freshwater springs whose sources flow directly on the beach. The springs benefit numerous individuals, camping in the wild on the beach, who have put up little tents in the shade of the salt cedars. If the novel beach bar, **Mermaid Island (4)**, built on a boulder in the sea, is open, you can get yourself a hot or cold drink. If you want to take a longer break here, there are sun loungers and parasols to rent at the beach.

At the beach bar, the coastal path continues on. Not quite a quarter of an hour later, meet up with the **Timios Stavros** Chapel **(5)**, situated somewhat below the trail, where you can take a break on a bench and enjoy a view of Loutro. Past the chapel, descend to a little pebble beach; early mornings, you can enjoy it on your own. Another pebble cove follows immediately after. From there, the path ascends again to a height of about 50 m above the sea and then finally reaches the eastern village limits of **Loutro (6)** at the Hotel Oasis. In front of the hotel, turn left to descend to the Taverna Pavlos on the seaside promenade and, from there, meet up with the ferry dock at the southern end of the little settlement in 5 minutes.

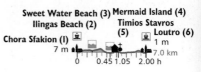

Fascinating gorge walk west of Loutro

When it comes to connecting with nature, the Aradena Gorge walk is most certainly one of the best in western Crete. In the picturesque village of Loutro, a coastal trail sets off, passing splendid bathing coves. From Marmara Beach, climb up along a challenging alpine path through the imposing canyon to reach the abandoned village of Aradena. A cross-in-square church, well worth seeing, is one of the few buildings still standing in the once major mountain village. The reason that the settlement has been abandoned for the last three generations is said to be the result of a bitter blood feud. Perhaps for many of the inhabitants, it was too cumbersome to have a home which could only be left or reached via a single trail through a gorge, even though the kalderimi is cobbled and perfectly laid. The steel bridge has only been in existence since 1986. From the bridge, 138 m in height, you can enjoy an impressive view into the gorge – if you fancy an adrenalin rush, you could also bungee-jump from the bridge into the canyon (www.bungy.gr). The crowning climax of this adventurous circular walk is the panoramic return descent to the Libyan Sea, during which, you should be sure to allow for a stopover at the taverna in Finix.

The precipitous stretch between Lykos Beach and Marmara Beach.

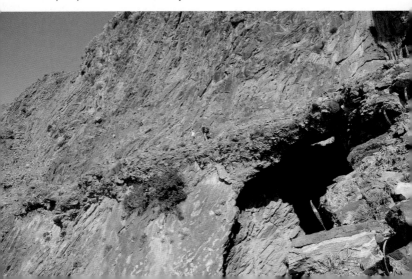

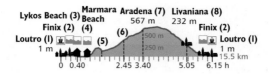

Lykos Beach (3) Marmara Beach Aradena (7) 567 m Livaniana (8) 232 m

Finix (2) (4) (6) Finix (2)

Loutro (I) 1 m (5) Loutro (I) 1 m

500 m
250 m
15.5 km

0 0.40 2.45 3.40 5.05 6.15 h

Starting point: Loutro, 1 m. From Chora Sfakion, ferry service up to 5 times daily in the summer months to Loutro (a 20-minute voyage). The first one sets sail from Chora Sfakion at 10.30 and the last ferry from Loutro returns between 17.00 and 18.10, depending on the season. You could also start from Chania (synchronised with the arrival of the ferry, a good bus connection).

Height difference: 750 m in both ascent and descent.

Grade: the walk leads to Marmara Beach along the well-laid and well-marked *E4*, during which, shortly past Lykos, you have to scramble up the cliff and then face a stretch that follows which is somewhat precipitous and exposed. The trail through the Aradena Gorge, *green/red* waymarked, is sometimes interrupted by sheer, steep drop-offs; here, too, you must sometimes use your hands while scrambling. The gorge walls provide shade, depending on the time of day; the descent from Aradena runs continuously exposed to the sun.

Refreshment: you can find tavernas in Loutro, Finix, Lykos, Marmara and Livaniana; there is also a kiosk selling drinks in Aradena.

Important Note: if you are not staying in Loutro, the time frame for the walk depends on the ferry schedule. The total walking time of 6.15 hrs has been generously calculated, but needing less than 6 hrs. to complete the walk is not very likely. We recommend, therefore, that you only take short rest stops, totalling a maximum of 1.30 hrs.

Alternatives: 1. Aradena – Livaniana – Marmara – Aradena: approaching by car, drive to Aradena, descend to Livaniana, then, below the church, take the fork towards Marmara and, after that, ascend from the sea, passing through the gorge, and finally climb up all the way to Aradena. By doing this, you will reduce the walking time to a total of only 4.30 hrs.

2. Aradena – Marmara – Loutro: take a taxi or the bus (end of May–Oct, daily 9.00) from Chora Sfakion to Aradena. From the kiosk next to the bridge, at first head towards the church but then, below it, take the narrow tarmac road to the right and descend through the gorge to reach the sea. From Marmara Beach, either take the water taxi (at 17.00; Poseidonas Boat, tel. +30-28250-91257 and +30-6988-981255) to Loutro (there, connections to the ferry for Chora Sfakion) or, from Marmara, follow the *E4* to Loutro. For the descent to reach Marmara, you can reckon with about 2.15 hrs and, from there to Loutro, another 1.10 hrs.

3. Marmara – Aradena – Livaniana – Loutro: You could also begin the walk in Marmara; from Loutro, in the high season, the water taxi Poseidonas sets sail at 11.00 to Marmara Beach (travel time, 15 minutes). Walking time is thereby shortened by a good hour (since the water taxi doesn't leave until 11.00, the time frame for the walk is not, however, significantly longer).

4. Marmara – Aradena Gorge – Marmara: If you would be content with a only a trial run into the Aradena Gorge, take the water taxi to Marmara, climb up a stretch into the gorge, turn around again at the halfway point, and while away the time on the beach in Marmara until the water taxi makes its return trip back to Loutro (17.00).

From the ferry dock in **Loutro (1)**, ramble along the seaside promenade to the first set of tavernas and, 75 m on, keep an eye out for a stepped trail branching off between the Hotel Daskalogiannis and the Hotel Madares (that is, do not take the steps in front of the Hotel Daskalogiannis). Some minutes later, the trail meets up with the *E4*; turn left onto the *E4* and continue ascending the slope (*yellow/black* waymarkers). Shortly past a gate, reach the ridge of the peninsula separating the two bays of Loutro and of Finix; the ruins of a Venetian castle are lying to the left. Cross over the peninsula while enjoying a view of the mountain village of Livaniana; to the left, you can spot the notch for Aradena Gorge. The path drops down to the bay of Finix, but then ignore a turn-off towards the houses at the little boat landing. Instead, skirt around the bay along the upper rim. Shortly past the **chapel at Finix (2)**, the *E4* crosses diagonally over a gravel track and then ascends for a couple of metres of height along a chain-link fence. A *blue*-marked turn-off to Livaniana is ignored (the return trail later on). Past another gate, descend along a gravel-paved access trail towards Lykos, following the trail towards

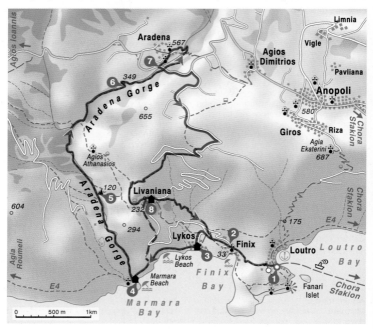

the sea. At the same height as a goat pen, below which, a car park is located, the trail veers to the left and a stepped trail leads to the tavernas at **Lykos Beach (3)**. Our trail leads directly across the terraces of Nikos Small Paradise and of the Taverna Akrogiali next door.

Now continue on along a chain-link fence for a stretch directly at the seaside. Past a small sandy beach, the path climbs steeply up a cliff where we have no choice but to use our hands while scrambling. Past a cave-like overhang, the path leads along a narrow and precipitous, cornice-like stretch. Ignore a second turn-off towards Livaniana and, shortly afterwards, descend to **Marma-**

You don't have to scramble up the ladder; the steep stretch can be skirted around via an alpine path.

ra Beach (4). If you are making good time, you can take a short bathing break on the little pebble beach. Upon closer inspection, the beach is actually also the mouth of the **Aradena Gorge**. From the seaside, follow the stream bed, at first broad and gravelly, into the gorge and find yourself immediately surrounded by rusty-red coloured rock faces, towering more than 200 m high. In autumn, the Chasteberry, growing up to 4 m in height, displays its lilac-coloured flowers; in spring, red flowering oleander bush casts its spell. Skirt around two bottlenecks, sporting boulders as big as a lorry, along a rocky alpine path on the right-hand side; waymarkers are an additional aid, during the further course of this stretch, in finding the perfect way between the boulders. Sometimes, short, steep spots have to be scrambled over, but in between times, stretches are met which lead pleasantly along the dry stream bed. After a good half an hour in the gorge, pass two striking **rock spires (5)**, 120 m. Afterwards, the gorge widens briefly to form a basin. Ignore a third, waymarked turn-off to Livaniana and a half an hour after that, beneath a rock face, an alpine path heading towards Agios Ioannis turns off to the left through a crevice. We bear right instead and then tackle the next steep stretch via zigzags.

A good 20 minutes past the turn-off leading to Agios Ioannis, reach the former **crux (6)**, 349 m, of the gorge. Until about ten years ago, this steep section could only be negotiated by climbing ladders. Now it can be skirted around on the left hand side of the gorge, via an alpine path, protected by railings and sometimes stepped. The railings are battered and missing in some sections and the path is somewhat precipitous here. A good 10 minutes later, the detour leads back to the stream bed of the gorge. Towering high above us, we can spot the steel bridge at Aradena which boldly joins

The restaurant Old Phoenix.

the two rims of the gorge walls together. Before the bridge was built, the gorge could only be crossed here along an ancient **mule track**, which was elaborately laid using supporting walls. Meet up with this trail after passing beneath the bridge and ascend along it on the left-hand side of the gorge.

Arriving at the rim of the canyon high above, reach the ruins of a house at the Aradena village limits. Past a gate, bear left and, 10 m further on, meet up with a narrow tarmac road; follow this through a grove of olive trees into the nearly abandoned village. 150 m further on, reach a second gate at a chapel for the cemetery. Immediately afterwards, leave the narrow road behind by turning left and then search for a way through the labyrinth of passageways leading through village ruins that exude a morbid charm. If you would like to pay a visit to the **cross-in-square church**, 75 m on, turn left at the first fork in front of a flat, rendered building with brown shutters. The church, hailing from the 14th century, was built on the ruins of an early Christian basilica right on the rim of the gorge. After visiting the church, at the main gate, turn left and, 20 m on, turn left again and finally meet up with the kiosk at the steel bridge in **Aradena (7)**, 567 m.

After a little refreshment, cross over the bridge spanning the gorge and take in a bird's eye view of the stream bed in the gorge lying 138 m down below. Behind the cross-in-square church, the White Mountains appear in all their grandeur, including Pachnes, at 2453 m. Not quite 400 m further on, turn right onto the access road towards Livaniana/Finix. The sign says 7.5 km to Livaniana, but many bends can be shortcut on the way. At the outset, the tarmac road winds through cushion plant scrubland while ascending slightly. Pass small fields which have been wrung out of this stony wasteland. Now pass a long farm building with a corrugated iron roof and, shortly after, reach a **rise**, at a good 600 m, where you can enjoy a downwards view of the Libyan Sea.

Pass yet another large building and, at a right-hand bend, ignore a *blue*-waymarked turn-off to Anopoli. A breathtaking view opens up of the southern coast and the village of Livaniana. Follow the road past two more hairpin bends and, directly past the second one, turn off onto a mule track (waymarkers). 10 mins later, the track meets up again with the tarmac road. Ascend along the tarmac road straight ahead until it meets up again, about 100 m further on, with the mule track, at first, rough and somewhat precipitous as it continues on. Suddenly, the Aradena Gorge appears again. The mule track, well-laid and cobbled here, leads for a stretch along the rim of the gorge; we lose altitude quickly as we descend in tight bends. At the end of the cobbled section, continue in the same direction and walk for a short way along a field-stone wall until afterwards, the **cemetery** at the upper village limits of Livaniana comes into view. 15 m above the cemetery's church, reach a junction; turn left to descend to Livaniana down below (turning right, you could climb down into the gorge again and continue the descent to Marmara).

From the church, *blue* waymarkers lead downwards into the village. At the junction, 3 minutes past the church, continue straight ahead to a concrete-paved street 25 m away: take it to reach the taverna at the lower village limits of **Livaniana (8)**, 232 m. (For Alternative 1, from the stepped trail, three minutes below the church, turn sharp right onto the *blue*-waymarked path to Mamara). From the taverna, keep descending along the street and, 200 m further on, ignore the tarmac-paved turn-off to Finix. A good 50 m past the turn-off, take the *blue*-marked path towards Loutro/Finix/Lykos. This leads immediately above two flat buildings and then ascends, now well-laid, along the slope in bends, while constantly allowing a view to the sea. Half an hour past the taverna, meet up with a fork and keep straight ahead (a right turn leads to Lykos). Cross diagonally over a gravel track. 200 m further on, shortly before Finix, reach the E4 at a spot already met on the approach route. A little later, pass the trail turning off to the right which leads to the restaurant Old Phoenix (possible stop for refreshment, see also Walk 30), then, passing the chapel at **Finix (2)**, continue on to return back to **Loutro (1)**.

The descent trail to Finix leads along a barren slope.

Magnificent descent from the highlands to the sea

After an ascent through the Anopoli Gorge, a fantastic descent into the car-free resort village of Loutro, with a good choice of places for refreshment, as well as fine panoramic views of the coast and two remote chapels along the way; all in all, an excellent combination for an very interesting day's excursion. Even the element of water plays a major role: not quite an hour before the end of the circular walk, situated in a splendid spot at the foot of a cliff face and only accessible on foot, Sweet Water Beach is an inviting place for a bathing break. Do not be put off by the long walking times and the many metres of height to be negotiated – there are also shorter alternatives.

Starting point: Chora Sfakion, 7 m. Good bus connections from Chania.
Height difference: about 900 m in both ascent and descent.
Grade: this is sometimes a strenuous ascent through the Anopoli Gorge,

»Trail squatters« on the Anopoli high plateau.

where you have to scramble over and around boulders on the way. The trail from Chora Sfakion, passing through the Anopoli Gorge, is *blue*-waymarked, the descent to Loutro, with *yellow* squares on a *white* background. Hardly any shade; be sure to take sunblock and bathing gear along!
Refreshment: several tavernas in Chora Sfakion; Taverna Tria Adelfia in Kambia; Taverna Platanos in Anopoli; numerous inns in Loutro (we recommend the Taverna Madares and the Café Loutro next door), as well as a simple beach bar on Sweet Water Beach.
Alternatives: 1. Chora Sfakion – Anopoli – Loutro: return by ferry from Loutro (five to six times daily; depending on the season, the last ferry between 17.00 and 18.10). Walking time is reduced to 4.20 hrs. (grade of difficulty: red).
2. Anopoli – Loutro – Chora Sfakion: starting from Chora Sfakion, take a taxi to Anopoli (€25) or by bus (end of May–Oct, daily at 9.00; information available in Chora Sfakion at the information booth on the roundabout). Walking time is reduced to 4 hrs. (grade of difficulty: red).
3. Anopoli – Loutro: by bus or taxi to Anopoli, return from Loutro by ferry to Chora Sfakion. The walk is cut down to only the worthwhile descent lasting 1.30 hrs. (grade of difficulty: blue).

In Chora Sfakion, a pine wood in front of the rugged, sheer cliffs on the coast lends a green touch.

Begin the walk in **Chora Sfakion (1)** at the roundabout on the village limits where the tourist information booth is also located. At Taverna Nikos, follow the line of restaurants until reaching the Café Akrogiali; in front of it, a concrete-paved trail ascends to the right. This forks about 200 m on in front of a couple of steps. Turn left here (*blue* arrow) following the traces of a path and then climb up a flight of steps to the secondary road leading to Anopolis. Turn left on this road and, 100 m past the last house, keep a sharp eye out for a *blue*-waymarked path that climbs up the rocky embankment. Just after two short bends, the path, cobblestone-paved only sometimes along the way, turns out to be the ancient connecting trail between Chora Sfakion and Anopoli. At the same time, a beautiful backwards view opens up of Chora Sfakion and the harbour.

10 mins later, the path merges onto a gravel trail. Not quite 100 m further on, ignore a track turning off in a sharp angle. As soon as the gravel trail turns sharp left while descending the slope down to the road, turn right instead, along a path (waymarker) that continues climbing down into the Ilingas Gorge, opening up before us. Here, the trail is cut somewhat into the rock face and

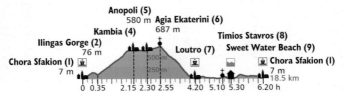

145

begins to drop, rather loose underfoot, down into the stream bed of the gorge. On the eastern side of the gorge, you can already spot the continued route of the trail. Along the last stretch, the old trail course has broken away and, while scrambling down almost eight metres, you will probably have to use your hands at times. In the broad, dry stream bed of the **Ilingas Gorge (2)**, 76 m, ascend for a short stretch until, about 75 m on, the villages' connecting trail continues to the left. Here, the trail has been laboriously reinforced with supporting walls as it ascends through the Anopoli Gorge, a branch, so to speak, of the Ilingas Gorge. In the dry stream bed, sometimes narrow and rocky, the cobblestones of the ancient *kalderimi* are only preserved in fragments. At two steep sections, one following soon after the other, each about 2 m in height, you have to scramble while using your hands. Further scrambles follow through bottlenecks. As soon as the rock faces begin to lose in steepness, the trail climbs out of the stream bed and continues ascending on the left bank. Still a good distance ahead of us, mobile phone transmission masts appear; we will pass these by later on.

At a pump house with an electricity pylon next to it, meet up with a gravel trail and take this to ascend further up the gorge. Pass another, smaller, pump house and, 5 mins after that, at the same height as some animal pens, climb up the broad track to the left. 75 m further on, the track veers to the left; leave it behind by continuing straight ahead along a stony path, heading towards a third pump house. 15 m before reaching it, turn left to climb up the embankment. A section of the ancient trail course continues above the pump house and then, at a hairpin bend, touches on the secondary road. 10 mins later, the trail meets up with a fork at a chain-link fence, next to the **mobile**

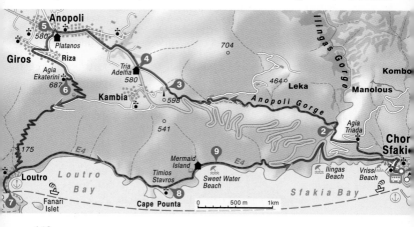

phone transmission masts (3), 590 m. Pass through the gate and, on the other side of the fence, bear right onto the gravel trail. The ascent is now behind us; we have reached the Anopoli high plateau and can enjoy the view of the White Mountains, dominated by the highest peak, Pachnes, at an altitude of 2453 m. Past a grove of olive trees surrounded by fieldstone walls, the trail meets up with the road in **Kambia (4)**, 580 m (a couple of paces to the left, heading along the road, leads to the Taverna Tria Adelfia, one of the first possible spots to take refreshment).

Turning right onto the road and a good 10 mins later, just past the bakery and the church, reach the village centre of **Anopoli (5)**, 580 m, at a major roundabout where the Taverna Platanos offers a rest stop. Lo-

Pachnes, Crete's second highest peak, above the Anopoli high plateau.

cated in the middle of the roundabout is a bust of the resistance fighter, Daskalogiannis, who was born in the village, and is the namesake, amongst others, for a ferry providing service along the southern coast and for the international airport at Chania. At the taverna, turn off onto a tarmac road heading towards Agia Ekaterini. A couple of paces on, the road veers to the right and soon ascends onto a mountain ridge. Past a bend to the right, ignore a trail turning off to the left and continue straight ahead. Before the semi-abandoned district of Giros, the narrow road veers sharply to the left and then ends at the foot of the chapel, **Agia Ekaterini (6)**, 687 m. The excursion climbing up to the summit chapel is worthwhile; with our backs to Pachnes, we can enjoy a bird's eye view of the semi-circular bay of Loutro down below.

At the end of the narrow road, pass through a gate and begin the climb down to Loutro. In tight zigzags, lose altitude quickly and, 25 mins later, meet up with a trail that is approaching from Kambia. Turn right onto this trail until reaching the next left-hand bend; a few paces further on, continue along a path. Almost the entire time while we are descending along this path, which is sometimes very loose underfoot, we are rewarded with a panoramic view

147

During the descent from Anopoli, a bird's eye view of Loutro opens up.

of Loutro. After descending for about an hour, meet up with the turn-off to Lykos, 175 m. Turn left here to finally cross the village limits of **Loutro (7)** at the ruins of a house. A stopover in the village, picturesquely nestled along the bay, is a must. So, keep to the right (to the left, the *E4* leads to Chora Sfakion) and, at the Hotel Oasis, descend to the Taverna Pavlos on the seaside promenade. Here, we are spoilt for choice between numerous restaurants and cafés (if you wish to end the walk in Loutro, continue on to the ferry dock at the end of the promenade). After a break, ascend back to the ruins of the house at the northern edge of the bay and now follow the **E4** towards Chora Sfakion. At first, the well-laid path leads about 50 m above sea level as it follows the coastline, but then it drops down to the seaside. Now pass two pebble beaches and then the secluded chapel of **Timios Stavros (8)**. From the chapel, it only takes about 15 mins to reach **Sweet Water Beach (9)**, which, because of its location at the foot of the towering coastal cliffs, rising up to 800 m in height, and the freshwater springs found here (Greek: *glika nera*; sweet water), is one of Crete's most extraordinary beaches.

From the beach, ascend along a narrow mule track through a scree-covered slope to reach the secondary road Anopoli – Chora Sfakion, which leads, in half an hour, to the village limits of **Chora Sfakion (1)**. Past the Pension Kelaides, a stepped trail descends to the seaside promenade down below, flanked by tavernas; from here, return back to the roundabout and the car park situated above it.

A short walk to ancient ruins and to a day-tripper's restaurant

Loutro is simply beautiful. Not only the picturesque setting on the crescent-shaped bay, but also the terraces of the cafés and restaurants, right on the sea, are pure Mediterranean stereotypes. In addition, the short excursion by ferry opens up an enchanting panoramic view of the rugged, sheer cliffs towering over the coastline. You can put your legs to work by taking a short circular stroll to a charming restaurant above the little pebble beach at Finix, but the brief ascent here should not be taken lightly when the midday sun is ablaze. In ancient times, the sheltered bay at Finix (also known as Finikas or Phoenix) served as the harbour for the important mountain village of Anopoli.

Starting point: Loutro, 1 m. From Chora Sfakion, ferry service to Loutro four or five times daily in the summer months. The first one sets sail from Chora Sfakion at 10.30 and the last ferry from Loutro returns between 17.00 and 18.10, depending on the season.

Height difference: about 200 m in both ascent and descent.

Grade: the circular walk almost always leads along sometimes stony paths; at the beginning, a short, relatively steep ascent. During the descent that follows, a short stretch requires some route-finding skill. Hardly any shade; be sure to bring along your bathing gear!

Refreshment: numerous tavernas and cafés in Loutro, the restaurant Old Phoenix in Finix (you could also spend the night here; www.old-phoenix.com).

Linking tips: the walk could also be combined with Walks 27 and 29.

The little pebble beach at Finix and the shady terrace of the day tripper's restaurant.

From the ferry landing in **Loutro (1)**, take the seaside promenade, flanked by tavernas, at the narrow pebble beach until it ends at the restaurant Pavlos. From there, pick up a concrete-laid trail through a passageway and immediately

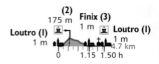

ascend along a narrow cobbled trail reaching the Hotel Oasis after only a few paces. In front of the hotel, turn sharp right and take the path, stepped at the outset, to the village limits and then reach a gate. Past the gate, bear left and head towards a tiny church with a concrete foundation and then ascend along an ancient connecting trail, heading towards Anopoli (continuing straight ahead at the gate, the E4 leads towards Chora Sfakion).

Along the *kalderimi*, cobbled in some sections, ascend very steeply while gaining altitude quickly. With every metre of altitude won, the panoramic view of the picturesque bay of Loutro just gets better. After about a 20-minute ascent, we have already reached a height of about 175 m above sea level and we have to keep our eyes peeled for a **turn-off (2)**; a sharp right turn here ascends further towards Anapolis, but we bear left instead. From this trail, also very well-laid, a view immediately opens up of a steep cliff face sporting an almost perfectly square entrance to a cave. The trail leads for a few paces below this cave. Afterwards, enjoy yet another view of the houses at Loutro and of the ruins of a Venetian castle, enthroned on a peninsula. To the west, you can spot the mountain village, Livaniana and, below it, Marmara Bay, situated at the mouth of the Aradena Gorge (Walk 28).

But we shouldn't be too distracted by this panoramic view; we have to keep an eye out for the route as well. A good 5 minutes past the cave, watch out for a **metre-high boulder**, crowned by a cairn. Here, a path descends to the left, but we continue straight ahead instead, at first, more or less keeping to the same height, along a narrow, indistinct path heading in the direction of Livaniana (cairn). Down below, the few houses scattered in the bay from

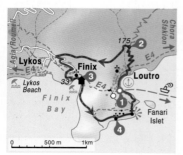

Finix come into view. Not quite 10 minutes past the boulder, the course of the trail becomes somewhat difficult to follow; the path veers sharp left at first, then immediately to the right and, finally, well-laid and distinct, descends along the slope.

In front of a couple of dog kennels, meet up with a gravel trail; turn sharp left and descend along it in bends. Just before the chapel from Finix, cross over the E4 diagonally

In the tavernas of Loutro, you can sit right at the seaside – this table, however, is private.

then head straight on descending along the gravel trail to reach the restaurant Old Phoenix in **Finix (3)**. The restaurant's terrace, shaded by bowers of bougainvillea, is just perfect for a rest stop; just below it, a pebble beach, flanked by salt cedars, is an inviting place for a swim.

From the restaurant, cross the beach to the neighbouring apartment house. Past this, a sign points left to an ascent towards Loutro, however, keep walking along the narrow concrete-paved trail on the coastline and continue on to another house, 50 m on. Before reaching it, go through an opening in the fence and, a few paces on, pass through a gate. Past the gate, a lovely, *blue*-waymarked coastal path sets off. Soon, catch a view of the southern tip of the peninsula, levelling off here, which separates the bays of Finix and Loutro from one another. At the end, cross over the peninsula while heading eastwards. Past a power pylon, meet up with a **chapel (4)**, its gable bell tower placed separately on top of a boulder. The old quarry stone walls of ancient Finix are lying next to it.

About 3 minutes past the archaeological digs, pass by Loutro's little **cemetery** and a bench standing in front of the cemetery chapel. A view opens up, taking in an offshore islet and, towards the east, far in the distance, Chora Sfakion. The path, now cobbled, passes through a gate and then continues, returning to the ferry dock in **Loutro (1)**.

151

The Samaria Gorge's »little sister«

If you are walking on Crete in early spring and the Samaria Gorge is still closed, you can still be well served with the Imbros Gorge as an alternative. The somewhat demeaning appellation »little Samaria« given to the gorge is actually advantageous because it isn't quite as crowded here as it is at her famous »big sister«. But still, you will rarely find yourself alone here as well; even organised walking tours include Imbros in their programmes. With 7 km of length, the gorge is much shorter, but therefore, not quite as strenuous. Plus, you will find a spectacular bottleneck here as well: if you spread your arms out in this bottleneck, you can touch both walls of the gorge at the same time!

Starting point: the bus stop at the Taverna Porofarango, 0.9km south of Imbros, 730 m. As an alternative, in the village centre of Imbros, at the Taverna Kalinorisma, there is a second waymarked trailhead from which the walk would be lengthened by a good ten minutes. Imbros is situated on the bus line Chania (daily: 8.15 and 14.00) – Chora Sfakion (daily: 6.45, 11.00, 13.30, 18.30) and Rethymno (7.00, 13.00) – Vrisses – Chora Sfakion (7.00, 11.00, 18.30).

Height difference: 565 m in descent.

Grade: a mostly pleasant to walk and, at times, cobbled trail leads through the gorge. Scrambling over sticks and stones, as is the case in many other gorges, is not necessary here. In the morning, the upper reaches are usually completely in the shade.

Refreshment: in Imbros, the Taverna Porofarango with a view into the gorge; at the gorge entrance, two kiosks selling cold drinks; in Komitades, several more tavernas, including the one hosted by Giorgos next to the church (here, simple studio apartments for lodging; tel. +30-28250-91005, www.taverna-giorgos-komitades-crete.com).

Opening times: the gorge is open all year round, €2 entry fee.

Return: 1. if you have approached by car and must return to it in Imbros, in Komitades take an unlicensed taxi (vehicles, mostly pick-up trucks, can be arranged with practically half of the villagers and, in almost every taverna, are offered obtrusively). Already at the kiosks at the exit to the gorge, you might be somewhat aggressively confronted and even provided with misinformation. If this is the case, don't lose your cool and simply continue the walk to the church in Komitades. Two of the houses next to the church belong to the friendly, family-run, tavena Giorgos – a prime location, and not only for refreshment. Anette, from Munich, and her Cretan husband Giorgos, can arrange a taxi for €20 for two people.

2. if you would prefer not to rely on a taxi, walk from Imbros to Waypoint 3 and, from there, take the same trail to ascend back again to Imbros (walking time, there and back, 2 hrs).

3. if you have approached with the bus to Imbros, from Komitades, take the road that leads in 1.3 km to the T-junction (Taverna Posidonio) on the main road Chania – Chora Sfakion and wait for the bus there that goes to Chora Sfakion. This arrives at about 11.00. If you are too late, try hitch-hiking or continue walking along the road for the last 3.5 km to descend to Sfakia.

Olive cultivation at the gorge exit of Imbros.

On the southern village limits of **Imbros**, at the **Taverna Porofarango (1)** and the entrance sign for the gorge, descend along the path that, at the outset, is flanked by a railing into the stream bed of the gorge. The gorge itself is initially barely recognisable as such. Some minutes later, reach the ticket office (quite often, the entrance fee isn't demanded until reaching the second ticket office at the gorge exit). The sometimes cobbled *kalderimi* leads in or along the broad, gravel stream bed of the gorge, flanked by stately mountain cypresses, Holm oaks and Cretan maple trees. A quarter of an hour past the ticket office, the trail leads beneath an **overhanging rock face**, and afterwards, the feeling of walking through a gorge gradually takes over; the rock faces begin to draw nearer and to climb vertically upwards.

Afterwards, reach the gorge's **famous bottleneck (2)**, 461 m. The rock faces here are a mere 160 cm apart, even narrower than the one at the Iron Gates of the Samaria Gorge, however, it is not quite so spectacular,

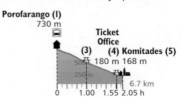

153

The upper reaches of the Imbros Gorge seem more like a broad valley but, during the continued descent, the walls of the gorge squeeze in quite closely (photos below).

since the rock faces are not nearly as high. Nevertheless, the spot is impressive enough; it is so narrow that only a little light can enter here. A few minutes later, the gorge becomes slightly wider and allows space for a little **rest area (3)**, 445 m. Above the bench with a wall hanging, many walkers have become immortalised by leaving a passport photo of themselves!

Past the rest area, the gorge widens even more, but the walls of the gorge, coloured in a scale from ochre to sienna red, tower higher and higher up. At a rock arch about 12 m in height, the gorge narrows somewhat again. A quarter of an hour after that, reach the exit of the gorge. Here is another little picnic area with benches.

About 5 mins later, pass some kiosks offering refreshment. At this point, ignore the left hand turn onto an ascending track; instead, continue on along the dry, stony stream bed. At the **ticket office (4)**, shortly afterwards, follow signs pointing right to reach two tavernas: Meltemi and

Imbros Gorge (the *E4* continues straight ahead and, 5 mins past the official exit of the gorge, meets up with the road). Our path leads along a fieldstone wall through a grove of olive trees. At the next junction, keeping slightly to the right once again, pass the tavernas, Dionysos and Imbros Gorge to reach the tarmac road from **Komitades (5)**, 168 m. Turn right along the road to reach the village centre with a church and, two houses further on, the Taverna Giorgos, where you can make arrangements for a taxi.

Congenial rest area (above); always along a pleasant trail (left), pass through the narrowest point (right).

From the hinterland of Frangokastello onto the high plateau of Kallikratis

For walkers lodging in Frangokastello, the question arises which of the two gorges, relatively close to one another in the hinterland of the coast, should be tackled first: the Asfendou Gorge or the one at Kallikratis? Both are fairly easy, well-marked, and of the same length, but which is the most attractive? A positive point in favor of the Kallikratis Gorge is that at the upper exit, you will find a pleasant café, offering bracing refreshment for the return route. The scattered settlement of Kallikrates itself is located in a picturesque setting atop a high plateau that is encircled by a wreath of mountains.

Starting point: Kapsodasos, 178 m, on the northern edge of the plain at Frangokastello. Approaching from Chora Sfakion, just past Agios Nektarios, bear slightly to the left, drive through Patsianos and, at the sign for the village limits of Kapsodasos, turn sharp to the left, ascending along a narrow road. Parking possible 700 m on, past a sharp right-hand bend, at the side of the road. Bus service from Chora Sfakion – Frangokastello, twice daily in high season.

Height difference: 550 m.

Grade: a well-laid, ancient trail connecting the villages, sometimes somewhat steep, leads through the gorge. No scrambling necessary! Route finding is very easy; the stretch through the gorge is a section of the *E4*.

Refreshment: the Little Café in Kallikratis (closed Mondays); in the German-run restaurant, amongst other refreshment, you can enjoy a good cappuccino and tasty, home-made lemonade.

Worth seeing: in Frangokastello, a glimpse of the Venetian castle from 1371 is worthwhile. Only a few paces away from the castle, you can take a refreshing dip at the beach; this drops off very gradually into the sea.

In the right-hand bend above **Kapsodasos (1)**, a path (*E4*-waymarked) descends after a few paces into the oleander-lush stream bed of the Kallikratis Gorge from which you can get a view into the gaping opening of the gorge's

mouth. Just after, two gigantic boulders must be skirted around to the left. A quarter of an hour later, the trail traverses a talus slope and, past that, crosses over the stream bed of the gorge for the first time. The well-laid and sometimes cobbled mule track ascends along the right flank of the gorge, usually with the V-shaped notch in the upper

The route is a leg of the E4.

The lower reaches of the Kallikratis Gorge.

regions of the gorge in view in front of you. Sycamore trees add a touch of green to the rocky wasteland and, in spring, Jerusalem sage bears yellow flowers. About 15 minutes past the talus slope, just before the *kalderimi* changes over to the other flank, you could head seawards to a delightful **viewpoint (2)**, 365 m: directly at the mouth of the gorge emptying into the sea, the Venetian castle of Frangokastello appears.

The gorge widens for a short stretch to form a funnel-shaped basin. In the further course of the route, sometimes you bear left, sometimes right, follow-ing the stream bed of the gorge that is chock-full of large boulders, and continue into the ever-narrower can-yon; one stretch of the trail runs (concrete-paved) along the rock face on a cornice-like ledge.

Afterwards, the walls of the gorge spread out noticeably. Only ascend-ing slightly now, the mule track merges into the **narrow road (3)**, 665 m, ascending here from Fran-

Very inviting – the Little Café.

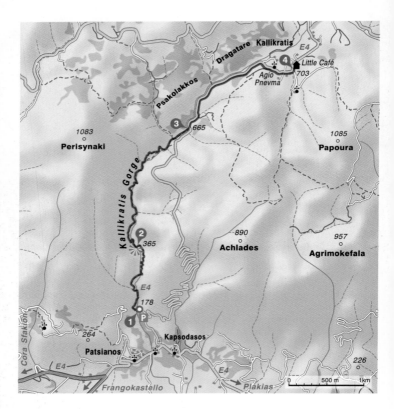

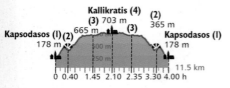

gokastello. Follow this, heading straight on and, not quite ½ hr later, reach the Little Café at the entrance to the village of **Kallikratis (4)**, 703 m.

In the event that you have not pre-arranged to be picked up, return from Kallikratis via the gorge (or along the secondary road) back to **Kapsodasos (1)**. (You could, instead, try your hand at hitch-hiking back again; although there isn't much traffic here, usually someone will stop to give you a lift.)

Along the mill trail into a picturesque mountain village

In the hinterland of the aspiring seaside resort of Plakias, two watermills have withstood the test of time. In particular, the »Old Mill«, with its monumental aqueduct, conveys an idea of how complicated it was to grind grain into flour in the past. A chapel is hidden away nearby. The tavernas located in the cosy mountain village of Mirthios above the »Mill Valley« are very popular with walkers and day-trippers due to their excellent homemade meals and the fine views they offer.

Starting point: Plakias, 2 m. A bus line connects Rethymno, on the northern coast, with Plakias, four to five times daily.
Height difference: 170 m in both ascent and descent.
Grade: a simple circular walk along broad farm trails and narrow paths. A stream must be crossed via a ford, where you may get your feet wet, depending on the water level. Very little shade.
Refreshment: numerous cafés and restaurants in Plakias. In Mirthios, the Taverna Plateia serving good Cretan food and boasting a lovely belvedere-like terrace, from which you can enjoy a view of the Bay of Plakias down below.

The walk begins at the combination bus stop and taxi rank in the village centre of **Plakias (1)**. Follow the seaside road towards the jetty and, just after a few paces, cross over a little bridge spanning a river (the mill stream). 75 m further on, past the Taverna Sifis and a little supermarket, turn right onto a very narrow street. At a junction about 300 m further on, bear to the right and then cross over the river once again via a second bridge.
At the next junction, turn left (straight ahead is the trail for the return) and

The Old Mill in the Mirthios Valley.

161

Panoramic: the terrace of the Taverna Plateia.

then immediately pass by the **youth hostel (2)**, where the narrow street becomes a gravel trail. Keeping to the main trail, in a grove of olive trees, pass a **library**, run by Brits (which is, according to their own advert, the »southernmost lending library in Europe«). A few minutes after passing Studios Adonis, meet up with the **first mill (3)**, of which, only a few quarry stone walls remain. The gravel trail leads somewhat above the mill stream that is flanked by dense patches of reeds. To our right and up above, we can spot the houses of Mirthios, which is the destination for the walk. Not quite 100 m past the tumbledown mill, turn left at a fork and then, at the next fork, turn left onto the trail climbing down towards the river. (At the first left-hand bend, a trail forks off to the right, but peters out in the undergrowth as it heads upriver.) Not quite 10 m past the left-hand bend, a path leads to the mill stream; here, the course of the stream can be crossed via a **ford** of laid stepping stones; in early spring, depending on the water level, this may prove to be not very easy. On the other bank, take a gravel trail to continue upstream. The trail narrows into a path and, below a second mill, meets up with an arched bridge, allowing you to cross over the stream. Below the imposing wall of the mill, the so-called **Old Mill (4)**, 60 m, and to the right, there is a little sign posted for Mirthios.

Ascend steeply to the aqueduct which was once used to bring water here to run the millstones. On the other side of an arch in the aqueduct, take a path for a short stretch along the narrow water channel and then continue the ascent along a

162

well-trodden trail. The path merges into an intersecting trail; turn right onto this trail. At the seaside down below, you can spot Plakias. At a junction 50 m further on, keep on the level, that is, bear slightly to the right (*blue* waymarkers). Five minutes

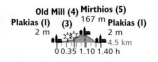

later, past a watering trough for goats, the path merges between two gates into a farm road with an ancient water channel running along next to it. Another five minutes more, turn left onto a concrete-paved track and ascend relatively steeply to the houses of **Mirthios (5)**, 167 m. At the lower limits of the village, bear right along an intersecting trail to reach, after a few paces, the settlement's ancient wash house. There is also a trough fountain with potable water here. From the wash house, ascend along a broad stone stairway to reach the village main street where, to the left, the Taverna Plateia offers an invitation for refreshment.

After a rest break, descend back again to the wash house, bear slightly to the left and descend steeply along the narrow tarmac road. Always keeping straight ahead, soon after, along a concrete-paved trail, finally reach the **youth hostel (2)** at the village limits of Plakias; from there, cross over the bridge spanning the mill stream to return to the seaside road in **Plakias (1)**.

The Bay of Plakias, as seen during the ascent to Cape Kako Mouri (Walk 34).

To the fine, sandy beach at Damnoni

The sandy beach at Plakias counts as one of the best bathing spots on the southern coast, so it is no wonder that what was once an insider's tip for backpackers has increased slowly, but surely, in popularity as a bathing destination for the run-of-the-mill tourist. Also, Damnoni Bay, to the east of Plakias, has been »discovered« in the meantime and much of it has been taken over by a major time-share complex belonging to the Swiss firm Hapimag. Despite this fact, the beach is still beautiful and the walk, skirting around the surprisingly pristine and rugged cape between Plakias and Damnoni, is still quite appealing.

Starting point: Hotel Plakias Bay at the south end of the beach in Plakias, 8 m. A bus line connects Rethymno, on the northern coast, with Plakias, four to five times daily. From the bus stop in the village centre of Plakias, follow the seaside road southwards for 1.3 km until reaching a dead-end street sign shortly before the Hotel Plakias Bay (added walking time: there and back 40 minutes).
Height difference: 220 m.
Grade: the walk follows gravel trails and paths, the descent to Kalypso is somewhat rough. The route is provided with *blue* waymarkers until shortly before reaching Kalypso. Along the return route, beginning at Damnoni, several junctions require a little more concentration. No shade on the way. Take along your bathing gear and some sunblock!
Refreshment: in Plakias, there is a good assortment of restaurants and cafés; in Damnoni Beach, the tavernas Violakis and Damnoni.

Begin the walk at the southern end of the beach (naturist section) of **Plakias**. From the beach road, ascend to the **Hotel Plakias Bay (1)** up above. To the right, next to the reception entrance, a path starts off, signed for Damnoni/ Kalypso. At the fork 20 m past the hotel, continue straight ahead through a gate. Not quite 200 m further on, turn sharp right to climb up along a gravel trail (the trail straight ahead will be our return route later on). Right away, enjoy a charming and fantastic panoramic view taking in Plakias Bay, above which, the villages of Mirthios (to the right) and Sellia (to the left) are perched; in between the two, the notch marking the Kotsifou Gorge can be spotted (see photo on page 163). Cross over a trail that intersects diagonally and, 3 minutes later, turn left onto a path (*blue* waymarker) heading towards a steep rock face. Reach a fork at the foot of the rock face and continue ascending straight ahead along the path running parallel (be careful, the path forking away is also waymarked in *blue*). Past a metre-wide gap through the rock, at about 135 m above sea level, begin to de-

Kalypso Cretan Village
Hotel
Plakias Bay (I)

Damnoni
Beach (4) Hotel
(2) Plakias Bay (I)

8 m
6.0 km

0   0.45 1.15 1.50 h

The fjord-like incised bay at the cape has been taken over completely by the Village Resort Kalypso.

scend again. The path veers to the left in front of striking crags and then continues the descent along tight bends. Soon, take a look at the dark, bizarre formation of the coastal cliffs at the foot of the cape. A short section of the trail is secured here by a cable fence. Then the path meets up with a road; turn right to descend along this road. Not quite 5 minutes later, reach the grand entrance gate of the **Kalypso Cretan Village (2)**, 43 m. Pass through this gate. At the point where the road turns to the right, a good 250 m further on, into the bungalow resort, leave it behind at a car park and take a **stepped trail**, secured laboriously with concrete walls and which you cannot possibly miss, to climb up to the top of a rocky cliff. On top of the cliff, a broad gravel trail sets off and slightly descends along the southern

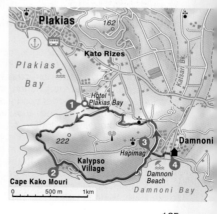

Along the precipitous mule track on the cape.

flank of the cape. On your left hand side, pass a cave that is usually occupied by goats. Shortly afterwards, a view of the Damnoni Bay opens up. Pass an access road leading to a boat landing in a little minor cove and then reach a fork in front of the resort complex **Hapimag (3)**. Bear right here and, at a water sports centre, meet up with **Damnoni Beach (4)**. To find some refreshment, continue on to pass a swimming pool, cross over the course of a stream via a footbridge and then you have the choice between the Taverna Violakis or the Damnoni; both boast spacious terraces shaded by Salt cedars.

After a break and/or a pause for a swim, return again to the fork near the bungalows of the Hapimag complex and then turn right onto the gravel road. A good 5 minutes later, meet up with a major **junction**. At this point, cross over the tarmac road and then, to the left of a power pylon, open a gate and, on the other side, pick up the traces of a path (at the outset, rather unclear) which heads towards a mobile phone transmission tower. 50 m further on, pass a cattle trough.

About 10 minutes past the junction, meet up with another, rather ill-defined, junction and bear left. Soon, continue over a little saddle and, passing this, descend to an unpaved road. Turn left along this road and descend. At the following junction, 100 m further on, turn sharp left and pass through two gates, one right after the other, and pick up a path which leads through a newly-planted grove of olive trees. In the grove, the path (here it is somewhat indistinct again) veers slightly to the right, descending, and then meets up with an intersecting trail. Turn left onto this trail and, a few paces further on, meet up again with the path used during the approach. This brings us back to the **Hotel Plakias Bay (1)**.

Through the Megalopotamos Valley to a marvellous beach

In the late 60s, the palm-dotted beach on the southern coast of Crete was a short-term destination for hippies and societal drop-outs, but today, Preveli is a popular target for excursionists – not least, because in every travel guide for the island, this fine, sandy beach is justly regarded as the loveliest bathing spot that Crete has to offer. This walk acquaints us with the valley of the Megalopotamos River; in spring, lush with greenery: a marvellous riparian forest skirts the banks. In the area around the mouth of the river, a dense grove of Cretan Date Palms are growing and, in the hinterland, olive trees and fields are scattered about.

Preveli Beach (3) (5)

Starting point: the Venetian bridge by Kato Moni Preveli, 42 m. From the north-south connection Rethymno – Agia Galini, approaching from the north and 7 km before reaching Spili, turn off towards Plakias. The road runs through the spectacular Kourtaglioto Canyon. 6 km before reaching Plakias, follow the signs in the direction of Preveli and, 2 km further on, reach the bridge. In summer, there is bus service to Moni Preveli from Rethymno (thrice daily) and Plakias (several times daily). The driver will stop near the Taverna Gefyra if you ask him to.

Height difference: a good 200 m.

Grade: not a difficult circular walk along roads and country lanes as well as narrow paths. The approach route is *red* way-marked and sometimes slightly precipitous. The descent to the beach is relatively steep. Take along your bathing gear!

Refreshment: Taverna Gefyra at the starting point/destination of the circular walk; a simple beach bar at Preveli Beach, where you can also order simple meals (only open in the summer months).

Alternatives: 1. From mid-June until Oct, ferries set sail daily from Plakias, Damnoni and Agia Galini to Preveli Beach, so you can start the circular walk from there as well.

2. From the beach bar, another 30 m brings you to a path laid in a beautiful setting, through a lush palm tree grove on the western bank of the Megalopotamos. The path ends, 10 mins later; if you wish to continue on to the rock pools (see photo, page 169) in the untamed and unspoilt gorge, you will have to scramble over boulders.

3. From the Venetian bridge, if you continue in the direction of Piso Moni Preveli, 2.3 km further on, a road forks off to a pay and display car park (WP 5). From there, you can descend, in 15 minutes, to the beach.

Worth seeing: 2.5 km from the Venetian bridge, reach the monastery Piso Moni Preveli, perched high above the Libyan Sea. In the monastery church, amongst others, the iconostasis and valuable reliquary cross are noteworthy. A small museum displays icons and other sacred objects. Like many other monasteries on the island, the Preveli Monastery, at present only inhabited by a handful of monks, played an important role in the Cretans' centuries-long struggle for freedom. Opening times: March 25–May 31, daily 9–18.30, June 1–October 31, from 9–13.30; a small entrance fee is charged for the visit (www.preveli.org).

At the **bridge (1)** (known to all as the Venetian Bridge, although it was not built by the Venetians but instead, was erected later, in 1852, during the Turkish occupation), use a ford to cross over the Megalopotamos. Just after, bear right and, a few paces further on, reach the **Taverna Gefyra**. 100 m past the taverna, the narrow road becomes a gravel trail. Take this, at first along the left bank, heading down the valley; we are accompanied by ancient olive and carob trees. The river is flanked by a dense riparian forest of Cretan maple, cypress and oleander; the scenery set around us is of steep, towering coastal cliffs. Not quite 10 mins later, cross over a stone bridge spanning a tributary of the Megalopotamos. Afterwards, continue to the right along a broad road and, another 10 mins later, meet up with a farm road that is blocked off by a **metal gate**; a little chapel for the monastery is situated below it. Keep to the road for another 20 m and then leave it behind by turning right onto another farm road. A few paces on, this splits into two paths; take the right-hand path, leading along a fence heading down the valley. Arriving at the valley floor, cross over the course of a stream, then continue on between about 30 and 50 m of altitude above the river; a precipitous stretch can be skirted around via a path located a few paces above it. The path

eventually leads away from the river and then ascends to a rise up above. Cross under power lines and, at the same height as a little **transmission tower (2)**, 120 m, a view opens up of the southern coast and the Paximadia Islands lying offshore; to the left, a downwards view of Ligres Bay. Along the descent trail, steep at first, meet up with a rather obscure fork at a rock spur, from which you have a downwards view of the taverna at Ligres; bear right here. Continuing a good stretch still above the coast, meet up with an intersecting path. To the left, you could reach the Ligres Bay, but we turn right instead, pass through a gate, and 100 m further on, enjoy a picture-perfect panorama of **Preveli Beach (3)** and the mouth of the river, flanked by Date Palms. A stepped trail climbs down

The gorge of the Megalopotamos.

To cross over the mouth of the river at Preveli Beach, you have to take your shoes off.

to the beach below; on the opposite side of the river, we can already spot the stepped trail for the return route. But, first of all, a bathing break is an absolute must – in freshwater or saltwater, whatever strikes your fancy. After a good, long rest stop in the shade of a salt cedar, cross over the river at an appropriate spot. In early spring, when the water level is high, this may be a difficult undertaking, depending on the situation. Starting in May, however, the water level is seldom over knee-high. On the western side of the bay, there is a beach bar where you can gather some strength for the return route and then take a worthwhile excursion into the palm tree grove (Alternative 2). Past the bar, climb up the stepped trail mentioned above to reach a **terrace viewpoint (4)**, 76 m, from which, professional photographers take the ultimate postcard photo of the fabulous beach (photo on page 53).

5 mins later, reach a **car park (5)**, 114 m, with a ticket booth. Bear right and, at the eastern edge of the car park, there are two gates. Here, pass through the right-hand gate, then turn left onto a path that descends along a fence and, at the same time, once again enjoy the spectacular panoramic view of the Megalopotamos Gorge, flanked by palm trees. The path leads for a stretch along the sheer drop at the rim. Past a transmission mast, cross under the power lines again and, some minutes afterwards, the path drops down to a **chapel (6)**, surrounded by olive trees. A gravel road begins at the chapel and leads for a short time directly along the river and then for a short stretch below the tumbledown monastery grounds, destroyed by the Turks in the 19th century, of Kato Moni Preveli. At the end, the road returns to the »Venetian« **bridge (1)**.

To a little waterfall and the ancient necropolis of Lappa

Argyroupoli is a touristy village spruced up with quaint little cafés and several souvenir shops. Here, you can buy, amongst other things, avocado-based cosmetics which are produced from the oil of the fruit from the plantation, presently numbering 2000 trees, located somewhat on the outskirts of the village. Those interested in cultural history will be attracted to the ancient necropolis, and the waterfalls somewhat below Argyroupoli are popular destinations. This short circular walk takes in all three of these attractions. In addition, while rambling through the old village centre, you will discover relics from ancient times. Eye-catching is the Venetian portal arch in the main passageway bearing the thought-provoking inscription »All the world is but smoke and shadow«.

Starting point: the village square of Argyroupoli, 265 m. From the National Road near Rethymno, follow the signs via Episkopi to Argyroupoli. You can park at the village square in front of the church and the clock tower. By bus from Rethymno Mon–Fri around 6.00, return from Argyroupoli around 15.30.

Height difference: 200 m.
Grade: a simple circular walk along a narrow path at the outset; in the further course of the walk, along broad farm tracks; short stretches along main roads.
Refreshment: cafés in the old village centre of Argyroupoli; seafood tavernas at the waterfall.

Hawker at the village square in Agiroupolis.

From the village square in **Argyro-upoli (1)**, with the archway housing the Lappa Avocado shop to your left (see photo on page 171), head back 50 m along the road to Re-thymno and then, opposite a little

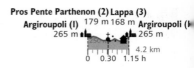

Pros Pente Parthenon (2) Lappa (3)
Argiroupoli (I) 179 m 168 m Argiroupoli (
265 m   265 m
                              4.2 km
0   0.30 1.15 h

supermarket, turn right onto a path which is cobblestone-paved at the outset and, at first glance, doesn't seem to be a walkable trail (*blue* waymarking). The path, flanked with fieldstone walls, begins somewhat overgrown and with sometimes damaged pavement as it descends into a stream valley which boasts jungle-like vegetation.

The path continues on the opposite bank of the stream, sometimes over steps, climbing up the valley slope in tight bends and, 5 mins later, merges into a road. Follow the road, bearing slightly to the left, and 10 m on, continue straight ahead. Far before us, the northern coastline appears with the gently curving Gulf of Aimirou, bordered to the west by the Drapanos peninsula.

At the next fork, turn left onto a gravel trail descending slightly through a grove of olive trees. The trail is concrete-paved as it continues further and then it merges into the secondary road Argyroupoli – Kato Poros. Turn left onto the secondary road. This leads above and along the course of a stream and then crosses over it. In front of a miniature church, leave the road behind by turning right onto a cobblestone trail (sign: »Church of Holy Five Virgins«).

The Oriental plane tree in Lappa is considered one of Crete's oldest.

Just a few minutes later, meet up with the **Pros Pente Parthenon (2)**, 179 m, the chapel of the five holy virgins. Next to it, there are several graves which have been set into the embankment. Somewhat further below, at the ancient necropolis **Lappa (3)**, 168 m, with even more graves set into the rock face, there is a shady picnic area with a five-armed trough fountain and, next to it, an ancient plane tree. After taking a break, climb back up to the secondary road, cross over it and then continue descending slightly along the cobbled trail. Not quite 5 mins later, the trail meets up with a tarmac road at yet another chapel. Turn right onto the tarmac road and at the fork not quite 100 m further on (mini market and a café), turn left onto the road heading in the direction of Asi Gonia.

The waterfalls of Argyroupoli.

10 minutes later, the houses of Argyroupoli appear again above the road. Shortly after, we are standing in front of cascading **waterfalls (4)**, 167 m, fed by a prolific spring gushing out of the rock face and tumbling down towards the valley over artificially created spillways. Half a dozen seafood tavernas have been established here for the Cretan day-trippers arriving in hordes at this popular destination, especially at the weekend. At the second taverna, climb up a large flight of stairs and immediately pass a chapel built into a cave where the waters of the spring are gushing along in a channel. At the Taverna Kastro, somewhat above the chapel, the trail forks. Ascend to the left along the narrow, concrete-paved trail to return to the village up above. Arriving at the lower village limits, just a little further up, we can already spot the bell tower of **Argyroupoli (1)**.

173

Through the untamed and unspoilt valley of the water mills

Only a few kilometres south of Rethymno, you will be surprised to find an evergreen valley, supplied with water the entire year round by a mill stream, which ran 20 mills and provided the livelihood for an entire village through the power of water. During Venetian rule, Mili supplied the entire region with flour. Most of the mills and quarry-stone houses have fallen into ruin today, but a rather morbid charm still haunts this ancient milling settlement. The trail through the mill valley has been renovated in 2014/15, thanks to EU funding, with most of the money being used for elaborate wooden railings and little picnic sites.

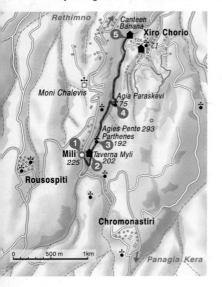

Starting point: Mili, 225 m. At the eastern village limits of Rethymno, leave the National Road behind in the district of Perivolia (not signed) by heading towards Amari. Then cross over the National Road and, at the roundabout 100 m further on, turn right towards Amari/Myloi/Chromonastiri and immediately afterwards, turn right again towards Chromonastiri. 4 km further on, ignore a turn-off to the right to Rousospiti and, shortly afterwards, do not turn right into the newly established part of Mili, but instead, continue straight ahead to reach an info point. A red city tour bus, from Rethymno and going to Mili, stops directly at the entrance to the mill valley. During high season, this sets off from Agnostos Stratiotis Square on an hourly schedule (tel. +30-28310-35530, www.rethymnocitytour.gr). The ticket is valid for the entire day (hop-on hop-off). From Perivolia in Rethymno, you could simply take a taxi to the starting point.

Height difference: 250 m in both ascent and descent.

Grade: for the most part, a shady ramble along well-trodden and sometimes cobbled, narrow paths. Numerous stream crossings over, at times, slippery stones require a certain amount of sure-footedness.

Refreshment: taverna in Mili, *kafenion* in Xiro Chorio, Canteen Banana.

Agies Pente Parthenes (3)   Canteen Banana (5)

192 m   35 m

Mili (1)   (3)   Mili (1)

225 m   (4)   (4)   225 m

4.8 km

0   0.45   1.40 h

From the info point (soon likely to be a ticket office) in **Mili (1)**, at first, take a quick look at the roofed terrace of the Taverna Myli, situated somewhat above the valley floor and impossible to miss; this is where our trail will pass by. A sign points out the descent into »Water Mills Valley«. 100 m on, bearing somewhat to the right, pass a chapel built into a cave which seems to seek protection by squatting under a rock face. In the valley floor, overgrown in dense greenery, a concrete bridge spans the mill stream. After the bridge, pass abandoned houses lying to the left to reach the **Taverna Myli (2)**, 202 m. From

For the trail through the gorge, the EU has financed a new wooden railing.

there, the idyllic path leads more or less at the same height along the right edge of the valley, heading downriver to the cemetery chapel of **Agii Pente Parthenes (3)**, 192 m; from the forecourt of the chapel, enjoy a view through the valley, reaching all the way to the north coast.

From the *chapel of the five holy virgins*, now begin an easy descent; fig, pomegranate and orange trees flank the edge of the trail and, in between, ivy is climbing up the plane trees. Pass several mills, along some of them, the water channel, running in an aqueduct, still remains. The path then descends in zigzags to the **mill stream** down below and, past another abandoned building, crosses over the stream. On the other flank of the valley, the path leads along the foot of a steep, ochre-yellow coloured rock face. After passing two arches of an aqueduct and crossing over the stream once again, reach the chapel **Agia Paraskevi (4)**, 75 m. Five minutes later, follow the path that leads again over the stream (straight ahead and 300 m further on, the chapel Agios Nikolaos). Past another aqueduct (above the stream bed and bearing a narrow water channel) the path merges into a concrete-paved trail at another info point located at the valley mouth. Along this, 200 m on, meet up with the **Canteen Banana (5)**, 35 m (turning right, you would reach the village square of Xiro Chorio in a few minutes). If, from the »canteen«, you choose not to return to the bus stop/car park at the starting point in **Mili (1)** by using the approach route, you could request that a taxi be sent to the romantic garden café to collect you.

From the taverna, by the way, you can spot the Villa Archontiko on the other side of the valley where the Venetian tax collectors bade the millers to open their purses to pay the piper.

Breathtaking views from Crete's highest peak

Apart from Psiloritis and Timios Stavros, the highest peak on the island also bears a common name from ancient times: Ida. At least four separate routes climb up to the summit. Starting points are the Nida high plateau and Livadia on the northern slopes of the massif (Walk 39) as well as Kamares on the southern flank and Fourfouras to the west. The ascent from the Nida plateau is the most popular one, but that doesn't mean that a visit to Crete's highest elevation is a simple ramble. Technically, the route, aside from a slightly precipitous stretch, is almost problem-free, but 1300 metres in ascent and descent through mostly rough karst terrain demands endurance and physical fitness. As a reward for the exertion, you will be greeted at the summit chapel by a spectacular panoramic view of the island – assuming, of course, that weather allows. You should be sure to take advantage of a relatively stable period of good weather; quite often clouds already begin to form around noon. Once a year, usually on a Sunday at the end of May/beginning of June crowds appear on and around Psiloritis; hordes of onlookers for the Psiloritis Race cheer on 300 extreme sportsmen as they climb up a tortuous course from the Nida high plateau to the summit. The best time achieved for the 35 km-long stretch, including a hefty ammount of metres of altitude, stands currently at 2.35 hours.

Psiloritis – a panoramic summit par excellence.

Starting point: the Nida high plateau, 1360 m. From Anogia, follow the signs in the direction of Ideon Andron. 2.5 km above the mountain village, the tarmac road passes by the Delina Mountain Lodge, and 14 km further on, you ignore a turn-off to the left heading towards Ski-nakas, and another 6 km after that, the road ends at a taverna on the Nida high plateau (total driving time from Anogia for the entire 22 km stretch is about 30 minutes). You can approach by bus from Heraklion to Anogia: Mon-Sat, thrice daily; from Rethymno, Mon-Fri, twice daily; from Anogia to the Nida high plateau by taxi. Since you can't return by bus on the same day, you should plan one or two overnights in Anogia.

Note: no matter where you are staying on the coast, the approach to the Nida high plateau takes at least 1.30 hrs when driving a hire car, therefore, there and back, 3 hrs. If the walk is planned as a day trip, due to the long ascent and descent, the time left over for tarrying on the peak is relatively short. To walk the route without any time pressure, we recommend spending one or two nights in Anogia.

Height difference: 1300 m.

Best time: for climbing to the summit, we recommend mid-June–end of October. Until end of May/beginning of June you can expect leftover snowfields. Apart from June, when springtime in the mountains awakens the *phrygana*, mid-summer is a good time; early mornings, it is still pleasantly cool even on the Nida high plateau.

Grade: because of the long walking time involved, this is a demanding alpine tour along a mostly rugged path. The route is waymarked throughout with *red* dots and the *yellow/black* waymarkers of the *E4*, so it does not demand much in the way of route-finding skill in good weather. No shade; be sure to take sunblock and plenty of drinking water along with you.

Refreshment and accommodation: nothing en route; a taverna at the starting point on the Nida high plateau. In the unfinished inn, you could also rent a simple

The ascent route past the Kolita alpine pasturage.

room (mobile +30-69716-50541). In Anogia, you can rent simple rooms at the Hotel Marina (www.marinahotelanogia.gr) and at the Pension Aris (www.arishotel-anogia.gr); if you are looking for comfort, try the Delina Mountain Resort (www.de-lina.gr) 2 km from the Nida Plateau.

Alternative: unlike the usual route, the alternative route, which is longer, opens up good views of the neighbouring peaks and the coastlines. The route has the disadvantage, however, that it is not as well-marked as the *E4* route via Kolita. We recommend taking the alternative route for the return, which means that approaching from the summit, you turn left at the cairn. At the beginning, the path is very indistinct and follows cairns for not quite 100 m to pass a hip-high hunter's blind and, 10 minutes after that, a traditional herdsman's shelter, built from quarry stones piled one on top of the other (*mitata*). From there, follow cairns over a gently rounded ridge and then climb down to reach a saddle. Past a crater-like sinkhole, a half an hour later, finally meet up with an *E4* post at the col (3).

177

From the large car park on the **Nida high plateau (1)**, next to an info board, ascend along a path that is stepped at the outset. The path crosses over an unpaved road twice in quick succession at a stone-built house and, 5 minutes later, at the mountain chapel **Analipsi (2)**, 1402 m, meets up again with the road. Climb up the road about 250 m until reaching a sharp right-hand bend. Here, turn off onto a rough alpine path (red waymarker) and, at the same time, cut to the chase. The path is steep, but well-marked with *red* dots, as it ascends along the slope. Soon, the alpine path is also marked by an *E4* post and the *yellow/black* waymarkers of the long distance trail. 20 minutes later, the path veers to the right into a long depression in the terrain and climbs up along it, at first, along the right-hand rim, passing through subalpine scrubland of cushion plants.

After a good three-quarters of an hour of plodding along the depression, reach a **col (3)**, 1890 m, sporting an *E4* post. To the northwest, Agathias, 2424 m, where our route will continue on the northern flank, blocks the view

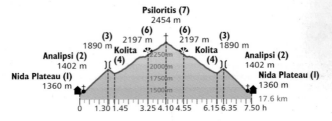

to Psiloritis. In the col, the trail forks; both routes are way-marked: diagonally to the left, a trail with *yellow/black* markings; the right-hand one, with *red* markings and with cairns (the Alternative). We follow the *E4* diagonally to the left and descend, at first in a southwesterly direction, to the alpine pasturage **Kolita (4)**, 1799 m, down below. You will end up seeking in vain, however, for an alpine hut or lush alpine meadows; in the hollow, you will only find a metal frame where there was once a trail sign. At the »alpine pasturage«, a trail, ascending from Kamares, merges into ours. From Kolita, follow the way-markers to climb up a valley; at the outset, the ascent is easy, but somewhat later, it gets steep

Crete's apex: the chapel on the summit of Psiloritis.

again. You can skirt to the left around the rocky knoll and, somewhat later, skirt around a large, funnel-shaped **sinkhole (5)**, 2141 m, to the right along its upper edge. From the sinkhole, climb up to a cairn a metre in height and, after a couple of metres of climbing back down, ascend again from this point through a broad valley to reach a second cairn up above (the alternative route turns off to the right here, but it is very difficult to spot). We have already reached an altitude of about 2200 m. Our route now ascends to an *E4* post at a **viewpoint (6)**, 2197 m, up above, from which we can get the first view of the summit chapel on top of Psiloritis. Here, the trail veers slightly to the left and traverses Agathias' rugged, stony northern slope. Three paths, one after another, ascending here from below, merge into our trail and, in the valley far below, you can spot the tarmac road leading to the shelter of My-gerou, the starting point of Walk 39. Shortly after that, the trail becomes somewhat precipitous. A broad ridge soon opens up downward views of the Cretan Sea to the north, as well as the Libyan Sea to the south. After the final ascent, meet up finally with the summit chapel Timios Stavros at the top of **Psiloritis (7)**, 2454 m. Next to it, there is a shelter that is always left open and a cistern containing, however, brackish melt water. After taking in a breath-taking view of the island, descend along the approach route to return back to the **Nida high plateau (1)** down below.

Psiloritis 2, 2454 m

The fastest route onto Crete's »rooftop«

The community of Livadia offered a very heartfelt welcome to walkers and pilgrims when, not many years ago, it tarmacked the 13 km-long, bumpy shepherd's path at the foot of Psiloritis, erected a shelter at the end of the path and, from there, paved the ancient ascent path to Crete's highest summit, at an altitude of a good 2000 m. The quickest and simplest ascent onto Crete's »mountain of mountains« can now, despite the long drive to the starting point, be negotiated in a single day. Every year, on the first Saturday following August 15, hundreds of Cretans ply their way to the summit chapel of Timios Stavros.

Starting point: Refuge Lakkos Mygerou, 1600 m. Approaching from Heraklion/Anogia, drive via Zoniana to Livadia. Just past the southern entrance to the village, at a little square with a marble obelisk, 5 metres in height, turn left and, a couple of metres on, bear to the right. At the next fork, the first sign points out the way to the »Refuge of Mygerou« (straight ahead). The narrow tarmac road ends, 13 km on, at the shelter.
Height difference: a good 850 m.
Best season: see Walk 38.
Grade: a long ascent and descent via a paved mountain path, climbing up to about 2000 metres above sea level. Some

short stretches during the continued ascent are precipitous and demand an excellent head for heights. The path is waymarked starting at Waypoint 3. No shade, so be sure to be protected from the sun and to bring along sufficient water!
Accommodation: the Lakkos Mygerou shelter is unmanned and is maintained by the community of Livadia. It is open year-round and is provided with a communal room and several billet beds, a fireplace, a water tap as well as a WC. At the summit of Psiloritis, next to the chapel, there is an emergency shelter.
Refreshment: nothing en route; tavernas in Livadia.

The walk starts off at the Lakkos Mygerou shelter at 1600 m.

Mostly pleasant and seldom disagreeably steep...

From the car park in front of the **Lakkos Mygerou (1)** shelter, a cobbled path, at the outset not too steep, heads at first towards the striking summit of Vouloumenou, 2267 m. During the ascent, breath-taking views open up of the shelter in the valley, soon lying far below.

After a 50-minute climb, reach a **basin (2)**, 1980 m, at the foot of Vouloumenou. Here, treat yourself to a respite to catch your breath and enjoy the far-reaching downward views of the northern coast. The path bears left from the basin to continue ascending the slope and, a good 10 minutes later, the cobblestone pavement comes to an end. Now the going is somewhat bumpy but the path, still sound enough for walking, heads toward a gently rolling ridgeline. Still a good way below this, the trail veers slightly to the right. At a hardly discernable fork, bear slightly to the right and, just past a metal post (without waymarking) shortly afterwards, meet up with the **E4 long distance trail (3)**, 2273 m,

... is the cobblestone trail to Psiloritis.

approaching from the Nida plateau (Walk 38). Turn right along the trail.

From the path, now waymarked in *yellow/black* as well as with *red* dots, you can already spot the chapel on the summit of Psiloritis. Some sections of the trail are precipitous, traversing the plunging northern slope of Agathias, 2424 m, as it climbs up to a **ridgeline (4)**, 2330 m, opening a view southwards of the Lybyan Sea and both of the Paximadi islands, lying offshore. Along the broad ridge later on, ascend to a little secondary peak that temporarily blocks the view of the main summit. Shortly past that, an ascent trail, approaching from Fourfouras, merges with our trail at a metal structure. Five minutes later, you are standing at the chapel, Timios Stavros, on the summit of **Psiloritis (5)**, 2454 m.

If the sky is clear, enjoy a view of the White Mountains to the west and, in the east, of the Dikti Mountains; especially dramatic is the downwards view of the Messara Gulf on the southern coast. After taking your fill of this lovely panorama, return along the approach route to descend back again to the shelter **Lakkos Mygerou (1)**.

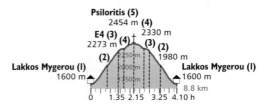

In front of the chapel on the summit of Crete's highest observation post.

182

6.20 hrs

To a Minoan sanctum high above the Messara Plain

As long as the weather is clear, the entrance to the Kamares Cave, 42 m wide and 19 m in height, lying a good 1600 m above sea level, can be spotted from many places in the Messara plain, and especially from the Minoan palace complex on top of Festos Hill. The Kamares Cave, on the southern slopes of the Psiloritis massif, counts as one of Crete's most famous caves; however, due to the long ascent needed to get there, the cave is seldom visited. The reason for its notoriety lies in the ceramic vessels that have been found there, dating back 3500 to 4000 years ago. The thin, delicate vases and bowls in red or white ornamental designs on a dark background earned their own name as a ceramic style: Kamares ware. If you are a fan of tackling great heights, you will be very well-served by this long ascent to the cave. Also, from a botanical point of view, this walk is very rewarding; along the way, there are magnificent kermes oaks and cypress trees; in spring, amongst others, sword lilies, arum lilies and Four-spotted Orchids are flowering here.

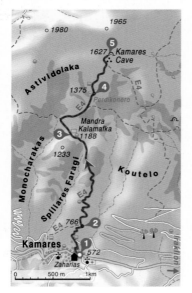

Starting point: Kamares, 572 m. From the Mires – Timbaki road, follow the signs in the direction of Kamares/Vori. In Vori, in the village centre, bear left and from there, reach Kamares which is located 17 km further away. Parking is possible near the Taverna Zaharias on the side of the road. There is a bus from Heraklion to Kamares providing service once a day, but you won't be able to return on the same day, so you have to plan to stay for the night.

Height difference: a good 1050 m in both ascent and descent

Grade: for the long, sometimes fairly steep ascent and descent, trekking poles are useful. The route is somewhat difficult to follow for the first few minutes, but further along, the alpine path is waymarked with *E4* posts set far apart from each other; in between, cairns are an aid for route-finding. Nevertheless, the course of the route is not always easy to spot straightaway. For the first 1.30 hrs, a concrete watercourse provides orientation.

Refreshment: Taverna Zaharias at the starting point for the walk.

The walk begins in **Kamares (1)**, at the eastern village limits on the road to Heraklion. Diagonally opposite the Taverna Zaharias, pick up a trail that is concrete-paved at the outset. 200 m on, when the trail ends, pass through a gate and ascend along the slope via a path which is indistinct as it starts off. Past a second gate, below a water reservoir, meet up with an intersecting trail and turn left onto it. About 15 m on, the path continues to the right and ascends further up along the slope about 150 m to reach an *E4* post above. At the post, turn sharp right and use yet another post, within sight, as orientation.

An aid to orientation during the ascent: the old watercourse.

We gain altitude quickly and can soon enjoy wonderful downward views of Kamares and the Gulf of Messara. Half an hour later, cross over a **watercourse (2)**, 766 m, for the first time. This serves as an orientation aid for the further route. While the watercourse leads steeply straight up onto a rocky knoll, the path negotiates the climb in numerous bends, but en route, it touches on the concrete watercourse time and again. At a trough fountain in the shade of a cypress tree, we can treat ourselves to a breather. Here, we have already gone over the 900 m above sea level mark. Starting at the **trough fountain**, the alpine path is well laid and, in the meantime, an open wood of mostly cypress and oak provides plenty of shade.

Sometimes climbing up directly along the watercourse and after an ascent of almost two hours, reach a rectangular watering trough and **Mandra Kalamafka (3)**, 1188 m, where a loud, gushing, pressure-adjusting chamber is situated. 40 m to the left of the trough,

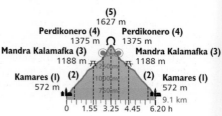

On the long-distance trail E4, high above the mountain village of Kamares.

herdsmen have set up a table with a little circle of stones around it to sit on. The path now continues along the watercourse while crossing through a forest of kermes oaks and, 10 minutes later, meets up with a second water chamber; here, leave the narrow channel behind by turning right (onto the E4). A black conduit is an aid for orientation. Possibly, signs have been placed on tree trunks with directions written in German: »Höhle« (cave). Meet up with an enclosed water source called **Perdikonero (4)**, 1375 m, in English, »partridge water«.

From here, continue following the black conduit to reach a walled-in water reservoir, the source of water for the conduit, situated beneath an overhanging rock face. Here, bear slightly to the right and ascend, more or less without a distinct path, across rocky ground and leading through a broad cleft in the terrain, during which, you have to rely more and more on cairns and faded *red* waymarkers. After a last, steep ascent, finally meet up with the spacious entrance to the **Kamares Cave (5)**, 1627 m. You certainly won't be alone here – the immense cave is home to flocks of Red-billed choughs and colonies of bats. Some metres in front of the cave, there is a little, level area where a view opens up of the Messara plain, 1600 m down below, and the broad sweep of the Gulf of Messara. After enjoying a break, climb back down along the approach route to return to **Kamares (1)**.

From the trout village through a canyon at the foot of Psiloritis

The summer retreat of Zaros draws our attention through its charming location on the southern side of Psiloritis; the tavernas lining the nearby spring-fed lake are also popular destinations for excursionists – a fish farm serves up fresh salmon trout for a meal. In the region around Zaros, abounding in water, spring water is bottled and can be bought in any supermarket on the island – perhaps you have a bottle of it in your rucksack at this very moment. The little lake is the starting point for an excursion into the Rouwas Gorge, also named after Saint Nicolaus. A relatively well-laid trail leads through the canyon, although some formerly helpful railings have been destroyed by rock fall. Nevertheless, the gorge itself is still relatively easy to negotiate.

Starting point: Votomos Lake, 420 m. Between Mires and Agii Deka, 0.4 km before reaching the early Christian basilika of Gortis, follow the signs and pass through the villages of Plouti and Panagia to reach Zaros (14 km). In Zaros, just past the village centre, turn right towards »Gorge/Lake/Idi Hotel«, pass the Hotel Idi and the Taverna Votomos and, 1.4 km past Zaros reach Votomos Lake. A bus from Heraklion to Zaros via Mires runs twice a day, but the return schedule is awkward for walkers, so you must spend the night in Zaros.

Height difference: 520 m.

Grade: crossing through the gorge demands a high degree of surefootedness; some short scrambles require the use of hands from time to time. In spring, in the upper reaches, you have to cross over the stream bed several times over slippery stones.

Refreshment: you can relax on the shores of the lake in the Taverna Limni (opens end of May) at the starting point for the walk. Fresh salmon trout is the speciality. Another major restaurant serving trout is the Votomos next to the Idi Hotel.

Accommodation: the Idi Hotel in Zaros (tel. +30-28940-31301, www.idi-hotel.gr)

The Taverna Limni on Votomos Lake.

is a popular spot for walkers.

Worth seeing: on the return journey, a visit to the archaeological digs of Gortis is worthwhile. Directly on the road are also the ruins of an impressive, early Christian, cross-domed church (Titus-Basilika) from 600 AD. North of there, in Odeon, you can read the renowned texts of law written in ancient Greek – these were engraved on stone blocks 2500 years ago (daily, 8.00–15.00, admission €4).

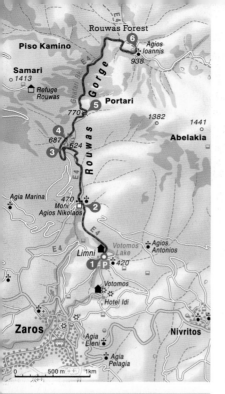

From the car park on **Votomos Lake (1)**, pass through an archway topped by a thick tree trunk and, along the left shore of the lake, reach the Taverna Limni. Just behind the terrace of the restaurant, a path starts off that is flanked by wooden railings and is stepped at the beginning (sign: »Agios Ioannis«). Along tight zigzag bends, ascend through a little pine wood, climbing up the slope. 5 minutes later, meet up with a metal gate and an intersecting trail. Turn sharp left onto the trail leading along a chain-link fence, while crossing over matted sage and thyme, and heading towards the cleft of the Rouwas Gorge which soon comes into sight. Next to the mouth of the gorge, the **Moni Agios Nikolaos (2)**, 470 m, lies crouched under a rock face. At a gate just before the monastery, continue straight ahead for a short stretch, cross diagonally over a rocky, dry stream bed and then climb steeply up the embankment to a secondary building of the monastery. The path now leads along the left bank of the rocky stream bed heading into the gorge. On a stone bench situated under a cluster of trees, treat yourself to a short breather. The path then changes over to the other bank of the gorge's stream bed. A good half an hour past the monastery, reach a striking **overhanging rock (3)**, 624 m. Afterwards, a pleasant trail leads down

Almost like a castle in a fairy tale – the Agios Nikolaos monastery at the mouth of the Rouwas Gorge.

In the meantime, the wooden ramp through the rocky bottleneck of the gorge has become extremely delapidated.

the valley, but leave this behind again, 100 m further on, by turning right. Ascend steeply up a scree-covered slope, loose underfoot, and at the end, ignore a turn-off towards Agios Nikolaos.

A stretch of trail follows, opening panoramic views. The path, stepped again and flanked with a ramshackle railing, ascends somewhat precipitously along the left side of the gorge. Shortly after passing two benches situated beneath a pine tree, reach a vertiginous **viewpoint (4)**, 687 m. We are standing a good 100 m above the stream bed of the gorge and can enjoy a view reaching far into the valley. The remains of numerous dead trees bear witness to a devastating forest fire which occurred in the 1990s and destroyed extensive stands of woodland in the gorge.

The canyon narrows here and you continue by scrambling over boulders polished smooth by the stream. Via a wooden ramp, the trail squeezes through a bottleneck in the gorge. Once above, cross over the **bridge (5)**, 770 m, constructed on a steel girder which, in winter, successfully defies a torrential stream. Shortly afterwards, meet up with a little rest area boasting tables built of stone. The steepest section of the route is behind us. Now keep steadily ascending along the torrential stream, slightly climbing, and cross over it several times. If you are here before May, you will discover if your shoes are truly waterproof.

The bridge spanning the narrow gap of the gorge has been washed away repeatedly by the torrential stream after the spring runoff. Now it is reinforced by a steel girder.

At the sign marking *kilometre 1*, bear slightly to the right and reach a little waterfall cascading into a rock pool. In spring, above the waterfall, numerous other rock pools are awaiting to invite you to a dip to cool off. 25 mins past the waterfall, after crossing over the stream many times, the forest opens up to a large clearing. There is a trough fountain with good spring water here and picnic benches situated beneath shady plane trees. Somewhat above this area, reach the chapel, **Agios Ioannis (6)**, 938 m, our turn-around point. From the fieldstone chapel, located on a high plateau, you can enjoy fine views taking in the surrounding mountain peaks.

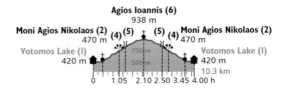

Ramble to a viewpoint in the central massif

On the way to the renowned mountain village of Zaros and to the Rouwas Gorge (Walk 41), usually you will drive through the hamlet of Panagia without stopping. Actually, this is a pity because you could pay a visit to a unique Byzantine church. From there, you could also take a stroll through groves of olive trees to a chapel of the Holy Cross, situated panoramically on the crest of a mountain ridge. During this tour, you also pass by another interesting church.

Starting point: at the eastern limits of Mires, from the through road, turn off towards Zaros (the turn-off is poorly signed) and, via Moroni, reach the church at Panagia, where the road veers sharply to the left. Parking is possible at the side of the road.

Height difference: not quite 200 m in both ascent and descent.

Grade: easy, short walk via broad farm roads; numerous forks require some concentration.

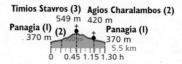

Refreshment: nothing en route; in Zaros (on the main road) the restaurant Vegera is considered one of the best in the region where mainly, but not exclusively, vegetarian meals are served (tel. +34-28940-31730, www.vegerazaros.gr).

In **Panagia (1)**, before beginning the walk, it is worthwhile to drop in for a glimpse of the eponymous, triple-naved Church of Our Lady (Panagia) from the 16th century which, apart from the Byzantine marble reliefs, also houses a column taken from an ancient temple. Opposite the church, a farm road sets off that, after a couple of paces, passes a trough fountain. Continuing straight on, about 300 m, meet up with a fork and turn right (*red* metal sign) and, 150 m more, take the trail to the left. The farm road leads along the right flank of a stream-fed valley, bedecked with reeds and Mediterranean cypress as well as kermes oaks and downy oaks, heading towards the Holy Cross chapel, perched on the crest of a hill. The course of the route, however, soon veers slightly to the right.

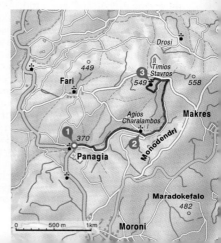

The Chapel of the Holy Cross in front of the southern declivity of the Psiloritis massif.

A couple of minutes later, reach the church **Agios Charalambos (2)**. Normally, the key is in the door so that you can take a look at the interior. Outside, a couple of steps ascend to a tomb next to the bell-gable; opposite the church, the ruins of former hermitages are standing.

From Charalambos, continue straight ahead along the cypress-flanked trail, ascending slightly and, at the fork 100 m on, bear left (do not follow the red arrow to the right). This leads through a short stretch of forest and then through a grove of olive trees where we keep to the right along the main trail and ignore the trails forking off to the left. Passing a gate, skirt around a barrier constructed of brushwood by bearing left. The farm road, now grassy, merges into an intersecting trail five minutes later, where you can spot the chapel, **Timios Stavros (3)**, 549 m, once again. Bearing left, now head directly for the chapel and leave the farm road behind by picking up a distinct path that ascends the last stretch to reach the chapel. From the chapel hill, an instantaneous view opens up of the Psiloritis massif with the mountain village of Zaros nestled at its foot. To the west of this, you can spot the entrance to the Rouwas Gorge. Southwards, let your eyes sweep over the extensive olive plantations of the Messara plain, stretching all the way to the Asterousia mountains.

For the return route from the chapel, take the gravel trail to descend and, at the first fork, keep straight ahead to meet up again with the trail already used during the approach. This brings us back to **Panagia (1)**.

Panoramic ascent on the eastern slopes of Psiloritis

Around Ano Asites, at the foot of the eastern foothills of the Psiloritis massif, mountain vineyards and olive groves make up the landscape. The unstaffed alpine hut, perched at a dizzying height, gives a sweeping panoramic view taking in the peaks of Eastern Crete, the northern coast and the metropolis of Heraklion. With a little bit of luck, you can spot Griffon Vultures circling overhead.

Starting point: Ano Asites, 470 m. From the Heraklion – Mires road, in Agia Varvara, turn off towards Prinias and 9 km further on, reach the village limits of Ano Asites. About 200 m past the sign for the village limits, a narrow road turns off to the left. Parking possible on the side of the road. By bus from Heraklion, Mon-Fri, four times daily, twice on Sat to Ano Asites (the last bus returns about 15.15).
Height difference: 580 m.

Grade: up until reaching Waypoint 2, along a broad farm track, then continuing along a fairly steep alpine path. Almost the entire ascent is well-marked (*yellow*), only the last 10 minutes demand a little route-finding skill. During the descent, you must pay close attention to numerous junctions.
Refreshment: a *kafenion* in Ano Asites.
Accommodation: info for the mountain hut see page 20.

In **Ano Asites (1)**, at a sign, turn onto the narrow road, tarmac at the outset. A couple of paces on, an *E4* waymarker appears on a power pylon (this is the only one) to prove that we're on the right track. About 150 m past that, the trail branches in front of a copse of gnarled olive trees; bear right here (possibly, a weathered sign is posted to the left). Now along a gravel trail, ignore a turn-off to the right shortly afterwards. Our trail heads directly towards Giristi, 1779 m, the highest peak on the eastern slopes of the Psiloritis massif. Groves of olive trees climb up the slopes of this mountain. Above the groves, you can spot the destination for this walk: the Prinos hut and, to the left of it, a small, white house is standing.

Ignore another turn-off to the right. The trail, waymarked in *yellow*, ascends relatively steeply along the right-hand flank of a lush, green valley where

The Prinos mountain hut lies a good 1000 m above sea level.

Mediterranean Cypress trees catch the eye. Along very steep sections, the trail has been concrete-paved. About 30 mins later, the trail forks in front of a **gate (2)**, 634 m. Leave the farm road behind by turning right through the gate (waymarker). 200 m on, bear slightly to the right to cross through a grove of olive trees and, past that, pick up a path. Pass through a gateway and, afterwards, the path ascends steeply, traversing a long, broad depression in the terrain. Cross diagonally right over a roadway and, a good 15 mins later, at the foot of a **rock face (3)**, 810 m, meet up with a tall Cretan maple tree (on the left-hand side of the tree, a cart track begins; this will be our return route).

The path leads along the rock face for a short stretch and then climbs up steeply over the depression, now narrower. 25 minutes later, the steepest section of the stretch is behind you. Now continue ascending relatively leisurely through low-growing prickly thrift. Here, the waymarkers are somewhat few and far between. The path leads to the right, passing kermes oaks and then merges into an intersecting trail (inconspicuous *red* waymarking). This bears left to bring us in a few minutes to the **Prinos mountain hut (4)**, 1050 m, lying within eyeshot. From a bench on the terrace, enjoy a far-reaching view.

After taking a break, climb back down to the maple tree at the foot of the **rock face (3)**. Here, turn right along the cart track to descend and afterwards, pass a watering trough for livestock. Ignore a trail forking off to the right and, 50 m below that, cross diagonally right over a trail (that is, do not

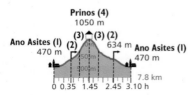

take the concrete trail to the left). Not until 150 m further on, do you bear left. A good five minutes later, the cart track veers sharp to the left and then reaches the **gate (2)** that we already met during the ascent. Straight ahead, descend back again to **Ano Asites (1)**.

A good, long beach walk along the Gulf of Messara

In Agia Galini, you don't really have to take to the air, as did the mythological characters Dädalus and Ikarus, to escape to freedom from the clutches of King Minos – their attempt to fly ended tragically anyway. This popular seaside resort on the southern coast is the perfect starting point for a delightful walk along the beach. The first stretch between Galini and Kokkinos Pirgos is simply picturesque: rambling along directly at the seaside, you pass along the foot of ochre to red-coloured coastal cliffs.

Starting point: the harbour in Agia Galini, 2 m. You can reach Agia Galini by bus from Heraklion (Mon-Sun, four to six times daily), Rethymno (four to five times daily), Matala/Pitsidia (Mon-Sat, three times daily via Mires or Festos). If approaching by car, you may be interested in the Alternatives.

Return: Pitsidia is located on the bus line Heraklion – Matala; also bus service to Agia Galini (via Mires or Festos).

Height difference: 80 m in ascent.

Grade: this walk leads, at times, without a distinct path, and along pebble beaches and rock plates, somewhat unpleasant to negotiate; the sandy beach stretching from Kalamaki to Kommos, can be walked barefoot. For this coastal walk, you should pick a day when the sea is relatively quiet because by stormy seas, the sometimes narrow pebble beach is impassable. From time to time, sections of the coastal cliffs may come tumbling down, but the waves usually wash away any obstructions fairly quickly. Shortly before reaching Kalamaki, the beach is blocked by a barrier of rock; here you have to skirt around via the steep embankment. Bring along your bathing gear and sun protection!

Refreshment: tavernas in Agia Galini, Kokkinos Pirgos, Kalamaki and Pitsidia.

Note: in the summer, the Loggerhead sea turtle comes ashore to lay its eggs at the beach at Kommos; camping is strictly forbidden.

Alternatives: you don't have to walk all the way to Pitsidia; you could, e.g., after a break in Kokkinos Pirgos, turn around to return to Agia Galini (there and back, a good 3 hrs). Or, you could start in Pitsidia, go as far as Kalamaki and then return again (there and back, a good 2 hrs).

At the harbour in Agia Galini.

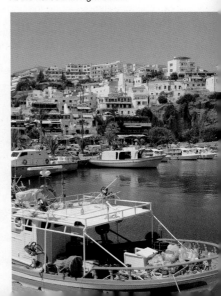

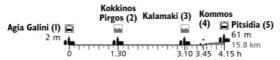

Agia Galini (I) Kokkinos Pirgos (2) Kalamaki (3) Kommos (4) Pitsidia (5)
2 m   61 m
                                                                15.8 km
0   1.30   3.10 3.45 4.15 h

At the harbour of **Agia Galini (1)**, stroll along the promenade, heading in a northeasterly direction, to reach the most popular beach of the seaside resort in a few minutes. Past the Taverna Kostas, cross over the steel bridge spanning the Platis River which empties into the sea here. Shortly after, the promenade ends and, at the same time, so does the sun lounger area, packed to the gills with bathers during the high season. Now continue directly along the pebble beach at the foot of the steep and rugged coastal cliffs. (If you prefer the going easier, you can take the gravel track running parallel above, however, you have to pay attention to find the right way back again).

Three-quarters of an hour later, reach the first **narrow strip**. Here, the ochre-yellow coloured coastal cliff makes room for only about a 2 m wide strip of pebble beach; when the sea is rough, this section is impassable! Another 45 minutes later, reach the harbour at **Kokkinos Pirgos (2)**, with its inviting Taverna Red Castle, nestled in the shade of Salt cedars and offering refreshment. Past the breakwater, an 8 km-long sandy beach begins. At first, stroll along the seaside promenade, passing by other tavernas and cafés, until the promenade ends abruptly. Past the trampled-down fence for the military airport, continue directly along the pebble beach until, shortly before reaching Kalamaki, the steep coastline begins again. There, you cannot continue directly on the beach for a short stretch. Along relatively solid, baked rock, climb up the steep embankment, about 12 m high, and then descend again

Aside from crossing over a lot of sand, the beach walk also leads over rugged plates of rock.

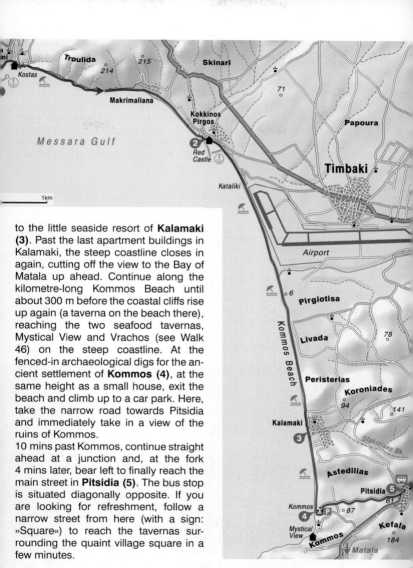

to the little seaside resort of **Kalamaki (3)**. Past the last apartment buildings in Kalamaki, the steep coastline closes in again, cutting off the view to the Bay of Matala up ahead. Continue along the kilometre-long Kommos Beach until about 300 m before the coastal cliffs rise up again (a taverna on the beach there), reaching the two seafood tavernas, Mystical View and Vrachos (see Walk 46) on the steep coastline. At the fenced-in archaeological digs for the ancient settlement of **Kommos (4)**, at the same height as a small house, exit the beach and climb up to a car park. Here, take the narrow road towards Pitsidia and immediately take in a view of the ruins of Kommos.

10 mins past Kommos, continue straight ahead at a junction and, at the fork 4 mins later, bear left to finally reach the main street in **Pitsidia (5)**. The bus stop is situated diagonally opposite. If you are looking for refreshment, follow a narrow street from here (with a sign: »Square«) to reach the tavernas surrounding the quaint village square in a few minutes.

197

Obligatory ramble to Matala's posh neighbouring beach

A daily pilgrimage takes place starting at Matala as hundreds of tourists climb over the mountain ridge to Red Beach, which is actually named Kokkinos Ammos and, since the hippie era, is one of the most famous in-crowd beaches on Crete. The fine, sandy beach shimmers in red only at sunrise and before sunset; during the day, it is a vibrant ochre colour. A little beach bar provides basic refreshment.

Starting point: Matala, 4 m. From Heraklion to Matala, bus service three to five times a day. The settlement can also be reached from Agia Galini via Mires or Festos. If you are approaching by car, there is a spacious car park at the beach at the entrance to the village.
Height difference: 170 m in both ascent and descent.
Grade: easy ramble with short, steep stretches of ascent and descent along a rocky path. No shade!
Refreshment: tavernas and cafés in Matala; a beach bar on Red Beach.

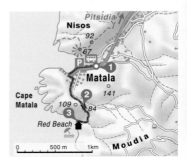

The Bay of Matala in front of the snow-covered Psiloritis massif.

In both low and high season, there is usually a lot of room on Red Beach with its fine sand.

The ramble begins at the village limits of **Matala (1)** in front of the »Hippie Memorial«, opposite the Hotel Zafiria. Heading into the village, pass the little village church, a good 100 m further on. Past the church, continue straight ahead over the village square and, shortly after, turn left at the Giannis Family Grill House onto a steep concrete-paved track climbing upwards. At the last house, a stony path with *blue* waymarkers sets off. Immediately, a marvellous view opens up of the caves from Matala. The path ascends relatively steeply up the slope, soon crossing over rugged bands of limestone rock. A path that is also waymarked in *blue* merges from the left. Continue along a chain-link fence. At a **col (2)**, 84 m, you can get a lovely view of the southern coast. Now pass through a gate. 50 m past the gate, the path veers downward towards **Red Beach (3)**, lying down below. At its western limits, it is tucked under the mighty limestone cliff. You don't necessarily need any bathing gear – the fine, sandy beach is, for the large part, a naturist area. The return follows the approach route back again.

(2) Red
84 m **Beach (3)**
Matala (l)   Matala (l)
4 m
2.5 km
0 0.30 1.00 h

To a viewpoint above the caves of Matala

The two seafood tavernas, Mystical View and Vrachos, are panoramically situated on the steep coastline of Kommos Bay. Whether the view of the sprawling sandy beach and the Psiloritis massif, blanketed in snow well into the spring, is actually a mystical one, every walker must decide for himself. In any case, bizarre panoramic views of the coast and a spectacular one of Matala are guaranteed during this entertaining walk.

Starting point: the »Hippie Memorial«, at the entrance to the village of Matala, 4 m; see Walk 45 for the approach.
Height difference: a good 160 m.
Grade: a circular walk along coastal paths; numerous sections without a dis-

tinct path. Be careful at the sheer drop at the rim! No shade.
Refreshment: the seafood tavernas Mystical View and Vrachos at the starting point/destination for the walk – boasting spectacular sunsets.

In **Matala (1)**, starting at the »Hippie memorial«, follow the road heading out of the village for not quite 100 m. At the Hotel Fragiskos, turn right to cross over a little bridge and immediately bear to the right. A gravel trail leads parallel to the course of the stream, flanked with reeds. Not quite 300 m past Fragiskos and about 50 m before the ochre-coloured, low building of the

From the terrace of the seafood restaurant, you have a truly beautiful view.

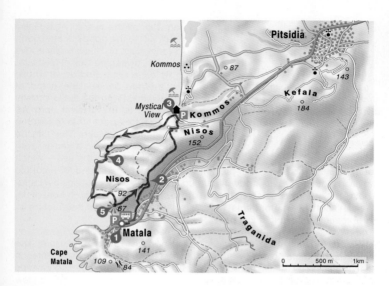

Hotel Calypso, two sandy traces of a path lead, one quickly following the other, to the foot of the limestone ridge; we take the second trace.

At the foot of the ridge, an alpine path begins (cairns) and traverses the steep slope diagonally. Not quite 50 m on, watch out for a *red* dot and, here, continue slightly left. A good 10 minutes ascent brings you to a **stone pyramid (2)**, 94 m, perched on the cliff-like ridge.

At the stone pyramid, turn right and, at a fork about 15 m on, turn right again. The path is sometimes not much more than a trace but just keep close to the rim of the sheer drop. Soon, the trig point perched on Nisos (152 m) appears before us. We don't, however, want to go there. After a relatively broad, but short, stretch of trail about 350 m before Nisos, the path becomes more stony; here, watch out for cairns and leave the rim behind by bearing left.

Below us, and to the left, a sandy, limestone track is running, to which we descend, more or less cross-country. Next to carob trees, meet up with the track which, after another 100 m, merges into a cart track. Continue straight ahead along this track for a couple of metres, descending, and then at a fork, bear right to continue the descent. A view opens up, taking in two tavernas, perched above the kilometre-long Kommos Beach.

The cart track descends in bends down to the restaurants; the final 150 m climbs down cross-country to a tarmac access road. Next to the taverna, **Mystical View (3)**, at first enjoy the view of the long beach, along which you

Fossilised seashell in the limestone plateau.

can walk all the way to Agia Galini (Walk 44, in the opposite direction). Psiloritis rises up majestically above the wide, sweeping Gulf of Messara; to Psiloritis' left is Kedros, at whose foot nestles the seaside resort of Agia Galini. From the steep coastal cliffs next to the taverna, turn left and walk for about 50 m to reach a fenced-in animal pen. This can be skirted around along a narrow path on the side facing the sea – watch out, the stretch is somewhat precipitous. Past the pen, ascend for a couple of paces to reach a well-trodden path up above, which soon leads over stratum of rock to continue along the rim of the steep coastal cliffs. In front of us, we can spot the **Paximadia Islands**. It is hard to believe that the western island reaches a height of 252 m.

The path winds through a row of huge boulders, which seem to have been strewn by a giant's hand, and widens for a short while into a road. Here, lime was mined in times gone by. As soon as the trail veers towards the interior, leave it behind by continuing straight ahead. The path keeps heading towards the sheer drop at the rim, bizarrely sculpted by erosion. At the rim, a view opens up of a smooth and barren headland, dropping gently towards the sea; descend onto the headland, more or less without a distinct path. The last leg is a descent along a rugged track to a **limestone cove (4)** that has been cut into the coastline like a miniature fjord. At this point, cross over a rocky stream bed. Past that, continue for a few metres above the waterline along the cantered limestone flanks. In the limestone, you may discover fossils of seashells. In some small, natural potholes, seawater has evaporated to leave salt deposits. About a quarter of an hour past the miniature fjord, Matala appears. Now ascend towards the interior along the humpbacked ridge, keeping to the left of a rocky crevice. Somewhat further up, the crevice can be easily skirted around. Shortly afterwards, meet up with the sheer drop at the rim of the ridge, from which, you can enjoy a brilliant **panoramic view (5)**, 70 m, of the beach, the bay and the houses of Matala (see cover photo). You are standing directly above the guardhouse for the caves of Matala.

At the rim of the sheer drop of the ridge, climb up along the traces of a path to the top of a **stone pyramid**, 92 m, about one and a half metres high. Continuing along the rim, not quite 10 minutes later, meet up with the other **stone pyramid (2)**, already met during the approach. From here, descend back again to **Matala (1)**.

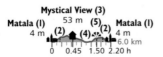

Mystical View (3)
Matala (l)   53 m (5)   Matala (l)
4 m   (2)   (4)   4 m
                          6.0 km
0   0.45   1.50   2.20 h

Through the Gorge of the Saints to an untamed and unspoilt bathing cove

The Gorge of the Saints counts as one of Crete's shortest and easiest to walk. The gorge has earned its name from the hermits who, in days gone by, lived their lives secluded from the world in the rock faces of the gorge. Today, the sheer plunging walls of the Agiofarango is a popular rock-climbing area and the pebble beach, which opens to the sea at the end, is a much-loved bathing spot for walkers and individualists who can do without sun loungers and beach bars. Unless water taxis are anchored offshore in the turquoise waters during your visit, this is a cosy little spot to enjoy.

Scrambling at the Goumenospilio Cave.

Starting point: the dusty road between Moni Odigitrias and Kali Limenes, 100 m. From the Mires – Matala road, not quite 2 km before reaching Pitsidia, turn off towards Sivas. At Siva's village square, follow the signs straight ahead towards Listaros and Moni Odigitrias. At the monastery, bear left and drive along the dusty road towards Kali Limenes for 3.4 km until meeting up with a trail branching off to the right. Parking possible on the side of the road. (If your vehicle is not too low to the ground, you could, depending on the condition of the surface, drive along the trail going down into the valley until you reach a car park).

Height difference: 100 m in both ascent and descent.

Grade: in view of the shortness of the route, this easy gorge walk can also be done in summer. Take along your bathing gear and sunblock; very little shade is available at the beach.

Worth seeing: either before or after the walk, you could visit the Odigitrias Monastery, built in the 16th century. In the monastery church, you can marvel at some icons.

Refreshment: nothing en route; tavernas in Listaros and Sivas. We recommend Ksa Sou, a traditional coffee house in Listaros, with a little inn attached.

The Agios Antonios Chapel.

From the **car park (1)**, on the dusty road, take the road that descends into the valley. At the valley floor, keep the sheep farm to your right. The trail follows along a stream bed that is only running water during periods of rain; along the banks, there are dense thickets of oleander. Past a fenced-in cattle trough, the rugged road ends at a car park just before the entrance to the gorge.

Now pass through a gate. Past the gate, a path leads between towering rock faces, which soon reach heights of 100 m; you can frequently spot rock-climbers. Pass a large cave; opposite to it, hidden behind oleander bushes, a picnic bench can be found. Shortly afterwards, meet up with the Byzantine chapel, **Agios Antonios (2)**; standing in front of a sheer, towering rock face, the chapel presents a picturesque photo motif. The chapel bell is hanging from an olive tree and an ancient well is standing in front of it.

About 100 m past the chapel, you could scramble up to the **Goumenospilio Cave**, which once served the monks as a communal meeting place. There is a comfortable hall inside and the roof is 9 m high in spots. Continuing along the broad, gravel steam bed, in the gorge, which is now opening up, finally meet up with the beach of **Agiofarango (3)**. This delightful bathing cove is enclosed on both sides by steep promontories and, here, several climbers are usually at their sport. After a good, long bathing break, return along the approach route back to the **car park (1)**.

Adventurous coastal route with a short visit to a gorge

The approach to Lentas along the narrow mountain road through the Asterousia Mountains is an adventure in itself. Far above the little seaside resort on the southern coast, you can already spot the humpbacked contour of the »Weeping Lion«, which closes the Bay of Lentas to the west. The walk follows the coastline, crossing over pebble beaches, to reach a bathing cove that is only accessible on foot.

Starting point: the village square in Lentas, 7 m. From the Heraklion – Mires road, in Agii Deka, follow the signs for Lentas. In Platanos, bear to the left. Before reaching Apesokari, turn right and then follow a road along many bends leading to a pass as it crosses through the Asterousia Mountains on the southern coast. If you approach by bus (from Heraklion via Agii Deka, Mon–Fri, once a day), you have to plan to spend the night in Lentas since the return from there is only possible on the morning after.
Height difference: 220 m.

Grade: an uncomplicated coastal walk without any great difference in height. A couple of slightly precipitous sections along the path to Petrakis Beach. In the Trachoulas Gorge, short, steep spots where you have to use your hands while scrambling. No shade; be sure to take your bathing gear. If you plan to spend some time at Trachoulas Beach, you should pack along a little sunshade sail.
Refreshment: tavernas in Petrakis Beach and Loutro Beach; from the numerous tavernas in Lentas, we recommend El Greco.

A landmark from far and wide on the southern coast: the »Weeping Lion« of Lentas.

Trachoulas Beach
Loutro Beach (3) (5) Loutro Beach (3)
Petrakis Beach (2)   (4) (4)   Petrakis Beach (2)
Lentas (l) 🏠 🏠   🏠 🏠 Lentas (l)
7 m   7 m
                                             10.2 km
0   0.35 1.10 1.50   3.05 3.40 h

Begin the walk in **Lentas (1)** at the rectangular village square, surrounded by tavernas and cafés. Between two cafés, a cobbled trail sets off in an easterly direction. 15 m on, the trail hooks off to the left and, a couple of paces afterwards, turns right to continue. At the tavernas, El Greco and Zorbas, signs point out the way to the beach, but we keep to the cobbled trail and, in front of the **Café Petros** (»homemade pastries«), meet up with a little square (the bus from Heraklion stops just above). Opposite the café, descend along the concrete-paved road to the right. In front of the Lentas Paradise Studios, the road immediately veers slightly to the left towards an abandoned house built from natural stone. Directly in front of the house, keep an eye out for a path that is difficult to spot, but is well-trodden (red waymarkers), which ascends from behind the house towards a low coastal hillock up above. Immediately, a marvellous view opens up of the »Weeping Lion«. To the east, a view opens up of a rock arch situated offshore and the silhouette of the Asterousia Mountains, dominated by the cone-shaped summit of Kofinas (Walk 50).

At the outset of **Petrakis Beach (2)**, cross over a dry stream bed. You could continue along the rather stony beach at first, but it is more pleasant to keep to the path following the shoreline embankment. Make a mental note of the tempting terraces of the two tavernas for the way back. From these, now continue along the coarse-gravel beach which is, nevertheless, good for bathing. At the end of the beach, you have to scramble at first over fallen rock and, past that, a sheer coastal cliff, dropping down, blocks a continued route along the shoreline. Here, bear to the left and climb up along a dry, rocky stream bed

On the coastline at Lentas, a little rock arch sticks out of the water.

(*red* waymarker), through a valley notch to reach the coastal road up above. Bear to the right to continue along the road and, only a few minutes later, catch a downwards glimpse of the new fishing harbour of Loutro. In front of a cluster of houses, ignore a trail turning off to Hamam Beach. Past the Taverna To Libyko (also boasting a shady terrace), descend along the road to **Loutro Beach (3)** down below.

Above the harbour, leave the road behind by turning left onto a dusty track. The track leads, in 10 minutes, to a **saddle (4)**, 82 m, where we can enjoy a downwards view of a gorge as it winds its way to the sea. At the col, a path begins, which descends in zigzags, rather slippery underfoot,

The little gorge of Trachoulas.

into the stream bed for the gorge. Bearing right, continue along the gravel stream bed towards the sea, skirt around smooth polished boulders without any problem, some short, steep sections must be scrambled over using your hands. Soon reach a bottleneck, the narrowest one, only 2.5 m between the rock faces of the gorge towering a good 50 m upwards. The gorge widens out again soon after, then reach **Trachoulas Beach (5)**. The only thing missing at the semi-circular cove with a fine, sandy beach, is some shade.

After a break for bathing, return along the approach route back to **Lentas (1)**.

Along a coastal trail at the foot of the Asterousia Mountains

The Asterousia Mountains drop down ruggedly to the Libyan Sea, but there is still room enough for a marvellous coastal path. Amidst the barren terrain, you will be surprised to find a stately pine wood. A highlight for the route is the chapel cave of Agios Antonios, which once served as a shelter for a hermit. Also, there is a lot to discover in the Koudouma monastery.

Starting point: Agios Ioannis, 35 m. From the Heraklion – Mires road, in Agii Deka, turn off towards Vagionia. Arriving at the village centre, bear left and, via Loukia, reach the twin village of Kapetaniana. Shortly before the village limits, continue driving straight ahead towards Ano Kapetaniana. The tarmac road ends at a car park at the village limits. Bearing slightly to the left, a broad, dusty road continues on; you can also drive this road with a standard vehicle, if you are careful (the better choice is to use an all-terrain vehicle). The road runs along the upper edge

of the settlement and, 150 m further on, reaches a junction. Here, bear right and descend (a small sign for Agios Ioannis). 7.5 km past Kapetaniana, above the houses of Agios Ioannis, pass a chapel. 300 m further on, reach a fork where a trail board has been erected.

Height difference: about 300 m.

Grade: a coastal walk along a well laid path with short stretches of ascent and descent; route-finding is simple. You will need a torch if you want to explore the cave.

Refreshment: cafeteria in Agios Ioannis.

At the fork, shortly before reaching the village limits of **Agios Ioannis (1)**, follow the gravel trail eastwards. Afterwards, pass two watering troughs. At the second one, turn right and meet up with the steep coastline, 25 m further on. From there, descend along a stepped trail to the mouth of the little **Eligias Gorge (2)** down below (the sandy bathing cove to the right is good place to take a break for a swim during the return).

On the other side of the stream bed for the gorge, climb up a stepped trail to reach a rocky rise above; from this point, you can already spot the entrance to the cave of Agios Antonios which still lies a good distance away. The path leads above the steep coastline, at first opening up panoramic views. Half an hour since starting off from Agios Ioannis, pass a number of caves being used as livestock pens. From there, the trail, flanked by a wooden railing, leads above the turquoise-coloured waters of a cove, Agios Antonios, and afterwards, meets up with a fork. At first, bear right to make an excursion to the hermit's cave, **Agios Antonios (3)**, 39 m. Pass through the cave entrance, which is shaped like a pointed Gothic arch, pass by the chapel and four water basins to penetrate into the furthermost reaches of the cave where you can marvel at the stalactites. Since ancient

Moni Koudouma: the monastery on the sea.

times, the local inhabitants have collected water dripping from these stalactites – rumour has it that this water possesses healing properties.

Returning to the main trail, turn right onto it and continue by climbing up the slope through an open wood of Turkish pines. At a **col (4)**, 121 m, pass by a little cross made of marble. A good quarter of an hour later, at another marble cross, a view opens up of the Bay of Koudouma. Along a path, which is sometimes loose and slippery underfoot, finally reach the **Koudouma Monastery (5)**. After paying a visit to the monastery courtyard, yet another bonus awaits: diagonally opposite from the monastery gate, a sign (in Greek) points towards **Osios Kosmas Erimitis (6)**.

Behind a neighbouring building, a pleasant path sets off, leading past a gate and reaching, 10 minutes later, the cave of a hermit, Avakospilio, with a chapel and bizarre dripstones. Unfortunately, from there, rugged coastal cliffs block the way to Agios Antonios, so that we must return along the path from the **Koudouma Monastery (5)** to head back to **Agios Ioannis (1)**.

Agios Antonios (3) Moni Koudouma (5)
                39 m   5 m   (4)
gios Ioannis (I)   (2) (4)   Agios Ioannis (I)
        35 m   (6) 121 m 35 m
                                (2)
                                        8.9 km
0   0.45 1.35   2.25   3.20 h

On top of the highest peak in the Asterousia Mountains

From the remote mountain village of Kapetaniana, a panoramic, high route, situated a good 800 m above the southern coast, leads to one of Crete's most striking summits. The conical mountain, which can be seen from far and wide, boasts a remarkable viewing perspective; when the weather is clear, you can spot all three of Crete's highest peaks. There's a lot of activity on the spacious Kofinas Plateau every September 14 when the very popular pilgrimage to the summit chapel takes place.

Starting point: Kapetaniana, 800 m. From the Heraklion – Mires road, in Agii Deka, turn off towards Vagionia. Arriving at the village centre, bear left and, via Loukia, reach the twin village of Kapetaniana. Shortly before both of the villages, at the junction, continue driving straight ahead towards Ano Kapetaniana and, 500 m further on, park your car.
Height difference: 500 m.
Grade: up to the foot of the summit, a pleasant, unpaved road (only used from time to time by herdsmen driving their pick-up trucks). The precipitous ascent to the summit has been recently secured with a railing, however, the walk still demands sure-footedness and an absolute head for heights. A narrow gully is negotiated by climbing up ladders. Route-finding skill is required for the descent from the Panagia Kera to the road. No shade!
Alternative: the walk is worthwhile even without the final ascent to the summit. Just follow the panoramic road until reaching the Panagia Kera – if you decide to leave out the shortcut through the stream courses, the route leads only via unpaved roads; at the end, the alternative can simply be graded blue (easy).
Refreshment: nothing en route.

From the summit plateau of Kofinas, a brilliant view opens up of the Libyan Sea.

At the car park before reaching the village limits of **Kapetaniana (1)**, three trails start off. We choose the dirt road that leads above the houses, continuing eastwards. At the fork, 150 m further on, bear left towards Moni Koudouma. The trail heads straight towards the cone-shaped peak of Kofinas. After passing a little valley notch, turn right at a fork and, shortly afterwards, pass the access road to a silo. A verdant valley with poplar trees sprawls down below the trail, appearing almost like a mirage in this otherwise barren and treeless landscape. This green oasis is skirted around along the upper edge and, afterwards, we ignore a trail forking off to the right. Also, in the further course of the route, always keep following the main trail.

Just before arriving at the foot of Kofinas, pass an abandoned **chapel (2)**, 832 m. In a sharp, left-hand bend shortly afterwards, the trail forks at the same height as a livestock pen outfitted with **stalls**. Bearing left, continue following the road. During the ascent to a col, which can be spotted from far away, we can also spot a chapel, the Panagia Kera, perched on a flank of Kofinas; near the chapel, a path begins which ascends to the peak. Kofinas has now changed its appearance in the meantime, instead of the cone shape, it is now transformed to a immense massif where a spacious plateau stretches up to the summit.

At the **col (3)**, 1027 m, meet up with a major junction. While the track descends straight ahead to the Koudouma monastery, we turn right to ascend onto an elongated ridge. Not quite ten minutes later, pass an **archaeological digs (4)**, 1069 m, where the meagre foundations of a Minoan temple are located. The trail continues heading directly for the rocky summit area of Kofinas.

At the junction, 100 m before the Panagia Kera , bear left to pass through a barrier and reach the track's end. Now continue along an alpine path, secured by a railing,

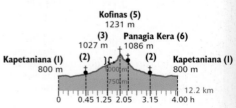

Climbing aids at the critical point on Kofinas.

which leads over rock, sometimes stepped, as it ascends steeply along the massif. 5 minutes later, climb up a steep rocky gully via small metal rungs. A precipitous stretch follows; you are standing almost vertically above the chapel. A little later, scramble up footholds to negotiate another precipitous section. 5 minutes later, we are standing in front of the chapel, Timios Stavros, and a couple of paces further on, at the cross marking the summit of **Kofinas (5)**, 1231 m. From the relatively narrow, but extensive, plateau on the summit, a brilliant view of the island opens up. Psiloritis towers above the Messara Plain, overflowing with olive and fruit trees, and westwards, in central Crete, the 2000 metre peaks of the White Mountains appear; to the east, you can spot the Dikti Mountains. The southern coast can be viewed to the heart's content; a striking landmark is found in the Weeping Lion of Lentas (see photo on page 205). Also, from the sheer drop at the rim, enjoy a breathtaking downwards view of the Koudouma Monastery (Walk 49). The chapel at the summit is set on the ruins of an ancient temple from the 7th century BC; nearby, numerous idols have been found, suggesting that a prehistorical shrine once stood here as well.

After enjoying the view for a good, long time, scramble back down again to the foot of the summit area below and then turn towards the **Panagia Kera (6)**, 1086 m. If we choose not to return along the approach route, from here, we can short-cut the road somewhat. To the right of the gate in the fence in front of the chapel, a goat path descends across the scree-covered slope to reach a mountain spring, **Koutsounari Keras**, with a watering trough next to it. From the spring, continue descending, more or less without a distinct path, to a stream lying about 75 m of altitude lower down. Cross over the stream on the diagonal and, shortly afterwards, pass a triangular-shaped boulder, about 3 m in height, where a **threshing circle (7)** is located, enclosed by stones. Past the threshing circle, climb down into another little valley with a stream where you can spot a goat path ascending to the **road** already used during the approach route – the terrain is easy for orientation and the gravel road cannot be missed. At a livestock pen with a corrugated iron container next to it, reach the road which will bring us back to **Kapetaniana (1)**.

To the ancient fortress above the Lassithi Plateau

From the ring of mountains surrounding the Lassithi high plateau, Karfi is the lowest and easiest to climb. In the col below the summit, the scanty ruins of a Minoan mountain settlement are situated. From the pillar at the summit, you can enjoy a marvellous panoramic view of the Lassithi high plateau and the 2000 metre peaks of the Dikti Mountains.

Starting point: Tzermiadon, 820 m. Approaching from the northern coast, beginning at Malia and Agios Nikolaos, follow winding roads crossing over passes to reach the Lassithi Plateau. Parking possible in one of the side streets near the Restaurant Kronio. By bus, you can only approach from Heraklion to Tzermiadon, however, the time schedule is so mistimed that you will have to plan to spend an overnight.

Height difference: 320 m.

Grade: except for a short, steep section in the area around the summit, the ascent is moderately difficult along cobbled trails and paths. The descent from the Nissimos Plateau leads over an easy to walk, concrete-paved road. The return route from Karfi's peak is well-marked with E4 posts.

Alternative: you could also, at the outset of the walk, follow the *E4* waymarkers onto the Karfi. In the event that you choose to descend back along the approach route, the walk can be graded »blue«. The walking time is then only slightly shortened.

Refreshment: in Tzermiadon, numerous tavernas, the Restaurant Kronio at the starting point of the walk is very popular.

The main summit of Karfi above the Nissimos Plateau.

At the junction in the village centre of **Tzermiadon (1)**, at the Restaurant Kronio, take the road towards Heraklion. Pass by arts & crafts shops, tavernas and the church to reach the village limits with a road signed »Archaeological Site/Timios Stavros« (*E4* trail board, this is our return route; see Alternative). 5 minutes later, turn off onto an unpaved farm road heading straight on. Flanked by walnut and quince trees, the road heads towards an estate with a red roof and two large garage doors. Past this house, bear slightly to the left and ascend to a metal gate up above; on the other side of the gate, a cobbled *kalderimi* begins. From time to time, *blue* arrow waymarkers point in the direction from whence we came. 20 minutes past the house, reach a signed junction where the cobbled trail veers to the right (sign: Karfi).

The trail climbs up to a **col (2)**, 960 m, where semi-dilapidated windmills are standing. From here, a far-reaching downwards view takes in the Bay of Malia; if the weather is clear, the panorama reaches all the way to the Psiloritis massif in central Crete. In days gone by, these windmills were used to grind the grain grown in the Lassithi high plateau. At the col, the cobbled trail merges into a gravel road. Turn right onto this road and immediately pass through a gate. Shortly afterwards, the striking summit of Karfi appears before us. At the fork, 150 m past the gate, the trail leads through a treeless terrain of cushion plant scrubland, heading directly for the humpbacked mountain and soon narrows down into a path. Still a way below the summit, meet up with an enclosed **spring (3)**, to the left of which, a trail forks towards Krasi. Standing just before the spring, bear diagonally left to continue head-

You can't miss the trail to Karfi.

ing towards Karfi. Extremely faded *red* waymarkers lead fairly steeply in an ascent to a col up above, but the path is relatively well-trodden and you can't miss the col. From here, you can spot Karfi's main peak, only some metres higher in altitude, topped by a circular pillar. The humble ruins of the walls marking a late-Minoan mountain settlement are located in the col. It is believed that a settlement for Minoan refugees was established here in about the 12th century BC.

From the col, now head for the trig point pillar perched on the **Karfi (4)**, 1141 m. From the pillar, a spectacular downwards view opens up of the mountain village of Kera, to the east, the Selena chain appears close enough to reach out and touch; it serves as a border for the northern edge of Lassithi. The plateau is dominated by the 2000 metre peaks of Dikti and Lazaros. Our return route is also easy to spot: at the foot of Selena, at the half-way point, so to speak, in a drop down to the Lassithi high plateau, you can see the Nissimos Plateau, through which, a road is running, clearly in view. Also, the chapel, Timios Stavros, is visible, perched on a hill above the plain; below the chapel, we will be descending to Lassithi.

From Karfi, at first descend again along the almost 40 m stretch to an *E4* post below the peak. Here, bear left onto a path that becomes distinct after a few paces. This heads directly towards the gently curved chain of peaks marking the Selena range and finally drops down to the **Nissimos Plateau**.

At the junction by the chapel **Agia Ariadni (5)**, 964 m, with the chapel to your right, cross over the high plain along a gravel trail heading straight on towards the hill where the Timios Stavros chapel is perched. At the junction almost on the southern edge of the plain, bear right and, a good 150 m further on, meet up with a concrete-paved road which turns sharp left and ascends towards Timios Stavros. Keep straight on, descending to the main road on the Lassithi Plateau, and return along the main road back to **Tzermiadon (1)**.

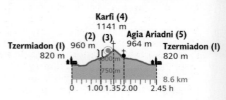

215

Easy walk through a gorge at the edge of the Lassithi Plateau

Up until 20 years ago, the Lassithi Plateau, located above the northern coast at about 900 m of altitude, was famous for its picturesque windmills, but today, the most significant attraction here on the widely cultivated high plateau is the Cave of Zeus near Psichro. Every day in high season, hundreds of tourists are brought by coach to climb down the 84 m deep, mystifying cave. Gorge walkers have also been well-served here ever since a signed road has lead to the entrance of the Havga Canyon. The mouth of the canyon merges into the high plateau at its eastern edge and the first stretch is easy to walk, however, 45 minutes into the gorge, the continued route can only be negotiated by experienced rock-climbers.

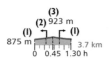

Starting point: the dam 2.5 km southwest of Agios Konstantinos, 875 m. Approaching from Malia or Agios Nikolaos, reach the Lassithi Plateau after about an hour's drive. In the village centre of Agios Konstantinos, about 150 m past the church, turn left onto a narrow tarmac street (sign: Havga Canyon). At the junction 75 m further on, bear left again and then immediately turn right and, 0.3 km on, at a fork, bear left onto a gravel road. Turn right shortly afterwards and then keep straight ahead, following the little brown signs, to reach a fenced-in artificial lake at a junction. Now follow the road straight ahead along the fence; at the end of the artificial lake, the trail veers to the left. A kilometre further on, bear right in front of a vineyard and, shortly after, meet up with a dam in front of the gorge entrance.

Height difference: 50 m.

Grade: a gorge that is easy to walk without any significant differences in height. The trail is waymarked with *E4* posts.

Refreshment: tavernas in Agios Konstantinos.

In the lower reaches of the Havga Gorge.

At the car park in front of the **dam (1)**, pass through a metal gate and then follow the gravel road towards the gorge entrance already in sight. The trail ends at a little livestock pen and then a path continues up the gorge. On a boulder situated in the middle of the stream bed for the gorge, a *yellow* arrow points to the left bank. At the outset, more waymarkers save us from the unpleasant route leading directly in the dry stream bed, while often crossing from one bank over to the other. 25 minutes later, meet up with a **fork (2)**, 902 m. To the right, a waymarked alpine path ascends to the chapel Timios Stavros up above, but

Huge boulders mark the turn-around point.

we continue along the stream bed heading up the gorge. Shortly after passing through an open wood of Holm oaks and Cretan maple, continue directly in the stream bed until finally reaching a **boulder impasse (3)**, 923 m, of gigantic blocks of stone. This is relatively easy to scramble over in the middle, but soon afterwards, continuing on is very difficult. So instead, we turn back at the barrier and return along the approach route back to the **dam (1)**.

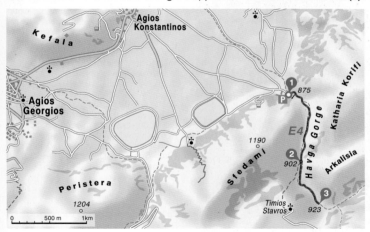

Short, but nice gorge walk that is very popular as well

Should you happen to pick a day for walking the Kritsa Gorge when no other walkers are there, you would still have company – in the gravel stream bed, dozens of cairns will greet you on your way. The gorge counts as one of Crete's most impressive and is especially enchanting due to several bizarrely eroded bottlenecks, formed by the running water.

Starting point: Kritsa, 253 m. At the southern village limits of Agios Nikolaos, at the major junction, follow the road to Kritsa, 9 km away. At the entrance to the village, turn right onto the road towards Lato and, 200 m past the sign marking Kritsa's village limits and past a bridge, turn left onto a farm road signed with

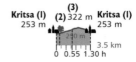

»Gorge« that heads directly towards the entrance to the gorge. You can park your car 300 m further on in front of a power pylon. By bus, you can reach Kritsa from Agios Nikolaos several times daily (additional walking time to the starting point is a good 15 minutes).

Height difference: 150 m.

Grade: in the gorge, sometimes you may have to use your hands when scrambling easily over boulders. The return route leads along broad farm roads and an ancient *kalderimi*. Route-finding is simple. Outside of the gorge itself, you will find very little shade.

Worth seeing: after the walk, a ramble through the narrow passageways in Kritsa is worthwhile. Before reaching the village, on the approach, one of Crete's most notable Byzantine churches, Panagia Kera, lies hidden away; the interior is completely decorated with very well-preserved frescoes from the 13th to the 15th centuries (Tues–Sun 8–15.00, entrance fee €3).

Refreshment: there are numerous restaurants in Kritsa.

Left: Some stretches are very narrow.
Right: The entrance to the Kritsa Gorge.

At the **car park (1)**, in front of a power pylon, turn left onto a path to descend. After a few paces, in front of a metal gate, turn left again and cross through a terraced grove of olive trees to descend to the stream bed of the gorge. Follow the stream bed up the gorge. Right away, you must scramble over huge, round boulders that have been polished smooth by the stream. At an especially imposing boulder, metal rungs on the right-hand side provide help for scrambling up. Immediately after, pass a **carob tree (2)**, 250 m, growing in the middle of the gorge.

Continuing on, encounter spectacular bottlenecks where only narrow openings allow you to slip between the rock faces towering up to 150 m in height. Metal rungs provide assistance for scrambling over a water-eroded stretch, sculpted into a **tube-like form**. Shorty after, some boulders, not yet smoothed by the water, catch our attention; these date back to a rock slip occurring only a few years ago – like all of the other Cretan gorges, the Kritsa Gorge is also still »in the works«. More boulder barriers and water-eroded steep sections must be skirted around. A good half an hour later, the gorge begins to widen somewhat. The most spectacular stretch is now behind us. About 100 m past a trampled-down fence (the remains of which can only be seen at the rim of the gorge) keep looking right to spot a cairn marking a **path (3)** which leads out of the stream bed for the gorge (straight ahead, a sign points out the way to Tapes).

A few paces further on, pass by a square foundation of concrete blocks. The path widens into a broad gravel trail which ascends through a slope of brushwood and Holm oaks. A trail, approaching from the left, merges into ours. A good 5 mins later, meet with an intersecting **gravel track**. Turn right along the track and descend slightly while enjoying a panoramic view of the Orno Mountains. Another 5 mins after that, the track veers to the left, but we continue straight ahead along an ancient mule track which is sometimes cobbled and is flanked by low fieldstone walls. Along this trail, enjoy a fine view of a broad valley, filled with olive trees, which is situated below Kritsa.

Past a gate, the path drops down gradually, then merges into a farm road which leads straight ahead through a grove of olive trees and climbs down to the **car park (1)** at the power pylon.

Panoramic circular walk through the Orno and Thripti Mountains

If you are acquainted with the island of Madeira, when you first spot the narrow watercourse at Kavousi, you will be reminded at once of the Madeira levadas which bring precious water from sources in the mountains to feed the plantations below. On Crete, this type of irrigation system was, and is, far less developed, but indeed, not only at Kavousi, but also, e.g., on the route to the Kamares Cave (Walk 40) and into Dead's Gorge (Walk 62), the remains of such watercourses can still be seen. The most spectacular watercourse can be appreciated during this circular walk; a stretch leads right through the middle of the breathtaking Mesonas Gorge. But this is not all there is: a cobbled mule track and, a not to be slighted, obviously ancient olive tree, are additional highlights of this adventurous circuit route. All in all, this is a fantastic circular walk, although, it's true, a major part of it follows broad roads.

Starting point: Kavousi, 100 m. The village is located on the National Road between Agios Nikolaos and Sitia. Bus service is available here, five times daily.

Height difference: 650 m.

Grade: a circular walk along ancient cobbled trails and unpaved roads. The stretch along the watercourse demands an absolute head for heights and sure-footedness. The cobbled trail and the channel route are waymarked in *yellow*; however, the track from Melisses to the pass is not.

Refreshment: numerous tavernas and coffee houses in Kavousi.

Worth seeing: the monumental olive tree at Kavousi is said to have an estimated age of 3250 years. This would make it the oldest tree of its kind (Olea europaea) in existence – a specimen exceeding this in longevity would, indeed, be very difficult to find in the entire Mediterranean region. The dimensions are extraordinary: trunk diameter, 4.90 m, trunk circumference, 14.20 m, trunk circumference at the base, 22.10 m. As a kind of homage to this hardwood Methuselah, the gold medal winner of the marathon, held during the Olympic Games of 2004 in Athens, was honourably crowned with a wreath braided from the branches of the Kavousi monumental olive tree.

The 3000 year old olive tree of Kavousi.

Panoramic view over the olive plantations of Kavousi to the offshore island of Psira.

The circular walk begins on the main road in **Kavousi (1)**. From the bus stop shelter diagonally opposite from the large, main church (here, a road turns off to Tholos Beach), at first, follow the main road for a short stretch towards Sitia, while passing by two tavernas. 200 m further on (if you are approaching by car, you can park here), turn right onto a tarmac trail (sign »Thripti/Archaeological Site/Ancient Olive Tree«, etc.); here, you can also find a trail board; however, it is not very helpful.

Shortly, 100 m on, leave the narrow road behind by turning left onto an unpaved trail, leading through a grove of olive trees and heading towards the entrance to the **Mesonas Gorge**, which slices through the Orno Mountains here as a deep rift. To the left, above the chasm, you can already spot the course of the ancient *kalderimi* leading to Melisses. Bear left in front of the entrance to the gorge and ascend to the mule track up above after only a few paces. The mostly cobbled *kalderimi* climbs up the left flank of the Mesonas Gorge, following tight bends; early mornings, the ascent route still lies in the

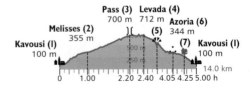

shade cast by the Orno Mountains. Right away, the trail allows downward views into the floor of the gorge and the first panoramic view opens up beyond Kavousi to the Gulf of Mirabello.

The cobbled trail traverses a stony, scree-covered slope and, a good half an hour later, merges into an unpaved road. Continuing the climb up the slope, 5 mins later, ignore a trail leading to a chapel located below which soon comes into sight. In front of us, the houses of **Melisses (2)**, 355 m, appear, surrounded by modest fields, fig trees and natural groves of olive trees. At the first house, past a metal gate, meet up with a fork where a sign directs us to the right towards Thripti. In the course that follows, keep to the main trail. Not quite 10 mins later, pass by two trails forking off to the left, one quickly following the other, and both blocked off by metal gates. At the fork about 250 m past the second gate, turn right. Still keeping to the main trail, enjoy a view of the Gulf of Mirabello once again. 50 m past a gate, reach yet another junction, signed for Thripti; bear right here.

The road climbs up along hairpin bends to reach a **pass (3)**, 700 m, up above. Here, too, keep to the main trail to continue. As you cross over the pass, leave the high valley of Melisses behind and, in front of us, Afendis Stavromenos appears with a transmission tower perched on its summit. From the pass, the road descends into a valley while opening up panoramic views. Not quite 20 minutes later, in a right-hand bend above some abandoned quarry-stone houses, cross over a stream bed. 150 m further on, a

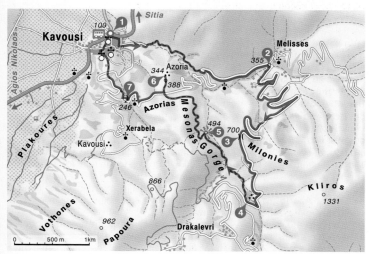

The old watercourse in the Mesonas Gorge.

gully (4) intersects the trail. Here, leave the road behind by turning right (*yellow* waymarking) and descending along a narrow maintenance trail for the water channel, rather dilapidated at first, leading down to the quarry-stone houses below. The next stretch is steep and somewhat precipitous. Below the houses, the gully cuts through a stream bed and, after that, the course of the channel keeps at about the same height and then descends to the narrow stream bed of the **Mesonas Gorge**. Some sections are secured with a rusty fence, but nevertheless, this stretch requires an absolute head for heights. The channel then crosses over the bed of the gorge along an aqueduct and, shortly after, is covered with a metal grid. Suddenly, instead of the water flowing through a conduit, it flows freely along an open channel. Now reach a striking projecting rock where the channel hooks to the left in a right angle. From the point where the channel hooks, a couple of strides lead to a cobbled **viewpoint (5)**, 494 m. While we take a short break, we can enjoy views of the Mirabello Gulf and the wind farm above Plaka. During the next stretch of descent, a short one, but steep and precipitous, the channel hugs up close to a rock face. Now meet up with a fig tree, standing in the middle of the maintenance trail.

A good 20 minutes past the viewpoint, the channel veers to the left and leaves the gorge behind; at this point, we are looking down upon a **farm track** below, to which we next descend. About five minutes past the veer to the left, keep an eye out for a *yellow* waymarker pointing out a path, loose underfoot, which leads to the track. Take the track straight on to continue the descent and, 75 m further on, meet up with a broad roadway that is ascending from the gorge. Here, a short excursion is possible to the excavation of a Minoan settlement (1200–500 BC). Follow the road to the right for a short way and then immediately turn left along an ascending path flanked by tumbledown stone walls. Just below the summit of a hill lie the ruins of the Minoan settlement **Azoria (6)**, 344 m, from which, we can enjoy a fantastic panoramic view of Kavoursi, down below our feet.

Returning to the main trail, turn right and follow it through a grove of olive trees. Always keeping to the main trail, meet up with a **chapel**, surrounded by eucalyptus trees. A few minutes later, finally reach the monumental **olive**

tree (7), 246 m. Despite its incredible age of more than 3000 years, the tree bears fruit annually. After showing appropriate esteem to this Methuselah, continue following the road and, 100 m further on, keep an eye out for a *yellow* waymarker. Here, turn right onto a cobbled path that, 5 minutes later, merges into a farm road. Cross over this road on the diagonal. Five minutes later, our path merges again with a farm road; turn right and descend along it. 25 m on, the path continues to the right. Surprisingly enough, the narrow channel has joined us again. The path crosses over the roadway again and then, at the upper village limits of Kavousi, meets up with a domed church. From here, descend along a narrow concrete-paved trail that forks 50 m below the church; here, bear to the left. Past the little chapel of Agios Georgios, finally reach the village square of **Kavousi (1)**, boasting cafés and tavernas with shady terraces. After perhaps taking a break, keep slightly to the right and, shortly after, pass the main church to reach the bus stop shelter on the main road leading through the village.

During the descent through the Mesonas Gorge, you almost always have a view of the Gulf of Mirabello.

From Koutsouras' communal park through Butterfly Gorge

The butterfly appellation somewhat confuses the issue; it's true that the gorge is named after this colourful creature, but they are no more to be seen here than in other places. The best time to spot one or the other species, numbering up to 50 different varieties on Crete, is from May until September. Nevertheless, the walker will be pleasantly surprised at the abundance of greenery found here. Well into the month of May, however, the stream bed may be running with a little too much current to allow a walker to continue through the little canyon to the chapel.

```
                    Agios
Koutsouras/  Dimitrios (4)  Koutsouras/
Communal Park (I)   123 m   Communal Park (I)
   6 m      (3)  †  (3)      6 m
                                  4.8 km
      0     1.05    2.00 h
```

Starting point: Communal Park Koutsouras, 6 m. The signed communal park of Koutsouras is located on the coastal road 20 km east of Ierapetra and about one kilometre west of Koutsouras. The bus line Ierapetra – Makrigialos stops directly in front of it (Mon-Sat, up to eight times daily; Sun, limited service). You can also reach Koutsouras by bus from the northern coast starting from Sitia.

Height difference: 120 m in both ascent and descent.

Grade: a gorge walk along a sometimes extremely overgrown path; however, waymarkers make route-finding easier. A steep section is negotiated by climbing a ladder.

Refreshment: the modern-style café/wine bar Koursaros on the through road 400 m east of the starting point.

At the outset of the walk, a successful reforestation project provides fresh greenery.

From the car park at the municipal park of **Koutsouras (1)**, follow the broad trail through a reforested pine wood which appears like an oasis compared to the rest of the southern coast. Behind a row of recently planted fan palms, a children's playground lies hidden; keep this to your left hand side. 10 mins later, in front of a mountain ridge with caves, meet up with a **water house (2)**, 24 m. From there, follow the stream bed, dry during the summer months, into the gorge via a path soon waymarked with *yellow* and *red* markings and weaving between boulders. A **ladder (3)**, 45 m, helps the scramble up a steep wall, about 4 m in height. After that, continue, higgledy-piggledy, through the river bed. Traversing jungle-like thickets of oleander and very tall reeds, cross over onto the right bank. There, the path continues in easy up and down walking, passing dead trees which bear witness to a forest fire. In front of us, still a good distance away, we can spot the destination for our walk, a white-washed chapel. The path changes twice from one side of the gorge's stream bed to the other. Now meet up with a somewhat dilapidated, narrow **channel**, whose function has been replaced by a large, black conduit. At a chain-link fence, leave the conduit behind and change over, once again, to the other bank of the stream bed. A fairly overgrown section can be skirted around at two *red* arrows by climbing up the slope. Now pass through a grove of olive trees and, from there, a farm road finally leads to **Agios Dimitrios (4)**, 123 m. Next to the chapel, a bench situated under a large cypress tree provides a nice spot to take a break; a trough fountain is also there for drinking water. After a break, return along the approach route back to the communal park at **Koutsouras (1)**.

Old watercourse in the Dasaki Gorge.

Through a grove of olive trees in a little canyon

The Pefki Gorge counts as one of the smallest on the island, but it is, neverthe-less, interesting. Above all, it is lovely to explore the gorge along a well-laid

circular trail which, at the same time, opens up a fantastic view of the mountain village of Pefki, framed by groves of olive trees and proudly presenting its landmark: a chapel perched cleverly on top of a conical hillock. Thanks to the »Zur Wein-laube«, there is also a quaint café in the village. If you are staying in Makri-gialos or if you are approaching here by bus, you could also visit the gorge starting from its lower end.

Starting point: Pefki, 386 m. Approach-ing from Ierapetra, in the village centre of Makrigialos, and shortly after passing Sunwing Resort, a road branches off to Pefki, 7 km away. 30 m past the sign for the Pefki village limits, a sign (Gorge) points to the left towards the gorge. Park-ing possible on the side of the road at the sign for the village limits. As an alterna-tive, you could reach the gorge, starting from Makrigialos. You can reach the re-sort town by bus from Ierapetra as well (up to eight times daily; only twice on Sun) or from Sitia (Mon–Sat, four times daily, twice on Sun).

Height difference: a good 230 m.

Grade: circular walk along mostly pleas-ant farm tracks and cobbled trails. The stretch through the gorge along a narrow path demands sure-footedness. The most important junctions are signed and E4-waymarked.

Refreshment: in Pefki, the *kafenion* »Zur Weinlaube«, where you can sample local country wine from the barrel.

Alternative starting at Makrigialos/ Analipsi: from the bus stop at the Sun-

wing Resort in Makrigialos, descend along the main through road towards Ier-apetra and, 400 m further on, turn right onto a narrow, concrete-paved road (sign: »White River Cottages/*E4* Pefki«). A good 5 minutes later, the concrete trail crosses under a bridge and, at the fork 400 m further on, bear left; a little later on, continue past the White River Cottages. At both of the following forks, one soon following after the other, bear right each time and then ascend steeply, following signs towards the »Gorge«. Above a cou-ple of holiday bungalows clad in natural stone, the concrete pavement ends at a junction; keep straight on, continuing along a gravel trail and, 400 m further on, meet up with an intersecting trail. Turn right onto this trail and ascend, in a good 5 minutes, to reach a light-blue coloured hydrant at an altitude of 212 m above sea level. Here, you have the opportunity to either follow the main route to the left to-wards Pefki and then, at the trough foun-tain, descend into the gorge or you could continue straight on from the hydrant and climb down into the gorge.

At the village limits of **Pefki (1)**, descend along a concrete-paved trail into a grove of olive trees (*E4*). At a fork, not quite 100 m further on, turn left and then immediately left again, 5 m after that: here, an ancient mule track begins. At an arbour a little later on, meet up with an intersecting concrete-paved trail. Turn left onto this trail and, a couple of paces further on, the descent through the olive grove continues.

Five minutes later, the path merges into a farm road. A backwards look treats you to a thrilling view of Pefki and, towering above it, Afendis Stavromenos, with the chapel at the summit. Bearing left, 3 minutes later, the farm road ascends to a trough fountain and a picnic bench at the tumbledown walls of **Milos (2)**, 313 m; the aqueduct for the ancient water mill is still well preserved. Turn right to continue descending along the farm road. To your left, the contours of the Pefki Gorge begin to take shape; the trail leads along the upper rim of the gorge. Not quite 5 minutes past Milos, leave the farm road behind by turning left onto a path (sign: »Gorge«), and shortly afterwards, enjoy a view that stretches through the gorge all the way to the Libyan Sea.

At another **trough fountain (3)**, 303 m, you will also find a bench; here, meet up with another junction. Turn left here to descend into the gorge (straight ahead is the return route). At a steep spot, cross over the **stream bed** for the gorge; after rainfall, a waterfall cascades down here and fills a rock pool with its waters. A **boulder (4)** blocking the way can be skirted around to the left (if you prefer, you could scramble under it to get through). Afterwards, way-markers lead us along the right-hand bank of the stream bed for the gorge to two **metal stairways**, along which, two steep sections can be climbed down (to the left, you have a possible excursion down to a spring).

Not far from the gorge's exit, meet up with a broad gravel trail. Turn right onto this trail and descend for a good 100 m; then, at a **fork (5)**, 188 m, cross over the stream bed of the gorge, which is overgrown here with a thicket of

The white houses of Pefki squat down at the foot of Afendis Stavromenos.

reeds. Bearing left, the broad trail ascends along the western side of the gorge to reach another fork up above where a light-blue coloured **hydrant (6)**, 212 m, is located. Here, turn sharp right towards Pefki (whilst the *E4* continues straight on, descending to Makrigialos). The gravel trail, a good 150m on, becomes a mule track, sometimes stepped. This ascends via tight bends to climb up along the western side of the gorge. Arriving at the upper rim of the gorge,

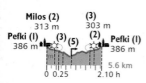

enjoy views of the eastern flank of the gorge and of Pefki, surrounded by groves of olive trees. The path, secured by a railing, leads for a stretch directly along the sheer drop at the rim and finally meets up with the **trough fountain (3)** and the approach route. From here, return along the approach route back to **Pefki (1)**.

Through a breathtaking canyon into a trim mountain village

Due to its remote location above the southeastern coast, the canyon at Perivolakia has long counted as one of Crete's least known, despite the fact that it is relatively easy to access along a well-laid and well-marked path. The fortress-like monastery of Kapsa, which is opened to the public, is enthroned above the gorge's imposing entrance. After ending the walk, you could spend some time relaxing in a little cove, nestled amidst Salt cedars; all in all, this is a daytrip abounding in diversity.

Starting point: Moni Kapsa, 3 m, 35 km east of Ierapetra. From the coastal road, 0.6 km past the Sunwing Resort in Makrigialos, turn off onto a secondary road towards the Kapsa Monastery. In front of the monastery, you can park above the pebble beach under the shade of Salt cedars. Driving time from Agios Nikolaos is a good 1.5 hrs.

Height difference: a good 300 m in both ascent and descent.

Grade: a long ascent along a sometimes well-laid alpine path; numerous short, steep stretches, which are slippery underfoot and somewhat precipitous, demand sure-footedness. Route-finding is easy; the gorge sets the course of the walk and the route is also waymarked with *red* dots and posts (a *red* dot on a *yellow* square). As long as you start off early in the morning, the lower reaches of the gorge are still in shade.

Refreshment: in Perivolakia, the quaint *Kafenion* Aposperida offers, aside from hot and cold beverages, also snacks.

Alternative: the route can also be converted to a circular walk. At the church in Perivolakia, follow the sign in the direction of Moni Kapsa. Past the settlement, *red* waymarkers lead for a stretch in an ascent of the slope and then via farm trails and a goat path, descend to the monastery, enjoying views. Walking time

A ladder helps negotiate a steep section.

is only marginally longer than the return route through the gorge.

Worth seeing: the monastery is open to the public daily from 6.30–12.30 and 15.30–19.00 (»no shorts«). From the double-naved church, boldly carved into the rock face, you can climb up steps to a hermit's cave.

The monk's monastery Kapsa at the exit of the Perivolakia Gorge.

From the car park at the foot of the **Moni Kapsa (1)**, cross the secondary road and immediately reach the entrance to the Perivolakia Gorge. At an information board, a path leads into the stream bed of the gorge, filled with oleander. Right away, we find ourselves standing in the middle of an extraordinary canyon flanked by towering walls almost 100 m in height and peppered by countless caves. At first, the waymarked trail leads along the left bank of the stream bed for the gorge, but in the further course of the walk, the route will change banks several times. About 20 mins later, traverse a scree-covered slope. The next stretch leads over smoothly-eroded outcrops of rock. Afterwards, the path runs beneath an overhanging rock to the other side and then ascends through a gully along the left flank of the gorge. Further up, cross over a field of boulders. Now meet up with a steep section, about 5 m in height, negotiated by climbing up a **ladder (2)**, 89 m. The path continues climbing steeply up the gorge, sometimes loose underfoot (be very careful on the return!), along sometimes somewhat precipitous spots. A short stretch is secured by a cable.

A good hour later, meet up with the upper entrance to the gorge. Still a good distance away, you can spot a high voltage power pylon perched at a

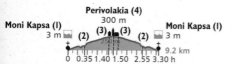

height that we will reach later on. After a long stretch leading directly through the stream bed of the gorge, cross under a **rock arch**, a very narrow passage, above which, a massive boulder has become wedged.

The walls of the gorge begin to level off somewhat while our alpine path heads directly towards a striking **crag (3)**, 283 m, enthroned above the upper entrance to the gorge like a sentinel. At the foot of the crag, pass through a tumbledown gate. Shortly afterwards, just before meeting up with a private property, bear left to reach a roadway. Turn right here and head towards the houses of **Perivolakia (4)**, 300 m. At a bridge, meet up with the village street; turn right to reach the *kafenion* near the church.

After a break, descend back again through the gorge to return to **Moni Kapsa (1)**.

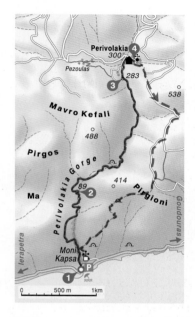

Below: In the lower reaches of the Perivolakia Gorge.
Photo page 234: The village of Perivolakia is hiding behind the striking crag.

Crete's marvellous coastline in the far east

About 5000 Date palms line the popular and, in summer, rather crowded, beach at Vai – the most beautiful palm beach on the entire island of Crete is, perhaps, yours alone only in the wee hours of the morning. If you haven't hit the trail until later in the day, that's not too bad either, along the coastal walk to Palekastro, you'll find plenty of remote bathing spots, without palm trees, however. If a GPS device is not part of your walking gear, you should plan plenty of time for this coastal walk; aside from bathing breaks, most certainly you will need a quarter of an hour here, 15 minutes there, just to pick up the sometimes indistinct route again.

Starting point: the palm beach of Vai, 1 m, 9 km north of Palekastro. In summer, bus service twice daily from Sitia via Palekastro.
Return: the first bus reaches Vai shortly before 12.00; the afternoon bus from Palekastro, leaves already around 16.30 to return to Sitia, therefore, the time element needed for the walk and the return by bus is relatively short. From Palekastro, it is better to organise private transport.
Height difference: about 340 m in ascent and 300 m in descent.
Grade: aside from some short stretches of ascent and descent demanding sure-footedness, the coastal trail is technically relatively easy; the difficulty of the walk lies more in route-finding. Apart from the recently repainted red waymarkers, marked posts (*red* dot on a *yellow* background) help in orientation. No shade; bring along your bathing gear.
Refreshment: : tavernas in Vai, Maridati and Kouremenos; it's very nice to sit in the Taverna Batis on Chiona Beach.

Cretan date palms flank the picturesque beach at Vai.

In **Vai (1)**, next to a restaurant on the southern end of the beach, pick up a stepped trail, flanked by a railing, and climb up to a **viewpoint** perched above, which provides a picture-postcard view of the marvellous beach. Our coastal path begins here just on the other side of a gate. 3 mins later, the little cove of **Psilos Ammos** comes into view. A path leads to the little, fine, sandy beach (just about 30 m long) down below. We bear slightly right, however, and follow the *red* waymarkers leading above the cove. The first waymarking post appears and, in the course of the walk, other such posts, unfortunately spaced very far apart, will provide an important aid to route finding.

Past Psilos Ammos, a sand dune is traversed briefly. Past the dune, the very indistinct path leads along the right edge of a little valley notch. Passing through mastic thicket, rock-rose and patches of juniper, you have to keep your eyes peeled for waymarkers; sometimes your search for a route may be aided by cairns.

A good 20 minutes later, a rocky coastal cliff, tumbling seawards, must be skirted around by heading inland. After that, take a short excursion through a dry stream bed to reach a little, stony beach, unfortunately, not especially suited for bathing, but where the continued route

Psilos Ammos, Vai's little neighbouring cove.

can be previewed: further on, a **steep headland** blocks the way directly at the coast, to the right of it, a sweeping saddle can be spotted where we will be climbing up. Now returning again to the main trail, soon meet up with a waymarking post to continue over an outcropping of rock, layered in plates, and then ascend, for a short stretch, steeply up to the next post. From there, follow the very indistinct path towards the **saddle (2)**. From the saddle, descend along zigzags onto a stony valley floor down below. Now an excursion through the stream bed to the beach, **Megali Kefala (3)** is a must. As soon as the stream bed becomes extremely overgrown with *phrygana*, you can skirt around this area via a path to the right. Steep, rugged cliff faces encircle the fine, sandy cove which is a good 100 m in length; the water is crystal clear and, at the southern end, a couple of overhanging outcrops in the rock face provide some shade.

Returning again to the main trail, climb up from the stream bed towards the left and surmount the next coastal cliff. Far above, another post, to the right and next to a pointed crag, marks the spot where we will meet up with the ridgeline. At the outset, well-placed cairns and *red* dot markings lead, for a

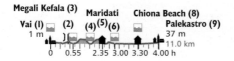

237

Olive cultivation in the valley of Maridati.

short stretch, up the slope and then slightly to the left, crossing through a notch; finally reach the **ridgeline** up above. Here, a view opens up taking in a couple of islets lying off-shore in the Bay of Grandes, as well as the Plaka Peninsula in the background.

Now at first heading directly along the broad ridgeline, continue the route. A good 100 m past the way-marker post, pass through a gate in a fence. The path soon leads about 20 to 25 m below the ridgeline on the side of the ridge facing inland.

At the end of the ridge, another valley opens up; descend now into this valley. The descent is fairly steep and loose under foot, however, relatively well-marked. Shortly before reaching the valley floor, we can get some orientation by spotting a waymarker post perched on top of a boulder, measuring a metre high. From there, we could take a short excursion through the stream bed to yet another **bathing cove (4)**. This one is not quite as attractive as Megali Kefala; however, keeping in mind the scrambling section we have just left behind, perhaps a stop for a dip is a worthwhile venture. The left side of the cove is framed by magenta-coloured Bunter sandstone rock.

Returning to the main trail, from the metal post, climb up to the left along a rocky secondary slope. The climb is steep for another 3 mins until the path descends, veering slightly to the left. Continue following *red* dot waymarkers to cross over a dry stream bed and, along the other side of the slope, ascend steeply once again. Soon scramble to the right of a striking protruding rock through a breach in the cliff face. Waymarkers point the way through cushion plant scrubland to a **viewpoint**. To our feet, lies the Maridati Valley, with a grove of olive trees, above which, we can look over the Bay of Kouremenos and all the way to the flat-topped mountain of Kastri; also, the villages of Agathias and Palekastro come into sight for the first time.

The following short, but very steep, descent into the **Maridati Valley (5)** is more than meets the eye. During the descent, use a large taverna for orientation. To the left of the taverna, spot a holiday home with a flat roof and a gate in front of it. Climb down to this house and then follow a farm road leading directly past the house (if the house is occupied, please respect the owner's privacy); the road crosses over the valley and then merges at the Taverna Maridatis into an unpaved access road for the beach.

If you don't plan on another bathing break, turn right along the road and, a good 5 mins past the taverna, watch out for *red* dot waymarkers (the turn-off is easy to miss). To the left, a narrow path leads, for the first metres, through a dense thicket and then, following power lines, climbs up a mountain ridge that serves as the southern border for the Maridati Valley. Along the ridge, leave a battered fence behind and, at a power pylon, about 100 m further on, cross over another wire fence. The path heads directly towards a couple of villas. 20 m before reaching the first one, the path veers to the left and then descends along a low ridge. Climb down the last metres, without a distinct path, to the access road for the fishing harbour. Bearing right, a few paces lead to **Kouremenos Beach (6)**. From there, turn left onto the seaside road, at first concrete paved, later, cobbled, and flanked by a promenade, which leads parallel to the beach. Salt cedars provide a little shade, and refreshment can be had, for example, in the garden café Grandes (with a lovely terrace).

The promenade becomes a gravel trail. At a fork, bear left and, 5 mins later, shortly before reaching the flat-topped mountain of Kastri, cross over a bridge spanning the **Kalogeropotamos (7)**. After that, skirt around a bungalow complex surrounded by a stone wall by walking along the side facing inland. Shortly past the access road for the bungalows, meet up with an intersecting gravel road. Turn left along the road and cross through a grove of olive trees until, 5 mins later, the road reaches the tarmac road to **Chiona Beach (8)**. Turn left and, 200 m further on, meet up with the lovely beach, boasting inviting seafood tavernas; by turning right instead, reach the village square in **Palekastro (9)**, after a half hour walk. The bus stop is opposite the church.

The fishing harbour at Kouremenos.

To a Minoan summit sanctum above the east coast

At a mere 255 m of altitude, Petsofas certainly doesn't count as one of Crete's highest mountains. Its completely open setting, however, makes it a perfect panoramic viewpoint taking in the eastern coast, broken up by coves, beaches and headlands, as well as the flat-topped mountain of Kastri. The Minoans maintained a sanctum at Petsofas' peak, but only a couple of ruined walls have withstood the ravages of time. Archaeologists discovered several terracotta figurines of weasels and tortoises; some of this collection is exhibited in the archaeological museum in Agios Nikolaos.

Starting point: the secondary road, Palekastro – Chiona Beach, 10 m. From the village centre of Palekastro, take the road towards Agathias. At the village limits of Agathias , bear left and, 500 m further on, reach the turn-off for a gravel trail, signed for »Rousolakos«. Parking possible at the side of the road (walking time from the bus stop for the church in Palekastro, 20 minutes).

Height difference: 250 m in both ascent and descent.
Grade: a short walk, at first along broad farm tracks and, afterwards, a moderately steep ascent along a good path. No shade! The junctions in the grove of olive trees are sometimes signed and/or way-marked with arrows.
Refreshment: nothing en route; tavernas in Palekastro and Chiona Beach.

Starting at the **secondary road (1)** from Palekastro to Chiona Beach, follow the gravel trail (sign: »Rosolakas«) in a grove of olive trees. A good 200 m on, ignore a left-hand fork and, at the junction not quite 100 m further, bear to the right. Another 150 m and the trail forks yet again; turn right (sign: »Peak Sanctuary«) heading for the houses of Agathias. At another junction, three minutes later, turn onto the left-hand trail towards Petsofas and afterwards

Chiona Beach with the flat-topped mountain, Kastri.

pass by a **miniature church (2)**. At the fork immediately after, turn left to continue along the gravel trail through the olive plantation. 5 minutes later, another sign points to the right for the »Peak Sanctuary«.

The trail ascends easily and we can now take a look at our continued route as it climbs up over Petsofas' northern flank via an alpine path. Turn left once again and then meet up with a **goat pen**. Now pass through a gate into the pen and then exit the pen, 50 m further on, through another gate. The olive trees are now lying behind us. The alpine ascent path begins, traversing the mountain ridge; a *red* dot marks the trail head. At the same time, a marvellous view opens up of the towering flat-topped mountain, Kastri, to the north of Chiona Beach and, beyond it, of the wide, sweeping Bay of Kouremenos; in front of us, the flush islets of Nissi Grandes and Nissi Savoura are lying out to sea. Soon, the barren Plaka Peninsula makes an appearance.

Afterwards, the path veers to the right and, a good 5 minutes later, we finally reach the column on the summit of **Petsofas (3)**, 255 m. A couple of metres below the summit, a square fragment of a foundation wall bears witness to the ancient sanctum once situated here; the shards of pottery scattered about are probably of a much more recent origin.

From the summit, return along the approach route back to the **secondary road (1)**.

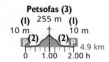

To a bathing cove only accessible on foot

Despite the good access road, Chochlakies is in the process of becoming a ghost town; only a handful of houses are still inhabited and it appears to be only a matter of time until the kafenion closes its doors. Just past the grove of olive trees behind the village, meet up with the entrance to a gorge. The trail through the impressive canyon leading to its mouth, opening wide to the sea, is neither very complicated nor very long.

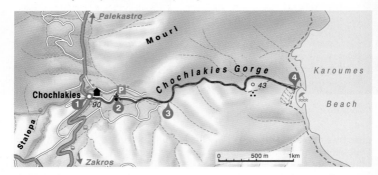

Starting point: Chochlakies, 90 m. The village is located on the secondary road between Palekastro and Zakros; limited parking possible on the side of the road (if you are approaching by car, you could drive to the cemetery which has a large car park). A bus stop for the line Sitia – Palekastro – Zakros is situated directly at the starting point; from Sitia, Mon, Tues and Fri, around 6.00, 10.15 and 14.15; return from Zakros, 7.00 and 15.40; in Chochlakies, the bus arrives about 15.55.
Height difference: 190 m.
Grade: The gorge trail is relatively easy to walk and is waymarked throughout with *red* arrows.
Refreshment: a coffee house in Chochlakies.

From the village limits of **Chochlakies (1)**, a narrow road, next to the little bus stop shelter, leads into the settlement. 20 m further on, pass the little *kafenion* located on the left-hand side of the road; don't blink because you might miss it. At the village limits, you can spot a **cemetery chapel (2)**, rather on the outskirts of town, where the concrete trail ends, a good 5 minutes later.

A couple of paces before reaching the chapel, keep left at the car park and then, along a gravel trail, pass a pavilion. A few metres further on, a directional arrow points to the right. Continue on through a grove of olive trees and, 5 minutes later, cross over a stream bed via a **concrete-reinforced**

ford. About 10 m further on, turn
left. Another good 100 m after that,
you have to pay close attention: a
few paces past a right-hand bend,
leave the farm road behind by turn-

ing left onto a path (very faded red waymarker). Past a gate, about 3 minutes
later, we have left the olive grove behind.

The path bears slightly left, heading towards the **gorge entrance (3)**, now
impossible to miss. In the usually rather broad stream bed, you must, at this
point, keep your balance while walking over smooth, round, black stones.
Sections that are not so steep (at the most, one and a half metres in height)
can either be skirted around or scrambled over with little problem, usually
without the aid of your hands. From time to time, the waymarked trail has to
squeeze between boulders.

About 50 minutes later, the gorge's walls begin to lose in height and the sea
comes into view. To the right of the stream bed, a path leads through extensive patches of spiny rush growing at the gorge's mouth, A couple of paces
finally brings us to two ancient Salt cedars at **Karoumes Beach (4)**. After a
break beneath the shade of Salt cedars on the lovely beach enclosed by
promontories and/or a break for a refreshing dip, return along the approach
route back to **Chochlakies (1)**.

Spiny rush at Karoumes Beach.

Along the E4 traversing a high plain above the eastern coast

Portrait of St. George, the dragon slayer, in Agios Georgios.

This stage of the long-distance trail runs mostly along a well-preserved kalderimi which, in the past, served as the connecting route between the villages of Zakros, Skalia and Ziros. The usually cobbled trail leads through a barren terrain of coastal cliffs, crossing the little high plateau of Mavros Kambos, while ascending to a chapel perched high above; the ruins of the abandoned Skalia are located even further up.

Starting point: Zakros, 208 m; parking possible near the village square. The approach runs from Sitia via Palekastro to Zakros; by bus, from Sitia, Mon, Tues and Fri, around 6.00, 10.15 and 14.15 (return from Zakros, around 7.00 and 15.40).
Height difference: 460 m.
Grade: not a difficult route along cobbled and gravel trails that are good to walk. Route-finding is easy; the stretch follows the *E4* waymarkers.
Worth seeing: the museum in the lovely, renovated water mill is open from 10.30–13.00; (closed Mondays and Wednesdays).
Refreshment: in Zakros, numerous coffee houses and snack bars.

Leave the village square of **Zakros (1)** behind by taking the road towards Kato Zakros/Xerokambos. Not quite 100 m further on, at the café/bar Neromylos, turn right onto a broad concrete trail (sign: »*E4*/Zakros Source«). At a fork located at a trough fountain, you could pay a short visit (50 m) to the Water Mill Museum. Otherwise, keep bearing to the left through a narrow village passageway and soon merge with a tarmac road. Turn left along the road and, 20 m further on, leave it behind by turning right onto a concrete-paved trail. About 200 m on, meet up with a huge cistern bearing crooked pipes on its roof. The *E4* continues towards Skalia by turning left and ascending, but if you wish, you could first continue straight ahead here to make a little excursion to the **Zakros source (2)**, 261 m. A rock slab trail (this is also a botanical nature trail) leads below the Afendis Christos chapel and then ends, 200 m further on, at the copious spring. The area around it has been redeveloped with EU funding.

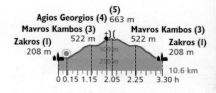

Returning to the main trail, continue the ascent towards Skalia and immediately meet up with a gate. Past the gate, bear diagonally to the right and a gravel trail leads, after two bends, to a **water reservoir**. A bench has been placed in front of the reservoir from which you can enjoy a lovely view of Zakros. From the reservoir, a cobbled trail continues now, which will set the direction of the route for the next hour. The trail climbs, sometimes very steeply, through treeless cushion plant scrubland; from time to time, E4 posts mark the trail, but indeed, route-finding couldn't be simpler.

On the high plateau, **Mavros Kambos (3)**, 522 m, meet up with a signed junction: to the left, a sign points out the way to Mount Vigla, but we turn right along the E4 to continue, now crossing over the plateau via a farm road. Not quite 10 minutes later, about 100 m past a gate, leave the farm road behind by turning left onto a path (E4 waymarkers) which soon reveals itself through its cobbles to be our mule track.

The trail leads along the left side of another small plain and then ascends to **Agios Georgios (4)**, 626 m. A memorial to the 40 resistance fighters who lost their lives in a battle against the Turks in the 18th century is located next

The high plateau Mavros Kambos along the E4.

The Agios Georgios Chapel.

to the chapel. A couple of strides away, the water for an enclosed spring gushes out of the rock face. On the rise above the chapel, a short excursion through the abandoned village of Skalia is worthwhile; the village is a victim of the ongoing rural exodus which has been taking place since the 1980s. While the *E4* passes by the spring and then continues towards Ziros, we follow the road that begins at the chapel instead. At the fork 5 mins later, continue straight ahead, crossing over a **col (5)**, 663 m. At the following fork, bear right, heading towards a rocky ridgeline. Before reaching the ridgeline, the trail veers towards the right while opening up lovely views of the **Mavros Kambos (3)** plain; we will now return to the plain by descending. Once arriving there, return along the already familiar mule track back to **Zakros (1)**.

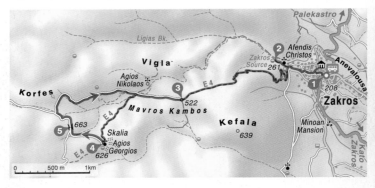

Circular walk through a breathtaking gorge to the Minoan Palace of Zakros

»Dead's Gorge« counts as one of the most famous and most popular canyons in eastern Crete; accordingly, the path there is a well-trodden one. At the same time, the trail through this natural marvel is the last stage for the long-distance trail E4. The Minoans built a palace at the mouth of the gorge 3600 years ago and they interred their dead in caves somewhat further up the gorge, located on the rock faces, some up to 200 m above the floor. A puzzling question arises here: How in the world did they bring the sarcophagi to the caves so far above?

Starting point: the village square in Zakros, 208 m. Reach Zakros by car from Sitia via Palekastro; by bus from Sitia, Mon, Tues and Fri around 6.00, 10.15 and 14.15 (return from Zakros, around 7.00 and 15.40).

Height difference: 260 m.

Grade: a well-marked path, relatively easy to walk, through the gorge; sometimes, you have to scramble over a couple of little boulders. The return route leads along roads that are completely lacking in shade. Route-finding is simple.

Bring along your bathing gear!

Refreshment: coffee houses in Zakros; tavernas in Kato Zakros; it is lovely to sit in the café/snack bar Amnesia at the southern end of the line of restaurants.

Worth seeing: the Minoan Palace; in summer, open daily from 10.30–17.30, in winter, from 8.00–15.00; entrance fee, € 3.

Shorter alternative: follow the secondary road to Zakros until reaching the car park, Entrance B (Waypoint 6). From there, you could descend to the stream bed of the gorge in a good 15 minutes.

The ruins of the Minoan Palace grounds at the exit of Dead's Gorge.

Gorge (2) 154 m (3) Kato Entrance B (6)
Zakros (I) 92 m (4) Zakros (5) 179 m (2) Zakros (I)
208 m 15 m 1 m 208 m
13.3 km
0 0.50 1.35 2.00 3.20 3.40 4.00 h

The walk begins at the village square of **Zakros (1)**. To the right, in front of the *kafenion*, signs point out the way to Kato Zakros and Xerokambos; but we turn left into a narrow street and, at the junction 25 m on, immediately left again (sign: »Kato Zagros/ Gorge«). Not quite 300 m further on, ignore a concrete-paved trail turning off to the left. At the village limits, the narrow street continues straight ahead through a grove of olive trees. On our left-hand side, we are following a stream bed that is flanked by a brush wood; soon, we will follow this into the stream bed. 20 minutes later, reach a **junction (2)**, marked by a number of signs. While the narrow road continues straight ahead, we turn left onto a gravel trail (*E4*). At the outset, the gravel trail leads somewhat above the lush, green stream bed. A couple of paces past a small, cubical water house, meet a junction and continue straight on. 200 m past that, bear left and, a couple of metres further on, turn left again. In front of a fence, the trail veers to the left and becomes a path that descends into the stream bed (all of the junctions are way-marked with arrows and signs). Arriving at the stream bed, the route is now waymarked with *red* dots.

The path immediately passes a mighty boulder while crossing through dense growth of oleander; in the spring, Cretan Cyclamen and Birthwort are flowering here. The scents of thyme, sage and oregano are in the air. The stream bed is crossed for the first time via a ford. Now, reach the **entrance to the gorge**. It's true that the towering rock faces are not in such close prox-

248

imity as in the gorges of Samaria, Imbros or Kritsa, but nevertheless, with patches of red-coloured rock and countless caves, they create a magnificent setting.

Soon, the path is joined by a narrow, concrete watercourse. Not long afterwards, pass a striking **plane tree**, seemingly growing directly out of the rock face. Almost unnoticed, the Xeropotamos Gorge (Walk 63) merges from the left; keep heading straight ahead for a stretch, directly along the concrete watercourse and, shortly after, reach a little **rest area (3)** in the shade of more plane trees where a stone bench and a trough fountain (without water) are located.

On your right-hand side, pass a pointed rock face that looks like the steeple of a church tower and boasts two caves. The walls of the gorge now close in some-

Along the trail at the upper entrance to the gorge.

what and, knowing that the Minoans buried their dead in the caves here more than 3500 years ago, they create a dramatic backdrop. The water-

course suddenly ends at a water shaft. 10 minutes later, a waymarked path forks to the right to a car park (Exit B) on the upper southern edge of the gorge (on the return route, we will pass by there). The stream bed for the gorge has now become packed with sprawling patches of Chasteberry which, in early autumn, bears lilac-coloured flowers, and well into the summer, the red flowering oleander casts its spell.

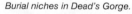

Burial niches in Dead's Gorge.

Pass by yet another waterless **trough fountain**. A couple of minutes later, meet up with a second **rest area (4)** beneath a tall fig tree. Afterwards, a wooden portal marks the entrance to Dead's Gorge for walkers who are approaching from the seaside; for us, this is the gorge's exit. A couple of minutes afterwards, meet up with a concrete-paved trail at a major **ford**. Before returning back to Zakros along the Old Road, turn left here and immediately reach the fenced-in, archaeological digs of the Palace of Zakros. A little later, at the Taverna Akrogiali, the concrete trail merges with the seaside promenade in **Kato Zakros (5)**. If it strikes your fancy, after a pause for refreshment, a relaxing rest stop on the beach and/or a visit to the Minoan Palace, return back to the **ford** and, from there, ascend along a road, at first concrete-paved. But after passing Stellas Traditional Apartments and other minor holiday resort complexes, the road becomes a gravel trail. A good half an hour past the ford, meet up with a **pavilion**, 143 m, where yous can, once again, enjoy a view looking down into Dead's Gorge.

25 minutes later, the Old Road merges with the secondary road Zakros – Kato Zakros. Here is a large car park where a sign points out **Entrance B (6)**, 179 m (an alternative starting point for an exploratory walk into the gorge). Follow the main road for a good 5 minutes and then leave it behind again by turning right onto the Old Road which descends to another car park (Entrance A) and to the **junction (2)** already met during the approach. From there, return back again to **Zakros (1)**.

Beach café Amnesia in Kato Zakros.

Fantastic circular walk with a short scramble over a steep spot

In contrast to the regular route through Dead's Gorge (Walk 62), where the return route leads along broad roads, the circular walk, starting at Kato Zakros, consistently follows paths that are sometimes rugged. A small drawback for the walker lacking sure-footedness: a steep spot, about 8 m high, must be negotiated; this is not, however, a serious obstacle for experienced walkers. An extra bonus: the route not only leads through Dead's Gorge, but also includes another canyon worth walking, the Xeropotamos Gorge; and, along the way between the two gorges, you can enjoy panoramic views of the mountainous countryside above the eastern coast.

Starting point: Kato Zakros, 1 m. The little settlement can be approached by car via a 9 km long access road; parking possible before reaching the village limits.
Height difference: 245 m in both ascent and descent.
Grade: along a sometimes rugged path which, at first, leads over karst terrain; in the Xeropotamos Gorge, metal rungs provide aid in climbing down a sheer drop. Dead's Gorge is accessed via a relatively pleasant path. The circular walk is way-marked throughout with *red* dots and the most important junctions are signed. The first good one and a half hours are completely lacking in shade.
Refreshment: nothing en route; in Kato Zakros, numerous tavernas and the café/snack bar Amnesia at the southern end of the line of restaurants.

At the exit, shortly before Kato Zakros.

At the Taverna Akrogiali in **Kato Zakros (1)**, a concrete road begins, heading towards the interior, and immediately reaches a fork: to the right, you could continue on to the Pelekita Cave, but we turn to the left (this direction is signed with, amongst others, »Archaeological Site«, as well as various adverts for apartment houses). 250 m further on, pass by the fenced-in grounds for the archaeological digs, as well as the entrance for the Minoan Palace of Zakros. At the junction past the fenced-in area, bear left towards the Gorge. Not quite 200 m further on, leave the concrete trail behind and turn right onto a path to climb up the rocky embankment. At this point, aside from our circular walk, another circular walk begins, which leads to the Pelekita Cave

(Walk 64). Not much later, pass through the first gate. The rough path is well-marked with closely-spaced *red* dots. The route ascends through a karst terrain, covered in cushion plant scrubland, to reach a **viewpoint** up above, which offers an impressive view into Dead's Gorge. At a chain-link fence, walk a few paces to the left and find a gate, which allows you to pass through. While gaining height, you can also enjoy excellent views of the Bay of Zakros.

A good 20 minutes past the Minoan palace, on a high plateau, 106 m, reach a signed junction: to the right, you could head to the Pelekita Cave, but we turn left instead, heading towards Dead's Gorge/Azokeramos. The path leads a certain distance away from, and parallel to, the chasm marking Dead's Gorge. Afterwards, slightly ascending along the left edge of a mountain ridge, climb up to a flat-backed **saddle (2)**, 218 m. From there, you can spot the white houses of Zakros, towered over by the striking summit of Vigla, 712 m. The path heads towards the rotating blades of the wind turbines in the distance.

Cross over yet another pasture fence and, on the left-hand side, a little secondary branch of Dead's Gorge opens up. A good 10 mins later, meet up again with yet another signed **junction**. Leave the path heading towards Azokeramos behind by turning left (sign: »Dead's Gorge«). After a short descent, cross over the gravel bed of the secondary branch and pass through yet another gate. On the other side of the gate, the path now leads towards Zakros and its sprawling groves of olive trees. Pass another fence and then bear right; a mule track descends in tight bends into the gorge of the **Xeropotamos (3)**, 147 m, down below. In the stream bed, overgrown in brush wood and oleander, turn left. The gorge is relatively easy to walk at the beginning; from time to time, you must scramble over small boulders. The trail

continues to be well-marked with *red* markings and leads along smooth, polished boulders between the gorge's towering walls, up to 100 m in height.

A **critical point** can be skirted around to the right along the upper edge, then chains and metal rungs provide help in scrambling down a steep spot of about 8 m in height. The trickiest stretch is now behind us. Once again, you must scramble over a couple of smooth, polished boulders until the Xeropotamos finally merges into **Dead's Gorge (4)** at some noble plane trees. The transition from one gorge into the other is almost seamless. Meet up with a narrow, concrete water channel and follow this while bearing slightly left to reach a little **rest area (5)**, 92 m, with a stone bench and a trough fountain (without water). Now continue

In Dead's Gorge.

along a mostly well-trodden path running next to the concrete watercourse. The watercourse then ends at a water shaft. The stream bed is now packed with sprawling patches of Chasteberry. Pass another dried-up **trough fountain (6)** and then a second rest area. The walls of the gorge begin to open up again and, not quite 15 mins later, a wooden portal marks the entrance for Dead's Gorge for walkers who are approaching from the seaside; for us, this is the **gorge exit**. A couple of minutes later, reach a concrete-paved trail at a major ford. Pick up the trail and, bearing left, return to the Minoan Palace and, a little later, the seaside promenade in **Kato Zakros (1)**.

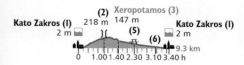

Kato Zakros (I) 2 m — (2) 218 m — Xeropotamos (3) 147 m — (5) — (6) — Kato Zakros (I) 2 m
0   1.00 1.40 2.30 3.10 3.40 h   9.3 km

On top of a panoramic mountain above Zakros Bay

Rugged paths through typical cushion plant scrubland, spectacular panoramic views of the coast from a summit viewpoint and, last but not least, one of Crete's most impressive caves, combine to accent this rewarding circular walk. Exploration of the Pelekita Cave, with a length of more than 300 m, and its incredible tufa formations, is reserved for experienced spelunkers with appropriate equipment. But in any case, you can descend for a couple of metres down into the wide maw of the cave.

Starting point: Kato Zakros, 1 m. The little settlement can be approached by car via a 9 km long access road; parking possible before reaching the village limits.

Height difference: a good 400 m.

Grade: a sometimes strenuous circular walk through karst terrain; at the outset, with steep ascents and a descent through rugged boulder fields. The circular walk is waymarked throughout, however, completely lacks in shade (except in the cave). To explore the cave, you will need a strong torch or a head torch; if you are not a competent caver, however, don't overestimate your capabilities; restrict your visit to the area around the cave's entrance.

Refreshment: in Kato Zakros, numerous tavernas and the café/snack bar Amnesia at the southern end of the line of restaurants.

Short walk: if you only want to visit the Pelekita Cave, turn right from the Taverna Akrogiali and follow the concrete-paved trail to exit the village. Past the boat landing and two little pebble beaches, pass through a gate and pick up a coastal path, at first rugged but, as you proceed, good to walk. In easy up-and-down walking continue on above the coast. The last 7 or 8 minutes of ascent to the cave is somewhat steeper. When compared to the rugged ascent and descent of the complete circular walk, this route is more like a ramble. Walking times there and back, a good 2 hrs.

The circular walk begins at the crescent-shaped bay of Kato Zakros.

The walk begins in **Kato Zakros (1)**, on the seaside promenade in front of the Taverna Akrogiali. Just as in Walk 63, do not turn right here towards Pelekita Cave (see Short walk), instead, turn left onto the narrow, concrete-paved street, pass the fenced-in grounds of the Minoan Palace, and, shortly before reaching the entrance to Dead's Gorge, meet up with an information board. Here, turn right along the *red*-waymarked path to climb up the embankment and, shortly afterwards, cross through a gate. At first, the path leads very close to the upper rim of Dead's Gorge and, 10 m to the left of our waymarked trail, presents a spectacular view into the canyon. Crossing through another gate, about 20 minutes past the informa-

tion board, reach a signed junction at the top of a **high plain**, 106 m; turn right here towards Pelekita Cave. The path crosses the entire plain towards a rugged mountain ridge and passes a solitary olive tree, standing forsaken in the middle of the plain. Shortly after, cross over a narrow, dry stream bed and, some minutes after that, plod up a steep karst notch. After negotiating this stretch, the path heads towards a mighty castle-like ring of rocks; skirt around this on the left-hand side.

Now continue for a couple of minutes over a high terrain and, soon afterwards, ascend steeper in the direction of a **crag**; skirt around this on the right-hand side. Up above, the rocky ridgeline of Lakomata begins to take shape with two humpbacked secondary peaks; the one to the right is called **Skopeli (2)**, 395 m. 10 minutes later, reach the column at the summit, right next to a miniature church. From a height of almost 400 m, enjoy a splendid panoramic view of the bay and the beach at Kato Zakros, as well as the surrounding coastal cliffs.

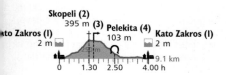

After the pause at the summit, continue by following the way-markers northwards, crossing a broad, treeless, high terrain, covered only in *phrygana*, while heading towards Tra-ostalos. In the middle of the

Skopeli peak with the miniature chapel.

plain, meet up with a signed junction at a waist-high boulder; this is the **turn-off** to **Traostalos (3)**, 376 m. Turn right in the direction of Pelekita and, at first, keep to the same height to continue. 10 minutes later, walk for a short way along a rust-coloured (stone-free!) dirt path; shortly afterwards, the descent begins, heading for the eastern coast.

Now cross over a boulder field. Past a lynchet, the sometimes steep descent continues through the boulders until, after crossing through another two level terraces, overgrown with cushion plant scrubland, a well-trodden coastal path appears. Before meeting up with this path, bear slightly to the left and continue following the *red* waymarkers directly to the entrance of the **Pelekita Cave (4)**, 103 m. The once mighty fig tree in front of the entrance has now passed on to the great unknown, but perhaps one of the new saplings can carry on. Lit by daylight, a zigzag path climbs down about 30 m into the cave; there, archaeologists have left their mark.

From the cave, now follow the well-laid coastal path southwards. For the first minutes, the path descends relatively steeply along the foot of mighty rock faces. Then continue in easy up-and-down walking at about a good 30 m above sea level while passing huge boulders. About one hour past the cave, cross over the little gorge of the **Kakos Potamos (5)**, 37 m. Before reaching the village limits of **Kato Zakros (1)**, pass through a gate, now following a broad trail, and then pass two little pebble beach coves and the boat landing to return back to the seaside promenade.

Contemplative coastal route in an attractive beach district

Lovely beaches are hard to hide. Nevertheless, the faceless, scattered settlement of Xerokambos provides a haven for individualists seeking peace and quiet, and so shall it remain in the years to come as, despite the new tarmac road, the »arid plain« in Crete's extreme southeast is simply too far off the beaten track. A well-marked trail leads through humble cushion plant scrubland along the rocky coast.

Starting point: Kato Zakros, 1 m. The little settlement can be approached by car via a 9 km long access road; parking possible before reaching the village limits.
Height difference: about 175 m.
Grade: the first 15 mins leads over sharp, rugged karst rock; in the further course of the route, the waymarked trail is relatively good to walk. Short ascents and descents through little ravines de-

mand some sure-footedness. No shade; in summer, usually too hot to attempt.
Refreshment: numerous restaurants in Kato Zakros; in Xerokambos, the tavernas Creta Sun and Kostas on the main road through the village.
Alternative: if you prefer not to take refreshment in Xerokambos, turn around again at Katsounaki Beach, walking time is thereby shortened by an hour.

From the information pavilion at the village limits of **Kato Zakros (1)**, walk back 50 m along the road and then cross over pebble stones to the southern end of the beach. Past a gate, a *red*-waymarked coastal path begins. Immediately, you have to ascend along a karst gully, perhaps needing the use of your hands to scramble up. The trail, rugged at the outset, leads along Cape Fagromouro, below the rocky coastal cliffs, while crossing over a plateau covered in *phrygana*, only interrupted by a dry stream bed cutting through it. Past the cape, Xerokambos appears in the distance, as well as the two offshore Kavali Islets. Not quite an hour later, in a rocky cove,

Sheer coastal cliffs at Rouso Spasma.

the sea cave **Lidospilia (2)** catches the eye – the cave seems to penetrate into the steep coastline like a tunnel.

The trail ascends for a short time, but then drops down again into a gorge-like notch and continues a good 40 m over the waterline, traversing above another cove. Red waymarkers point out a turn-off to the right, heading towards Ambelies, but we continue on along our path. The path soon passes to the left and below a striking breach in the rock face. The valley of the **Kalo Potami (3)** opens up in front of us; the river has cut a broad trench on its way to the sea. At first, the path leads for a short stretch towards the

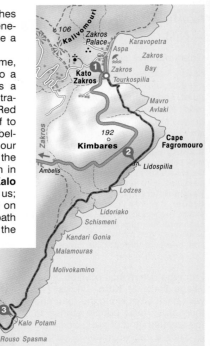

interior, but then it descends steeply into the valley and finally crosses over the dry stream bed in the broad mouth of the valley situated at sea level.

Crossing a stony, terraced beach, meet up with **Rouso Spasma (4)**. The little pebble cove catches the eye with its steep, beige to ochre-coloured escarpment. At the southern edge, there is a sheer drop at a rocky heap of fallen rock that towers

In winter, the shallow lagoon often attracts migratory birds.

out of the sea; here, you could climb down to the pebble beach – but only if you are an experienced rock climber.

15 mins later, meet up with a fence; a gate allows us entrance onto **Katsounaki Beach (5)**. This is the northernmost beach at Xerokambos and, with its fine, powdery sand, it is one of the very best. Please be sure to pay close attention when walking over the dunes – in the autumn, hundreds of white sea daffodils are flowering in this fragile ecosystem (photo on p. 33). From the eastern end of Katsounaki Beach, follow the trail along the now level coastline to a crescent-shaped pebble beach, flanked with Salt cedars, and then to another sandy beach. Further on, in the **Alatsolimni shallow lagoon**, flocks of migrating birds, amongst which are herons and flamingos, stop over for a rest from their journeys. At the end of the lagoon's beach, an unpaved road begins at a cubical cottage; the road merges, 5 mins later, into the village street of **Xerokambos (6)**. Bearing to the left, another 5 mins later, meet up with the Taverna Creta Sun and, just a little later, the Taverna Kostas. If you do not wish to hitch-hike back, return along the approach route to **Kato Zakros (1)**.

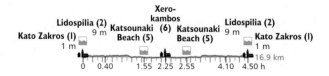

Index

Cover photo:
Bay of Matala.

Frontispiece (page 1):
The Psiloritis massif at the end of the melt water period in June.

All 206 photos are by the author,
except the photo on p. 212 (Florian Dlauhy).

Cartography:
65 small walking maps with a scale of 1:50,000 and 1:75,000
© Bergverlag Rother GmbH, Munich
(drawn by Gerhard Tourneau, Munich)
as well as two overview maps with a scale of 1:700,000 (inner pages)
and an overview map with a scale of 1:2,000,000 (cover)
© Freytag & Berndt, Vienna

Translation: Tom Krupp

Special thanks to Manolis Sergentakis and his staff for their warm
hospitality (Hotel Galini Beach, Kissamos), Manos Papadakis for the lift
to Vai (House Margot, Palekastro), Stella Ailamaki & Elias Pagianidis for
the excellent waymarking in the area around Dead's Gorge (Stellas Traditional Apartments, Kato Zakros), Nikos Falelakis for his active support
in finding new walks (Ravdoucha Beach Studios, Ravdoucha), Mike
& Tsatsa Spintakis (Mikes Restaurant, Pitsidia) and the Milia Mountain
Retreat (Milia) for their delicious vegetarian food and
Hans Zaglitsch (Deventer, Netherlands) for his photographic support.

2nd, revised and extended edition 2018
© Bergverlag Rother GmbH, Munich

ISBN 978-3-7633-4840-4

We heartily welcome any suggestions for amendment to this walking guide!
BERGVERLAG ROTHER · Munich
**D-82041 Oberhaching · Keltenring 17 · Germany · tel. +49 89 608669-0 Fax -69
Internet www.rother.de · e-mail bergverlag@rother.de**